ABOUT THE AUTHOR

Linsey McGoey is a writer and sociologist based in the United Kingdom. She has written for *The Guardian*, *The Times*, *The Spectator*, *Jacobin* and *Fortune*, is the author of *No Such Thing as a Free Gift* (2015) and a co-editor of *The Routledge Handbook of Ignorance Studies* (2015). She is an associate professor of sociology and Director of the Centre for Research in Economic Sociology and Innovation at the University of Essex.

The
Unknowers

HOW STRATEGIC
IGNORANCE RULES
THE WORLD

Linsey McGoey

ZED

The Unknowers: How Strategic Ignorance Rules the World was first published in 2019 by Zed Books Ltd, The Foundry, 17 Oval Way, London SE11 5RR, UK.

www.zedbooks.net

Typeset in Avenir and Haarlemmer
by Swales & Willis Ltd, Exeter, Devon
Index by Rohan Bolton
Cover design by Andy Allen

A catalogue record for this book is available from the British Library

ISBN 978-1-78032-636-8 hb
ISBN 978-1-78032-635-1 pb
ISBN 978-1-78032-637-5 pdf
ISBN 978-1-78032-638-2 epub
ISBN 978-1-78032-639-9 mobi

Printed and bound by CPI Group (UK) Ltd, Croydon CRO 4YY

In memory of my brother Drew McGoey

He who knows only his own side of the case, knows little of that.

– John Stuart Mill and Harriet Taylor, On Liberty

CONTENTS

Acknowledgements   ix

INTRODUCTION: THE POWER TO IGNORE   1

1   NARROW HISTORY   23

2   SEEING IGNORANCE DIFFERENTLY   50

3   ELITE AGNOTOLOGISTS   79

4   THE MURDOCH STRATEGY   99

5   SUSPICIOUS ATTENTION   125

6   KNOW-IT-ALL EPISTOCRATS   154

7   CONFLICT BLINDNESS   171

8   MASTERS OF INDUSTRY, MASTERS OF
    IGNORANCE   193

9   THE OSTRICH INSTRUCTION   227

10 GOOD EXPERTS   249

11 THE PRETENCE OF IGNORANCE   280

    CONCLUSION: THE GREAT ENLARGEMENT   306

    Notes   329

    Index   358

ACKNOWLEDGEMENTS

I've been researching and writing about the topic of strategic ignorance for over 15 years, with many debts accrued.

This book had a long period of development. It is rooted in a PhD thesis, 'The Value of Ignorance,' that I designed and carried out at the London School of Economics from 2004 to 2007. After LSE, I held research fellowships at the University of Oxford before moving to the Department of Sociology at the University of Essex. In each of these settings, my substantive research focus changed: at LSE, I studied corporate crime and pharmaceutical regulation; later, while working as a researcher at Oxford, I investigated 'big philanthropy' and its unintended social effects. A couple of years later, at Essex, my research shifted to a focus on the history of economic thought in the 19th and early 20th centuries.

Although the empirical settings were different, concepts that I had developed in my PhD were relevant to new empirical research areas, including notions such as regulatory 'anti-strategies' and 'strategic ignorance' (a term coined before me, but which I define in a new way).

ACKNOWLEDGEMENTS

The Unknowers expands upon these earlier concepts, developing a new theoretical approach for understanding the relationship between knowledge, ignorance and power in the modern age.

The stories and news events described in *The Unknowers* draw on different research methods, from investigative reporting to qualitative sociological interviewing. It is a book that marries the history of ideas, and particularly late Enlightenment political economic thought, with first-hand reporting on the power and value of ignorance to powerful people and institutions today. This focus draws on different professional qualifications, including my earlier work as a freelance journalist, followed by training at LSE as a sociologist, leading to a current post as Director of the Centre for Research in Economic Sociology and Innovation at Essex.

My doctoral research at the LSE examined the social implications of governmental efforts to ensure that pharmaceutical medicines are safe for use and affordable for different members of the public, and for this research, I carried out interviews with a number of high-profile people who were in the news frequently during the mid-2000s, when large pharmaceutical companies including Merck and GlaxoSmithKline were found to have hidden evidence about the harmful effects of some of their bestselling pharmaceutical drugs.

I interviewed many different stakeholders central to the story, including the CEO of the UK's drug regulatory agency, Kent Woods, and David Graham, a heroic whistle-blower and FDA employee commended in the media for disclosing the risks of Merck's bestselling drug Vioxx. Some of the people I interviewed agreed to speak on the record and others did not. Those who agreed to speak on the record, including Woods and Graham, are named in this book, as well as identified in earlier articles of mine published in journals such as *The Lancet* and *The Journal of Medical Ethics*. I'm grateful to the many physicians, regulators and lawyers who took the time to speak with me during interviews that took place over the mid to late 2000s, as well as to more recent interviewees, acknowledged in individual chapters, who participated in discussions over the past two years about the legal and social uses of strategic ignorance.

This book therefore draws on and republishes, with permission, some my earlier work, including 'On the Will to Ignorance in Bureaucracy,' *Economy and Society* (2007); 'Pharmaceutical Controversies and the Performative Value of Uncertainty,' *Science as Culture* (2009); and 'The Logic of Strategic Ignorance,' *British Journal of Sociology* (2012).

Other chapters in the book are indebted to the analysis and reportage of journalists who describe events where I was not present. This includes the Grenfell fire and Rupert Murdoch's appearance before Parliament. In Chapter 4, Nick Davies' important book *Hack Attack* was particularly indispensable. Any errors are my own.

A first draft of this book was written during a visiting fellowship at Sciences Po in Paris in 2017. Thanks to Jenny Andersson, Olivier Godechot and Mark Vail for their collegiality during this fellowship.

Thanks also to Fabian Muniesa and Catherine Grandclément, and to other interlocutors in Europe and elsewhere carrying out important research on ignorance, especially Matthias Gross, who is co-editor with me of the *Routledge Handbook of Ignorance Studies*, as well as to Michael Smithson, Peter Wehling, Mathias Girel, Nathalie Jas, Nicolas Larchet, Didier Torny, Marc-Olivier Déplaude, François Dedieu, Thomas Depecker, Grégoire Mallard, Adriana Mica, Katharina Paul, Christian Haddad, Nora Stel, Stuart Firestein, Stefan Böschen and David Demortain.

This book also draws on early co-authored articles with Emily Jackson about the legal circumstances of the Seroxat controversy. I'm grateful to her for discussions about legal matters, as well as to Alexander Sarch and Alexandra Cox for commenting on Chapter 9 of this book, where I discuss the role of ignorance in law. Once again, any errors are my own.

Thanks to Nikolas Rose, an inspiring PhD supervisor. Thanks to former colleagues at Oxford, especially Steve Rayner, Steve Woolgar, Andrew Barry, Javier Lezaun, Tanja Schneider, Ann Kelly, Jerome Ravetz, Peter Healey, Noortje Marres, Lisa Stampnitzky, Christina Fuhr, Will Davies, Sam Evans, Maja Korica, Devi Sridhar and Allison Stewart.

Thanks also to conversations with Barbara Prainsack, Scott Vrecko, Lynne Pettinger, Monika Krause, Fran Tonkiss, Bronwyn Parry, Amy Hinterberger, Donald Light, Brian Balmer, Jacqueline Best, Kean Birch, Dean Curran, Fuyuki Kurusawa, Nicolas Langlitz, Wendy Espeland, Sophie Harman, Filippa Lentzos, Sabina Leonelli, Martyn Pickersgill, Michael Power, Salla Sariola, Amos Laar, Kaushik Sunder

Rajan, Stefan Ecks, Ian Harper, Melissa Parker, Robin West, Ayo Wahlberg and Cynthia Gibson.

At the University of Essex, I'm grateful to many colleagues, students and friends. Thanks especially to Michael Halewood, Sandya Hewamanne and Kanyinsola Olanrewaju. Thanks to Sandy Macmillan at the Albert Sloman Library.

Thank you to Kim Walker, Jonathan Hoare and all the editorial and production team at Zed. Ken Barlow offered astute comments on drafts and was a kind and supportive editor.

Conversations with my partner Darren Thiel were an important influence on this book. I thank him more than I can say, including for his comments on drafts. Thanks also to my mother, my father, stepfather, stepmother, stepsiblings and my brother. This book is dedicated to the memory of our brother Drew.

INTRODUCTION: THE POWER TO IGNORE

In the summer of 2018, a little-reported news event in Britain offered an eye-opening glimpse into a political strategy I term 'strategic ignorance.'

The news was focused on a recent court battle involving children living in the 'Calais Jungle,' the informal name for a migrant camp near the port city of Calais, France. At its peak, the camp was home to thousands of migrants before French authorities raided the illegal settlement in 2016, dispatching many residents to detention centres. The effort to count the Calais Jungle residents at any one time gives a snapshot of the way that headcounts often tend to be political challenges and not simply numerical ones.

To quell public concern about the scale of the migrant crisis, French authorities put the headcount of migrants at its peak in the lower 4000s, while human rights and refugee support organizations put the number in the 9000s. Gaps between 'official' government statistics and 'unofficial' statistics are like the momentous pause before a singer's last crescendo: they are a type of meaningful silence – a loud unknown.

Sometimes, government-produced unknowns can be deemed illegal in courts of law. This happened in July 2018, when England's Court of Appeal overturned an earlier decision made by the High Court, which ruled a year earlier that it was lawful of Britain's Home Office *not* to have provided about 2000 children living in the Calais camp with reasons for why their application to join family members in the UK was rejected. A few months after the High Court cleared the Home Office of wrongdoing, a Home Office official sent an email with a revealing and likely accidental disclosure: 'our legal department had advised against full disclosure because of the risk of challenge.'[1]

The Home Office's *stated* reason for not providing children an explanation for their application's rejection was that French authorities had requested that British authorities omit this information. But that appears to be a lie. In reality, the French *did* request fuller disclosure, but the Home Office balked at this, because any explanation might have given the children legitimate grounds for legally appealing the rejection of their effort to join family. In a statement, England's Court of Appeal suggested that the Home Office's failure to disclose the truthful reasons for withholding relevant evidence was 'a serious breach of the duty of candour and cooperation.'[2]

This book looks at similar situations where non-disclosure is tactically deployed to avoid the repercussions of inconvenient evidence. The less they are informed, the British government appears to have speculated, the weaker the children's legal case. By keeping families in the dark, the government hoped to reduce its own legal burden. This time, ignorance was not blissful for the government: the Court of Appeal deemed the government's actions unlawful. It was an instance when Britain's system of law worked as the nation's visionary early leaders intended: as a check on government power.

The question is: how often does strategic ignorance actually work as a political tactic? The short (and unsatisfactory) answer is: nobody knows. Any attempt to conclusively quantify the success or failure rate of strategic ignorance in political affairs is thwarted by an obvious problem: we are doomed to miss the most successful cases, the situations where a strategy of non-disclosure works as it's meant to work and dispels the possibility of being found out.[3] It's the major hurdle which people who study the political value of strategic ignorance all face: the fact that imperceptibility is the greatest measure of the tactic's success. But that doesn't mean we should ignore it all together.

By 'strategic ignorance,' I mean any actions which mobilize, manufacture or exploit unknowns in a wider environment to avoid liability for earlier actions. But I also use strategic ignorance to refer to situations where people create or magnify unknowns in an *offensive* rather than a *defensive* way, to generate support for future political initiatives rather than to simply avoid liability for a past mistake.

For example, environmental groups concerned about the effects of hydraulic fracking sometimes strategically avoid disclosing their links to large international NGOs like

Greenpeace in order to build community support in rustbelt regions of the US or farming communities in Australia. In these regions, NGOs like Greenpeace or Friends of the Earth can be resented by politically conservative residents. The strategic effort to appear unlinked to larger NGOs helps to build grassroots support among rural farmers.[4]

Strategic ignorance is a cross-partisan phenomenon: liberals, conservatives, left-wingers and right-wingers all engage in it. It's also a very old tactic.

During the late 19th century, the American oil magnate John D. Rockefeller would hire lawyers to pretend to be furious small businessmen and farmers opposed to government legislation that sought to reduce Standard Oil's corporate monopoly. Far from being an open market, the American oil business in the 1870s and 1880s protected large incumbents at the expense of small upstart companies. Rockefeller paid off lawyers to pretend to be outraged farmers to 'foster the impression of a popular groundswell' against anti-monopoly legislation, compounding public ignorance about the lawyer's real identities, as well as Rockefeller's role in bribery and corruption at Standard Oil.[5]

In this book, I mostly focus on tactics of ignorance deployed by the political right. I examine the way that two centuries of thinkers labelled 'market fundamentalists' strategically ignore the role of governments in offering preferential treatment to wealthy citizens through protectionist economic policies. The common view in both academia and the media is that the US and the United Kingdom have 'free market' economic systems. But in reality both nations have often been strongly protectionist, especially during the US and Britain's rise to global economic dominance over the 18th and 19th centuries. But government protections have not been evenly applied. Typically, it is wealthier individuals and large corporate monopolies which benefit the most from state protections, especially during the East Indian merchant trade of the 18th and 19th centuries, the industrial 19th-century 'gilded age' in America and throughout the 40-year-long emergence of a new gilded age today.

I focus on the political right, but the left also ignores inconvenient facts, such as the mid-20th-century denial of forced starvation in the Soviet Union, something long ignored by socialist supporters in the west who refused to believe that mass killing was embraced by a government they esteemed.

'It is sometimes asked why Western observers were slow in recognizing the truth about the Soviet Union,' British political philosopher John Gray writes.

> The reason is not that it was hard to come by. It was clear from hundreds of books by émigré survivors – and from statements by the Soviets themselves. But the facts were too uncomfortable for Western observers to admit. For the sake of their piece of mind they had to deny what they knew or suspected to be true.[6]

It's a compelling and accurate point from a philosopher whose ideas I draw on throughout the book. But I also suggest Gray gets things a little wrong about the political usefulness of denial. In his book *Straw Dogs*, Gray offers the following quote from a French biologist named Jacques Monod (the point that Gray is making is that people tend to share a universal tendency to downplay the problem of human fragility and future uncertainties): 'All religions, nearly all philosophies, and even a part of science testify to the unwearying, heroic effort of mankind desperately denying its contingency.'

This book makes an opposite argument. Contingency is defined as a 'future circumstance which is possible but cannot be predicted with certainty.' I argue that over the past 200 years, influential figures in western cultures learned not only that it's possible to embrace rather than to deny the problem of human contingency, but also that there are enormous financial rewards in harnessing and magnifying the uncertainty and unknowns around us to achieve different financial and reputational advantages.[7]

Powerful individuals thrive on strategic ignorance and the deliberate exploitation of uncertainty. A good example of this problem is the way that the writing of the political economist Adam Smith has been distorted over the years.

Smith, the 18th-century Scottish enlightenment thinker seen as the father of modern economics, pointed out in his influential book *Wealth of Nations* that an entirely free market is an impossible utopia. He insisted that steps towards an ideal economy – an economy that, in his words, has 'perfect justice' and 'perfect equality,' should be taken gradually, with political leaders maintaining ever-vigilant 'suspicious attention' towards businessmen who steer laws in their favor.[8]

Today, market fundamentalists often abuse Smith's name to back policies that would have him rollicking in his grave.

But their efforts are open to challenge, because Smith's dream of 'perfect equality' is plain to read in *Wealth of Nations* – as long as we check the full edition, and not edited versions popular throughout the 20th and 21st centuries.

Other times, a historical evidence base is less clear. For example, the great 19th-century British political philosopher John Stuart Mill suggested in his autobiography that his wife, Harriet Taylor, co-wrote some of his essays, including *On Liberty*, one of the most influential political essays in modern history. '*Liberty* was more directly and literally our joint production than anything else which bears my name,' he writes. 'The whole mode of thinking, of which the book was the expression, was emphatically hers.'[9]

After Mill died, his friends pressured his stepdaughter to remove passages from his autobiography where he esteems female influence on his ideas, and although some recent editions correct these omissions, most university students are still taught Mill's ideas without learning of the co-authorship with his wife that he describes at length. It was Mill's liberal friends – defenders of free speech and freedom of thought – who censored his writing, an irony I discuss later.

REFUSING TO IGNORE THE POWER OF IGNORANCE

In this book, I argue that to ignore the power of strategic ignorance is irrational, and yet social scientists by and large have done exactly that.

We have dismissed the importance and universality of strategic ignorance among all individuals, as well as turned a blind eye to the distribution of ignorance in society, wrongly assuming that it is a *bottom-heavy* problem rather than a *top-heavy* problem – that the poor tend to be more ignorant than the powerful. I suggest that the reason for this tendency lies to some degree in the popularity and influence of utilitarianism, a 19th-century system of thought which continues to be the most dominant political philosophy in the world today.

As a body of thought and a policy guide, utilitarianism is an inspiring, humane and intelligent way of trying to meet human needs fairly. But it over-values knowledge epistemologically, especially the knowledge of highly educated individuals (a point Mill made), leading to blind spots built into modern systems of knowing.

Influential thinkers such as Jeremy Bentham, the British founder of utilitarian theory, tended to see knowledge as the best philosophical defence of liberal values, including the right to liberty. In this book, I suggest something opposite to this. I argue that acknowledgment of the universality of inalienable ignorance is the best defence of both liberty and equality.

Many natural scientists, by and large, do now admit and celebrate this fact, emphasizing that science is always ignorant at some level, and also that shared human ignorance is what helps to drive science forward.[10]

And yet the importance of this insight hasn't really pierced political theory. Philosophers will point to American political philosopher John Rawls' notion of a 'veil of ignorance' (I introduce the concept in the next chapter) as evidence that the unknown can be a fruitful academic tool for understanding why some people have less physical liberty or economic freedom than others. Rawls' idea is an important one, but the point I am making is different. I argue that ignorance is not simply useful as an analytical device in academic thought experiments, but also that it can be a useful moral device – indeed perhaps the most powerful device – for asserting the fundamentality of human equality.

Where the philosophers of the enlightenment pointed to their own mental faculties to emancipate themselves from feudal rule, I suggest we can point to the limits of those faculties to reclaim democratic rights in today's increasingly plutocratic age.

Today, 240 years after Immanuel Kant's essay 'What Is Enlightenment' proclaimed that we must 'dare to know,' another task is upon us: to interrogate 'truths' wrongly seen by many people today as irrefutable, like the assumption that Adam Smith venerated unrestrained self-interest and profiteering, or that Edmund Burke, the great 18th-century statesman, would object if he was alive today to contemporary colonial and anti-slavery reparations movements.

This book looks at what they actually wrote and the relevance of their ideas in our time. It's not meant merely as academic exercise (though it will be academic, with fairly long excerpts from books like *Wealth of Nations* – I hope the slog is worth it so readers can judge Smith's ideas for themselves). But also to suggest something that may appear unusual in our deeply divided age, when the integrity of truth seems threatened by callous and vested interests. Like many people today,

I worry that the truth *is* threatened – but I also hope attentiveness to strategic ignorance can help rescue the truth's liberating potential.

Against men like the industrialist Henry Ford, who used propaganda to vilify Jewish Americans and who proclaimed when challenged about his bigotry that 'history is more or less bunk,' it is possible to turn the ignorance of women and men like Ford against themselves, to uphold their propaganda as a mirror for our times and the threats humans collectively face – but whose penalty is *always* worse for the most impoverished and least free peoples in any period, a point that Burke made when he demanded justice for the Indian victims of East India Company traders. A commitment to accurate history, to better understanding of our past – to greater history – is the best defence against Henry Ford's heirs today.

Please view this book however you like, but if you'll permit one plea, it's this: don't presume that to unknow is nihilistic. Don't presume that to unknow is to challenge the value of truth. Rather, this book calls for trust in the power of revolutionary ignorance, to marvel, like enlightenment thinkers in the past, in the possibilities of daring to unknow.

BLISSFUL IGNORANCE?

Maxims such as 'ignorance is bliss' are common in daily life, and it can seem obvious that people try to shield themselves from uncomfortable knowledge. But until very recently, the psychological and sociological value of unknowing has been neglected. As the former editor of the *American Journal of Sociology* suggested recently, the social sciences continue to exhibit 'a certain sociological ignorance of ignorance.'[11]

We need better analytical tools to understand the usefulness and the power of ignorance and this book develops new concepts for doing so.

I build on but also deviate from earlier work from the field of 'agnotology,' a word that entered public consciousness about 15 years ago, popularized in important research by the historians Robert Proctor and Londa Schiebinger. Defined as the academic study of the deliberate production of ignorance, agnotology is a powerful lens for conceptualizing the wilful manipulation of facts and evidence that are evident in sectors such as big tobacco, not to mention big pharma, big oil, big tech, big agriculture and big food.[12]

Take pharmaceutical sales and marketing. The pharmaceutical industry is one of the most profitable sectors in the world – and in some cases those profits are defensible. Scientific innovation takes a lot of work and money, and this heavily state-funded industry helps keep many people alive. But the balance between preserving life and preserving revenue is not always an easy one. There are well-documented cases where pharmaceutical companies deliberately hid and distorted evidence about harmful drug effects: pick up any book from bestselling British science writer and physician Ben Goldacre for details of the way that greed in the pharmaceutical sector chaffs against the legal duty to produce and market safe drugs. His recent bestseller *Bad Pharma* got its name for good reason.

Even so, while pharmaceutical malfeasance often gets a lot of press coverage, it's not always clear how the companies manage to get away with it. My concept of 'ignorance alibis' helps to provide an answer, showing the way that unwitting scientific experts can be exploited to absolve a corporation's liability for the marketing and sales of unsafe pharmaceutical drugs.

An honest expert can be used for malicious ends, not by exploiting her knowledge, but by relying on her ignorance. This is because if the expert doesn't know something, it becomes plausible to insist that a phenomenon is not real, regardless of how many non-experts insist that it is. Experts, in other words, can be useful authorities on ignorance.

MICRO-IGNORANCE AND MACRO-IGNORANCE

Paying more attention to what I term *micro-ignorance* and *macro-ignorance* helps to illustrate the power of ignorance.[13] By micro-ignorance, I mean individual acts of ignoring. By macro-ignorance, I mean the sedimentation of individual ignorance into rigid ideological positions and policy perspectives that obscure their own mistaken assumptions from adherents, leading to new patterns of individual micro-ignorance.

This cycle – micro-ignorance leading to larger, more structural forms of macro-ignorance, which in turn compels individual forms of micro-ignorance – is common to all religious and secular thought systems, including capitalism and socialism.

A weakness of both systems, especially in their most extreme, polarized form, is a shared problem. Both are 'harmony ideologies' which purport to minimize and even completely defuse human conflict by aligning different individual goals if implemented successfully. This unrealistic attitude to social and economic conflict is the bane of both ideological systems. Especially when pitted against other, both ideological standpoints lead to strategic ignorance among dogmatic believers because each system is predicated on lessening suffering and conflict, and therefore obvious suffering tends to be necessarily ignored.

In a way, I'm simply re-stating John Gray's point about the Soviet Union in different language. When he suggests the facts 'were too uncomfortable for Western observers to admit,' my question is: which mechanisms enable people to deny available evidence about the most brutal aspects of the Soviet regime? Or in the case of market fundamentalists, to deny that unregulated labour practices let business owners get away, quite literally at times, with murderous labour practices?

In other words, what kind of 'ignorance pathways' explain the relationship between micro-ignorance and macro-ignorance and vice versa? This book takes up that question by exploring many of the social and political factors that underpin strategic ignorance about economic inequality and human suffering in our times.

In doing so, I draw on a wide range of writers across the political spectrum, such as Andrew Bacevich, a conservative military historian in the United States who has written about what he sees as America's failed wars in the Middle East since the 1980s. This book is not primarily about recent US and Britain-led military interventions, but I refer to them because they illustrate what many people see as persistent ignorance among many citizens of the UK and US to the cost of recent wars, both economically and in terms of lives lost. As Stephanie Savell of Brown University points out, 'most of us don't even think of ourselves as "at war."'[14]

Whether or not one thinks she exaggerates the scale of western apathy towards ongoing strife in the Middle East or not, there's a factor that has likely contributed to declining interest in the human cost of US-led global warfare: the fact that the US moved to the all-voluntary military force in the early 1970s. The end of mandatory conscription for adult males has led to a troubling trend that tends to be discussed more in conservative news outlets than progressive ones, even though the left usually thinks of itself as fighting for the rights of low-income groups: the fact that poorer Americans as well as non-white Americans are far more represented among military recruits than offspring from white wealthy families.[15]

A recent article in *The American Conservative* points out 'the Army now gets more soldiers from the state of Alabama, population 4.8 million, than it gets from New York, Chicago, and Los Angeles combined, aggregate metropolitan population more than 25 million.' This article makes important points about this regional split, suggesting that one reason why military hawks don't seem that bothered about committing soldiers to largely unsuccessful but seemingly endless interventions in the Middle East is because many elite policymakers have fewer of their sons or daughters sacrificing their lives personally.[16]

I'm not raising this point to make a policy argument about conscription, but simply to illuminate the value of a micro-ignorance and macro-ignorance framework for understanding changes in social attitudes. The ending of forced military service is one 'ignorance pathway' for understanding why public attitudes to the Iraq and Vietnam wars are different.

The main ignorance pathway I tease out in the book is not about war. Rather, I draw on the history of ideas from the late 18th century onwards to understand the origins and the implications of the assumption, still pervasive within many undergraduate economics and political science textbooks, that western economies grew wealthy from 'free' trade, an erroneous presumption that is blocking innovative approaches to major challenges of the 21st century, including the effort to produce safer and more affordable medicines, economically just working conditions and fairer taxation policies.

THE STRONGS, THE SMARTS AND THE GREATS: AN OVERVIEW OF THE BOOK

In opening chapters, I lay out the book's conceptual approach, first by describing how this book differs from earlier approaches to the study of ignorance, including recent work in psychology and political science, and then by introducing three new concepts – 'useful unknowns'; 'ignorance alibis'; and 'oracular power' – which help to illustrate the power of ignorance.

I also introduce a thought experiment: the development of a new typology for conceptualizing groups which I label the *strongs*, the *smarts* and the *greats*. These groups are not formal entities and do not have a formal membership. Rather, they are loose coalitions of individuals, often steered by charismatic figureheads, who are beginning to openly advocate in favour of curbing voting rights in democratic nations, often by claiming to possess exceptional powers of insight over average voters.

I argue that the *smarts* and the *strongs* try to acquire political and corporate dominance through monopolizing what I term 'oracular power,' defined as the capacity to determine where the boundary between knowledge and ignorance lies.[17]

In well-functioning democracies, oracular power is shared among constituents and elected representatives. The power of *strongs* and *smarts* is characterized by the opposite impulse, by leaders who resent having to listen to a plurality of voices, and who take steps to delegitimize the knowledge of their detractors, including disenfranchisement efforts.

Neither what I term the *smarts* camp nor the *strongs* camp is entirely new. Today's smarts have a lineage that extends through Walter Lippmann's criticism of voter knowledge in the 1920s, to utilitarian arguments against wider suffrage in the 19th century, to defences in favour of elite rule by thinkers like Plato in antiquity.

What *is* new is the emergency of a novel, fashionable word to describe this quite old idea: 'epistocracy,' which means 'rule by knowers.' Early chapters explore epistocracy in more depth, listing what I see as its many flaws, including its worst error: the fact that defenders of epistocracy routinely underestimate the problem of their own ignorance.

Authoritarian *strongs*, meanwhile, inherited from early 20th-century thinkers such as Georges Sorel the belief that truth, in an empirical sense, is irrelevant to the task of gaining and maintaining power. Sorel championed the idea that leaders should deliberately use myths, even knowingly false ones, to foment civic devotion, an idea that was influential on Italian fascist movements. His advocacy of post-truth politics did not die following WWII; traces of his theories can be seen in propaganda efforts from both camps, from both Soviet and western stakeholders during the Cold War.

Today, Sorel's ideas about myth-making and explicit disdain for empirical fact are reminiscent of Donald Trump's approach to the truth, but they also recall the manipulation and distortion of evidence that characterized the build up to the 2003 invasion of Iraq. The proclaimed newness of post-truth politics is a myth in itself.

The *greats* is my shorthand for various national and international democratic social movements across the world that are challenging political and corporate authoritarianism. Some of these movements have formal connections, while many do not, but they tend to share concern over the erosion of democratic rights and a desire for justice and reparations for people experiencing racial injustice and forced economic immiseration at a time of deepening wealth concentration.

The greats have a knowledge-based advantage that I argue tends to be overlooked. They have the fundamental, inalienable capacity to point out the limits of the strongs and the smarts' claims to possess special enlightenment. This capacity is inalienable because elite ignorance is inalienable. There is always something that the smarts and strongs do not know.

The inescapable fact of elite ignorance functions as a perpetual weapon of resistance for the greats. It also points to the emancipative potential of ignorance, and the way that illuminating the ignorance of elites can foster positive change, a point emphasized by feminist scholars like Audre Lorde in the late 20th century, and earlier by the 18th-century democrat radical Thomas Paine.

Writing in the 1770s, Paine called attention to the ignorance of Britain's rulers to encourage Americans in their fight for independence. 'Men who look upon themselves born to reign,' he writes, are 'early poisoned by importance.' He goes on: 'the world they act in differs so materially from the world at large, that they have little opportunity of knowing its true interest' – their governance decisions tend to be 'most ignorant and unfit of any.'[18]

Paine doesn't use the term 'elite ignorance,' but his meaning is similar to mine – although I add a twist. Paine introduces a common understanding of elite ignorance – the challenge of understanding hardships faced by less powerful groups. I agree this is a serious problem, but I define elite ignorance differently. I see it as the superior capacity to exploit ignorance to command greater institutional, individual and class-based advantages.

Clearly, not all powerful or elite individuals do this – many strive to transcend narrow self-interest, just as visionary enlightenment thinkers did in their day. But the more that social and cognitive scientists neglect the problem of elite ignorance, the more we shy from the type of 'suspicious attention' towards business practices that Adam Smith called for, the more unrealistic a picture of reality the social sciences become.

* * *

The middle of the book looks at strategic and elite ignorance from different angles, including Donald Trump's 2016 presidential win and the Brexit vote, where I explore the way that low-income voters are seen as more 'ignorant' than wealthy voters, even though evidence since has shown that wealthier voters propelled both outcomes.

Next, I examine phone hacking at News International, a scandal that rocked the United Kingdom ever since news first broke that staff at the tabloid newspaper *News of the World* had illegally hacked into the voicemail of a murdered schoolgirl named Milly Dowler.

CEO Rupert Murdoch claimed not to know anything about illegality at his organization. This insistence on his part reflected the long-standing ability of CEOs to 'know what not to know' when it comes to illegal and immoral practices at their companies.

To make this point clearer, I turn to history, exploring the business practices of 19th-century industrialists Andrew Carnegie and John D. Rockefeller – masters of industry who were also masters of ignorance.

Their life stories are useful for a few reasons. For one, their stories show that CEO strategic ignorance has a long heritage in global business practices.

Also, the lives of Carnegie and Rockefeller are relevant for another reason: they help to explore why Adam Smith's call to be 'suspicious' towards the self-serving activities of business merchants is neglected in mainstream economic theory today.

Today is a good time to re-examine Smith's attitude to profiteering among business merchants. Harvard psychologist Steven Pinker, in his recent bestseller *Enlightenment Now*, also turns to the late 18th century, but I argue that he gets Adam Smith wrong, and also that his historical omissions are pregnant with meaning. What Pinker *doesn't* say about Smith helps me to examine where the myth of America and Britain's laissez-faire origins have come from, and why those myths still thrive today.

Turning to the thought of Smith and other thinkers in his era, including Mary Wollstonecraft, Edmund Burke, Thomas Paine and Alexis de Tocqueville, I explore how leading intellectuals in the 18th and 19th centuries treated corporate regulation and corporate accountability.

Despite significant ideological differences among them, these thinkers are best known for their shared concern with limiting abuses of power by the government. But importantly, they were also preoccupied with limiting and punishing harm inflicted on the public by private stakeholders as well, especially the growing class of merchants taking advantage of new banking, industry and trade opportunities. The problem of corporate harm is one of the reasons why early political economists such as Smith, Burke and Tocqueville called for government regulation of industry activities.

Today, their beliefs have been turned upside-down; Smith and his followers have been romanticized as being far more laissez-faire than they actually were, a tendency that helps to confer respectability today on the illiberal ideas of later economists who espouse more extreme forms of market fundamentalism than Smith ever voiced himself.

This book is the first to examine the role of strategic and elite ignorance in distorting the legacy of Smith and his peers.

My focus on the 18th and 19th centuries is important for a few reasons. As well as being a time when economics first grew into a formal academic discipline, the 19th century is the earliest time when legal cases centred on the problem of 'deliberate ignorance,' also known as the 'Ostrich instruction,' first appeared in modern legal settings, introduced in British courts during the 1860s and applied in the US from the late 19th century on.

A century later, at the end of the twentieth century, the 'Ostrich instruction' featured in the successful prosecution of Enron executives. Jurors reached a guilty verdict based on the 'wilful blindness' principle – essentially, that because Enron's management had the means to identify criminal activity, executives were guilty even if they didn't *directly* carry out criminal acts themselves.

This leads to a question. Given that wilful ignorance has clearly been deemed an illegal act in both UK and US courts, why aren't there more cases of successful prosecutions?

The answer is that wilful ignorance is difficult to prove, which makes it the valuable corporate strategy it is. Enron was a relatively unusual case because the prosecution's emphasis on wilful ignorance was successful, leading Enron's management to receive prison sentences. Often this legal strategy fails.[19]

The book's final chapters explain why this matters today. Focusing on the global pharmaceutical industry, I show the ways that large corporations exploit strategic ignorance for financial gain. Pharmaceutical companies *do* occasionally face financial penalties when they commit illegal acts; in 2012, for example, GlaxoSmithKline, a British pharmaceutical giant, was ordered by American authorities to pay a $3 billion fine after it committed fraud – it is the largest fine ever levied on a pharmaceutical company in US history.[20]

It is a huge amount of money, but it's also a negligible amount next the profits that GSK pocketed from carrying out the fraud to begin with. Also, while GSK exhibited the same bad behaviour in the UK, that nation chose not to prosecute or fine the company. The legal infrastructure was different enough between the two nations for the same company to face fines in only one jurisdiction.

It is not innate ability, but the presence of favourable political networks and laws that makes strategic ignorance a more lucrative tactic in some countries and historical eras than in others. In my conclusion, I suggest that greater recognition of this reality can lead to emancipative ignorance.

CHAPTER 1

NARROW HISTORY

They had seen it in their nightmares: the possibility of the inferno that came true, the premonition of a fire killing their neighbours and family members. Over 70 boys, girls, women and men died in the fire at London's Grenfell Tower on June 14, 2017.

The Grenfell residents had seen smoke before.

In May 2013, they noticed it spilling from the sockets of different appliances, their fridges, televisions and laptops damaged by a series of ominous electrical surges.

'We had numerous power surges in the space of a minute, and in that process my computer and monitor literally exploded, with smoke seeping out from the back,' one resident wrote at the time.[1]

Residents had raised concerns over fire risks as far back as 2004. Those who clamoured the loudest for Grenfell's management to address their fears were treated the harshest. When he wrote a series of blogs expressing his concerns over fire risks, one resident was threatened with legal action. In July 2013, Kensington and Chelsea Council sent a letter directing him to remove the blog or face legal implications for his 'defamatory' posts.[2]

The blog stayed up, and three years later, in 2016, a grimly prescient post foretold the coming disaster: 'It is a truly terrifying thought but the Grenfell Action Group firmly believe that only a catastrophic event will expose the ineptitude and incompetence of our landlord.'[3]

Six months later, Grenfell Tower was engulfed in flames. In the weeks following, residents, journalists and activists wrote scores of articles dissecting the origins of the tragedy. One article used particularly apt wording stating that Grenfell resulted from many things: cost-cutting; greed; apathy towards the lives of others. But most of all it stemmed from the 'wilful ignorance of experts' who were determined not to perceive or resolve the peril that residents knew they were facing.[4]

CREDIBILITY DEFICITS

The Grenfell tragedy is a stark reminder of the ways people are judged to be inferior knowers. Grenfell residents knew their lives were at risk, but their lack of political clout or social status made them easy to ignore. They were subjected to a specific form of dismissal so widespread that it often happens without comment or rebuke – the presumption that someone lacks the knowledge to pass authoritative judgement about a given situation. In this case, Grenfell residents were deemed incapable of judging their own safety. They were presumed to be ignorant, a presumption that underscores a terrible irony. Grenfell *did* result from ignorance, but not from the residents. Rather, the will to ignorance was mastered by expert authorities who wielded the power to dismiss residents' concerns.

The Grenfell tragedy illuminates the persistence of something the philosopher Miranda Fricker describes as 'testimonial injustice,' the tendency for some individuals to experience *credibility deficits* – the undervaluing of a person's ability to understand or prescribe a sound course of action in a given situation. Fricker contrasts the notion of credibility deficit with *credibility excess*, the tendency to be perceived as especially intelligent or authoritative even if one has no right to be judged so.[5]

Often, credibility deficits are rooted in blatant stereotypes, such as negative perceptions of another person's intelligence or aptitude based on skin colour, gender or accent. The opposite instinct is also true. Whether we are willing to admit it or not, many of us have assumed someone must be a source of authority on a topic because they sound and look so: the expensively dressed middle-aged man who commands more respect than his counterpart with a working-class accent.

One of the clearest examples of testimonial injustice occurs whenever a person or a group of people is denied recognition and reparation for past injustices until someone who is *not* among or descended from the injured party admits that the abuse took place. Those who have first-hand experience of suffering or who grew up in families where accounts of violence were passed down are treated as incapable of giving a definitive understanding of the injustice. Often, the ill-treatment their families suffered only becomes real to a larger majority when a member of the majority admits that abuse occurred. And yet typically, members of the majority often benefit from persistent ignorance of the injustice in question, and for this reason undeniable abuse is somehow denied for decades, even centuries, and when it's finally recognized by a wider public, people suggest it happened so long ago that to speak of it is counter-productive.

A further illustration can be taken from the lethal policies carried out against native groups in Canada during the colonial period and beyond. In 2013, James Daschuk, a little-known assistant professor of health studies at the University of Regina, published a book called *Clearing the Plains* that detailed the severity of Canada's treatment of indigenous peoples. It became a surprise success: a bestseller read widely by the Canadian general public, reviewed in leading national newspapers, and awarded the most esteemed book prize in Canada, a Governor General's award.

Daschuk's book challenged conventional understandings of why people from indigenous communities died in much greater numbers than neighbouring settler communities after the establishment of the Canadian dominion in 1867. He documents a turning point in government policy: the appointment of John A. Macdonald, Canada's first prime minister and the individual most responsible, Daschuk and others argue, for the forced starvation campaigns that led many First Nations to die when the Canadian government wilfully breached treaties by refusing to deliver food to starving groups in the prairies. Macdonald also oversaw the establishment of residential schools, where at least 6000 children died – this number is only an estimate because Canadian authorities chose to stop counting the dead in 1920.[6]

'The first question one might ask is, why is this history so unknown?' political theorist Niigaanwewidam James Sinclair writes in a review of Daschuk's book. 'The documentation is clearly there, and First Nations historians have been relaying stories of starvation, legal impositions, and resistance for decades.'[7]

Ignorance of the past is compounded by the chequered education even the most highly educated Canadians receive. 'First Nations people know this story,' Daschuk said during a public talk in Ottawa. 'But what I'm really surprised about is that white Canadians haven't heard this story, because it's not taught in schools.'[8]

First Nations accounts have been dismissed as a sort of non-knowledge, an interpretation of the past that was never acknowledged *as* the past until Daschuk, a white scholar, testified to the truthfulness of their accounts. Although the injured group's version proves accurate in the end, the fact that it takes a dominant and often oppressive group to confirm that it took place only underscores the pernicious relationship of inequality that endures – and at times is even magnified – through attempts to redress injustice.

The brutality of Canada's starvation of indigenous groups is both known and unknown. Historians and media columnists often admit that treaties were illegally breached, but the involvement of national icons such as Macdonald is skirted over.

Jeffrey Simpson, a columnist for the nation's most eminent newspaper, the *Globe and Mail*, has dismissed recent criticism of Macdonald's legacy as 'presentism,' the application of moral standards to a historical period where they were absent. He argues that presentism 'always deforms history because it reads back today's mores and beliefs and assumptions into a time in which we did not live.'[9]

There is nothing particularly surprising about Simpson's viewpoint – it is widely shared. But what *would* be wrong is to assume it is grounded in a command of historical knowledge when really it is grounded in a command of historical ignorance. For Simpson to stand his ground about Macdonald, he needs to resist rather than to pursue knowledge that could undermine his understanding of the past. By using the word 'presentism,' for example, he implies that moral outrage over the treatment of native groups was absent in Macdonald's day.

But that is not the case. In Canada, ambivalence over the righteousness of Macdonald's treatment of native groups was evident in popular newspapers. An 1888 cartoon in *Grip*, a Canadian satire magazine, shows Macdonald huddled with Edgar Dewdney, Lieutenant-Governor of the Northwest Territories. 'Indians starving?' Macdonald asks. 'Oh well,' he answers himself. 'They're not "friends of Dewdney," you know. I'll see that *you* don't come to want, though, Mr. Contractor.'[10]

And long before Macdonald was ever in power in Canada, there was loud debate among European philosophes over the ethical treatment of earlier inhabitants of conquered lands.

Writing in the 1740s, Montesquieu was one of the earliest enlightenment thinkers to publicly consider whether the 'new' world's indigenous inhabitants should be treated as sovereign equals. Listening to stories of indigenous people from European missionaries, Montesquieu's answer is a self-satisfied hedge: 'All countries have a law of nations,' he writes in *Spirit of the Laws*, 'not excepting the Iroquois themselves, though they devour their prisoners: for they send and receive ambassadors, and understand the rights of war and peace. The mischief is that their law of nations is not founded on true principles.' This self-serving equivocality has characterized European debate over the rights of indigenous peoples for over four centuries.

It is inaccurate to suggest that concern over indigenous rights is merely a recent phenomenon, but many people, including celebrated scholars, do still argue this position. What renders their view of the past compelling is not the scope of their gaze but the convenience of their narrowness. To maintain that narrowness, believers must choose *not* to explore or admit facts that could destabilize a narrative they wish to see as inalterable. They must become masters of the unknown.

AGNOTOLOGY AND ITS LIMITS

The fact that dominant histories of the past tend to be selectively narrow, that the powerful often 'unknow' uncomfortable truths, is a reason to be cautious about recent mainstream media attention to the problem of 'agnotology.'

On the one hand, it's a good thing that news media are studying the problem of agnotology, but sometimes, this news coverage misunderstands the main point of earlier academic work, which is that *all* organizations (and all individuals) have incentives to disregard inconvenient information. Experts are not immune to the problem of strategic ignorance any more than 'lay' individuals are.

Take a recent article from British economist and journalist Tim Harford. Writing in the *Financial Times*, Harford uses the word 'agnotology' to explore political volatility in the Brexit and Trump era. He emphasizes the claim made by Leave campaigners who suggested the UK sends '£350m a week to the EU' and if the UK left, the money could be spent on the NHS. It's 'hard to think of a previous example in modern western politics of a campaign leading with a transparent untruth, maintaining it when refuted by independent experts, and going on to triumph anyway.' He suggests that to combat agnotology and the deliberate manufacture of ignorance, experts need to find better ways to engage 'incurious' voters: those who prefer 'football, *Game of Thrones* or baking cakes' to discussions about 'banking reform.' He ends the article with a plea to academics to find better ways to pique the interest of average citizens through presentations of 'official data from the likes of the World Bank.'[11]

His article is well-meaning and the problem he diagnoses is correct: deliberate misinformation did affect the EU vote. But his remedy is misguided, or at least overly one-sided. With Brexit, the problem isn't necessarily that people were incurious about the news. Harford doesn't provide empirical evidence to support this claim, and, indeed, voter turn-out for the Brexit vote (72.2 per cent) was higher than every general election since 1992, suggesting the opposite of incuriosity. While Harford is justified in criticizing propaganda, he doesn't offer any suggestions for holding the powerful to account; instead he flips the problem onto the public.

He also exaggerates the exceptionality of lies in the Brexit era. We often don't like to hear about it, but deception by the powerful is more common than he admits. A famous example stems from the Suez crisis of 1956. France and the United Kingdom were both alarmed by Egypt's nationalization of the Suez Canal Company, but there was little domestic support for military intervention. Britain and France plotted with Israel for Israel to launch an attack on Egypt that the French and British could then pretend to be surprised by, giving Britain a pretext to intervene, landing blows on Egypt while appearing to referee the battle. Conservative Prime Minister Anthony Eden called for a protocol of the plot to be destroyed, but leaks still dribbled out. It took 40 years, but evidence of the plot is now stored in Kew National Archives.[12]

'General elections are always dismal affairs,' the British economist John Maynard Keynes complained of the 1931 national elections, 'but I do not think I remember any election in which more outrageous lies were told by leading statesmen.'[13]

More recently, there are ongoing questions over whether former Prime Minister Tony Blair lied to the British public about the Iraq war. At the least, he disparaged the idea that oil demand was a motivation for the military invasion, even while his ministers admitted in covert meetings as early as 2002, a year before the invasion started, that making sure British companies could profit from Iraq's oil was an objective for the British government. In 2011, investigative journalists Greg Muttitt and Paul Bignell obtained documents detailing secret meetings between oil companies such as BP and Shell and Blair's government ministers and civil servants. Minutes from one secret meeting in October 2002 stated that Elizabeth Symons, then the Labour trade minister in Blair's government, 'agreed that it would be difficult to justify British companies losing out in Iraq.' Symons promised BP and Shell that she would lobby on their behalf and 'report back' to the companies about her efforts within two months. These covert discussions took place in 2002. One year later, Tony Blair called it 'absurd' that oil exploitation could be a factor leading to war, but his minister's earlier meetings with oil companies suggest otherwise.[14]

Even former chairman of the US Federal Reserve, Alan Greenspan, admitted that oil was an impetus for the invasion, writing in his memoir: 'I am saddened that it is politically inconvenient to acknowledge what everyone knows: the Iraq war is largely about oil.'[15]

The point I'm making is simple: the belief that the EU vote was characterized by a rare case of deception is troubling in light of the many historical examples that provide evidence otherwise. This reinforces a larger question asked throughout this book: which individuals are the most irresponsible 'homo ignorans' – the misinformed, or the ones deliberately misinforming?

Contrary to widespread belief, it is rarely the poorest or least-educated members of society whose ignorance produces the most catastrophic effects for other people. The poor might follow a demagogue or a propagandist, but the ability to spread lies relies on well-financed channels, as Chapter 3 shows.

THE LEGITIMACY OF QUESTIONING EXPERT AUTHORITY

People often presume a course of action is advisable because an expert says it is true, but this tendency can imperil human livelihoods, as the 2007–2008 financial crisis made clear. Oxford government professor Ian Goldin has made this argument well. 'The financial sector is home to the biggest and most powerful expert system, from banks to treasuries to the International Monetary Fund. The 2008 Financial Crisis highlighted the inadequacy of that system,' he writes. 'The denial of evidence is irrational, but it is not necessarily irrational to challenge experts and authorities.'[16]

It's an insightful point: just because there are a lot of decent and well-informed experts at the IMF and World Bank doesn't mean the organizations as a whole are above questioning or rebuke, especially given how wrong experts got things in the lead up to the financial disaster of 2008. When Harford suggests that 'official data from the likes of the World Bank' should be marshalled *against* agnotology, he turns a blind eye to legitimate concerns over expert ignorance at the World Bank and IMF.

As *Guardian* economics editor Larry Elliot observes, there has rarely been any admission from 'the IMF or World Bank that the policies they advocated during the heyday of the so-called Washington Consensus – austerity, privatisation and financial liberalisation – have contributed to weak and unequal growth, with all the political discontent that this has caused.'[17] The lack of institutional soul-searching at these organizations post 2008 is a sort of strategic ignorance, and in recent years, academics have published accounts of 'institutional ignorance' at the IMF.[18]

Goldin and Elliot's criticism is controversial not due to the outlandishness of their statements (their criticisms of the IMF are quite mild), but because of a problem that, for want of any better framing I've seen, I label the Bannon–Pinker conundrum – after two figures who have amassed widespread public followings for different reasons: Steven Pinker and Breitbart mastermind Stephen Bannon.

THE BANNON–PINKER CONUNDRUM

Bannon is at the forefront of propagandist efforts to demonize what he calls a 'globalist' conspiracy to undermine the interests of western nation states and what he sees as a superior Judeo-Christian world outlook. His anti-foreigner views are deservedly condemned by centrist political thinkers including Steven Pinker, who has criticized Bannon's ideas.

But the Pinker–Bannon conundrum is this: although Pinker disavows racism, he also tends to imply that *any* criticism of globalization, no matter how reasonable or evidence-based, is 'anti-progress' as he puts it.

In doing so, he makes it seem as if the effort to make global institutions such as the World Bank and IMF more representative of the interests of developing nations and global workers who have been the main losers of financial-ized global capitalism is as odious as Bannon's nationalist propaganda. Pinker closes down possibilities for improving the World Bank or the IMF's structure by implying that any criticism of the status quo is the same as Bannon's anti-globalist stance – but it's not.

Many of us who have long studied the World Bank and IMF don't want these organizations shut down, but we do want them improved, and that means doing what academics should do: questioning their evidence base, including, for example, the World Bank's decades-long position on labour deregulation in poor nations.

Pinker is at the helm of a new force in politics: celebrity intellectuals who peddle a sort of 'accept your lot' populism with upbeat, near-evangelistic fervour. Writing in the 1990s, the political economist Albert Hirschman gave a label to 'accept your lot' defences of the status quo: he called it the 'futility thesis,' the fatalistic certainty that new policies inevi-tably make matters worse over all, so better not to change things at all.[19]

Since at least the 18th century, when modern ideas about political economy first emerged, futility arguments have been leveraged to justify steep wealth inequalities, just as Pinker does in a problematic way in his recent book, *Enlightenment Now*.

Futility arguments harness the apparent immutability of structural forces in a way that makes people feel better about their own worsening economic circumstances, or at least more stoically resigned to the difficulty of changing the world. Turn inwards, the message goes: improve yourself and not your peers or your 'betters.' It's a spiritual message, leveraged today by status quo intellectuals who popularize feel-good, low-hanging metrics like absolute global poverty reduction.

Pinker is right to point out that across the world, less people live in absolute poverty, but he has an attribution problem I return to in later chapters. He hails 'free' markets in a way that ignores the importance of government regulations in reducing poverty, as well as the key role of protest and labour movements in curbing predatory business practices and state violence.

He also pays scant attention to the worsening problem of in-country inequality in both rich and poor countries, a problem getting worse across the globe. For nearly 40 years, for example, the income of the majority of American workers has stayed flat or worsened in real terms, while the rich get richer. In 2017, as the BBC reported, average life expectancy stopped improving for the first time since 1982, when figures first began – and this dismal statistic can be linked to government austerity programmes that continue to hit the poorest the hardest.

The occasional times that Pinker *does* acknowledge that in-country inequality is worsening, he insists the suffering of

American and British workers is a fair 'tradeoff' for global poverty reduction. He even suggests that any efforts to improve economic inequality are 'ungrateful.'[20]

I suggest that to discount in-country inequality is irrational, if not dangerous, because doing so invites extremists like Bannon to serenade exploited workers who have good reason to suspect the economic picture isn't as rosy or fair as Pinker insists.

PSYCHOLOGICAL BLINKERS

I'm not making these points simply to criticize Pinker's thesis, but because he exemplifies this book's larger argument: that even smart people use data selectively. Even smart people can be elite agnotologists, a point that J.S. Mill made of Bentham: 'There is hardly anything in Bentham's philosophy which is not true. The bad part of his writings is his resolute denial of all that he does not see, of all truths but those which he recognises.'[21]

Status quo populists have a similar problem today. Pinker, for example, does an excellent job in his recent book, *Enlightenment Now*, describing psychological theories of information avoidance. This includes concepts such as 'confirmation bias,' where people are more likely to embrace facts that square with their earlier worldviews over facts that disconfirm them. But perhaps understandably for a psychologist, he knows his psychology well but his sociology less so. He often ignores organizational power dynamics that make it harder for some individuals more so than others to perceive their own cognitive blind-spots or to blow the whistle on bad behaviour.

A similar problem can be seen in an important article from psychologists Gerd Gigerenzer and Rocio Garcia-Retamero, published in 2017 in the journal *Psychological Review*. They asked two separate groups of people, one in Germany and one in Spain, a series of questions related to both 'negative' events and 'positive' ones, to gauge whether the respondents (900 in total) would want to know the outcome in advance if they could. Negative events included:

> Would you want to know today when your partner will die? No: 89.5 per cent.

> Would you want to know today from what cause you will die? No: 87.3 per cent.

> Assume you are newly married. Would you want to know today whether your marriage will eventually end in divorce or not? No: 86.5 per cent.

Positive events included:

> Assume you video-recorded a soccer World Cup game because you could not watch it live. While you are watching the recording, a friend enters who has already watched the game. Would you want to know from the friend how it ended (as opposed to asking not to tell)? No: 76.9 per cent.

> Would you want to know in advance what you are getting for Christmas? No: 59.6 per cent.

Would you like to know whether there is life after death? No: 56.9 per cent.

According to the Gigerenzer and Garcia-Retamero, the results show a surprisingly *low* desire for knowledge, and a high penchant for remaining deliberately ignorant of both bad and good outcomes about our lives. They emphasize that this finding jars with mainstream assumptions within psychology that claim the opposite: that humans tend to share a 'general need for certainty' and preference for 'ambiguity aversion.'[22]

The design of their study was new, but their findings square with other recent experiments from game theory and behavioural economics that reach the same conclusion: people often prefer to act on the basis of ignorance rather than knowledge.[23] In their article, they make a sharp distinction between the psychological realm and the social realm. 'Agnotology looks at how external sources maintain public ignorance, even against people's will,' they write, 'deliberate ignorance, in contrast, entails maintaining personal ignorance.'[24]

I don't think this is the best way to look at ignorance. I have been writing about the utility of ignorance for about 15 years. Gigerenzer and Garcia-Retamero cite my earlier research on the sociology of ignorance in their work on the psychology of ignorance, which I mention not just to score points, but to give context to my criticism. Their work on the psychology of ignorance is extremely valuable, but their definition is misplaced, in my view, because it makes it seem as if people's willingness to either acquire new information or to ignore information is divorced from external pressures. In reality, external forces *always* shape personal ignorance. Social taboos shape decisions over which truths are shared publicly and which truths are shamed into silence; and social power (as well as the socially powerful) sets agendas for what is known and what is not known.

This is especially true when one looks at how ignorance and knowledge flow through government agencies and corporations. As I show, whistle-blowers in the public and private sectors try to report crimes to the public – only to be ostracized by their peers or threatened with their jobs, dealt 'hard' and 'soft' forms of punishment that impose silence on insiders through the cultivation of intense company loyalty and the ever-present threat of stigmatization and redundancy.[25]

The strength of different organizations – social, economic, cultural – is often reliant on *not* articulating the ways that internal practices conflict with public perceptions of the organization's activities. The economist John Kenneth Galbraith put it well: 'in any great organization it is far, far safer to be wrong with the majority than to be right alone.'[26]

This type of collectively induced unknowing can happen at multiple levels, from the aversion to knowing sordid details about close family members (such as their sex lives or their addictions), to the level of the nation, where citizens typically resent the effort to draw attention to global atrocities carried out by their own governments in both the past and the present. As political philosopher Gayatri Spivak points out, societies often derive a sense of national identity through what she terms 'sanctioned ignorance' of state crimes that could undermine a sense of national respectability or honour.

Sanctioned ignorance leads to distorted national self-understandings of the past that remain prevalent in textbooks and popular discourses not necessarily because of lay or 'voter ignorance' (a concept from political science explored further in Chapter 3), but because of *elite* ignorance, and the fact that most school and university textbooks still favour a reading of British history that is slanted towards celebrating its history of political liberalism rather than asking how its imperialism undermines the claim to having had a liberal past during the 19th century.

Many branches of philosophy and international relations continue to see 18th- and 19th-century political and economic liberalism as projects of 'inclusion,' devoted to extending human rights universally, rather than confront a harsher truth: that 19th-century liberalism was actually an illiberal period of continued conquest, including the British perpetuation of the 'coolie trade,' which led to the forced abduction and enslavement of tens of thousands of indentured workers from India and China. This occurred even as prominent philosophers at home such as J.S. Mill publicly praised Britain's exceptionality as a nation that abhorred slavery.

Legal slavery and indentured servitude *are* different and I'm not suggesting otherwise. But the practices share a lot of similarities. Tens of thousands (at a low estimate) of indentured servants were kidnapped and coerced to work against their consent, and also suffered routine flogging and even torture, abuse that took place both as an inducement to emigrate and during the periods when servants were 'bonded' to their employer in foreign lands, with little opportunity to avail themselves of their legal rights.[27]

Domestic politics were also oppressive for the majority of British subjects in the 19th century. It is not widely known, for example, that a large proportion of men in the United Kingdom only gained the right to vote in 1918; millions of working-class men fought in WWI without a say in their own government. The British often celebrate the enfranchisement of women following WWI but neglect the fact that 40 per cent of men only gained the vote then too.[28] The obfuscation of British history unfolds in subtle ways through the comparative omission of working-class and female perspectives in textbooks.[29]

It's a cliché that history is written by the victors, but that doesn't make the problem any less frustrating for people whose histories are side-lined, or for educators who aspire to truthful teaching, because the earlier suppression of information can introduce historical distortions that are passed on unwittingly as fact.

In Britain's case, the legacy of colonialism is still not appreciated enough in schools or universities, in part because of the effort to destroy evidence about colonial brutality, a problem journalist Ian Cobain details in his book *The History Thieves*.[30] Throughout colonialism, British officials drowned and burned incriminating files; then, in the mid-20th century, as colonies gained independence, aware that African leaders might question the absence of pertinent minutes or reports, British civil servants were told to fabricate false files to replace ones that had been removed.[31]

Governments that obfuscate their role in human rights abuses are often excused from having to answer for egregious actions, while national mythmaking also fuels elite ignorance at the academic level, because mythologized understanding of a nation's past comes to be slowly misperceived as factual reality, leading to misinformed policy solutions. A good example is the belief that the British state was largely uninvolved in building or regulating economic markets during the 19th century.

Long viewed as a 'free market' bastion, the UK is widely seen as having an economically liberal government rather than a 'protectionist' one during that period. Even someone as astute as the British journalist Paul Mason has made this mistake, claiming that in the 19th century 'the state stood back to let market forces rip and allow businesses to stand or fall' – whereas today, what marks out the current economy is the flow of ongoing government support to corporate beneficiaries. Mason is right that western governments today extensively subsidize the private sector, but he is wrong to suggest this is a new practice – that in the 19th century, the British government 'stood back' from business. The British government was strongly interventionist then just as it is strongly interventionist now.[32]

Domestic measures such as Britain's repeal of protectionist Corn Laws have been romanticized in a way that overshadows 19th-century subsidies to industry groups, including government subsidies to West Indies plantation owners which offset the already rock-bottom cost of hiring indentured labour, or the government compensation offered to former slave owners after slavery was abolished across British colonies in the 1830s. Throughout the century, the British government forcefully intervened in the shaping of both domestic and global economic markets, including the use of military force to impose unfair and unfree trade terms on other nations, like the Treaty of Nanking, one of a succession of 'unequal treaties' with China that led to a thriving illegal trade in indentured servants.

As journalist Pankaj Mishra points out, the violent underpinnings of 'free' trade are not entirely unknown: this history *is* taught today in former colonies such as India, and Indian economists such as Utsa Patnaik have carried out extensive research calculating the cost of colonialism to India. But when Mishra left India in his 20s and travelled in England and North America, he was surprised to find that 'violence had been carefully hidden from its long-term beneficiaries.'[33]

Later sections in this book explore various strategies of ignorance that help to explain *how* this violence was obscured over the 19th and 20th centuries, as well as the way that language tricks continue to enable organizations such as the World Bank to obscure labour exploitation today.

A NEW DEFINITION OF RATIONAL IGNORANCE

As well as drawing on recent agnotology literature, this book builds on earlier scholarship from a small and still neglected body of academic research from feminist and racism studies that has begun to analyse the value of ignorance to powerful groups.[34] This work on workplace racism, sexual discrimination and white-collar crime explores the ways that deliberate unknowing can be a common feature of everyday life.[35]

Take an example from the philosopher Charles Mills, a Jamaican-American scholar who has published important research on the way that ignorance can bolster white supremacist thinking and racial hierarchies. He points out that even in eras when racial injustice is blatantly obvious, calling attention to injustice can be dangerous because powerful groups have an incentive to punish people who speak out. He gives the example of an American black woman recalling life under Jim Crow racial segregation laws:

> My problems started when I began to comment on what I saw … I insisted on being accurate. But the world I was born into didn't want that. Indeed, its very survival depended on not knowing, not seeing – and certainly, not saying anything at all about what it was really like.[36]

Charles Mills is rare among major political philosophers for placing the study of ignorance at the centre of his understanding of political power in modern history, but there are other outliers. Indeed, Socrates was among the first great thinkers to appreciate the personal and political importance of ignorance, claiming that his wisdom lay in realizing what he didn't know.

Philosopher Hannah Arendt is another exception. Although she never used the term 'strategic ignorance,' she grasped that bureaucratic and corporate anonymity can provide release from individual liability, leading to systems of domination where 'no men, neither one nor the best, neither the few nor the many, can be held responsible.'[37] When it comes to corporations, there's a legal term for this type of impunity; it's known as the 'corporate veil.'

Finally, there's a small core of thinkers with political science and economic game theory who have specifically used the word 'ignorance' to understand the utility of unknowing, including Rawls' concept of the 'veil of ignorance' and political scientist Anthony Downs' notion of 'rational ignorance,' both of which were developed in the mid-20th century.

The veil of ignorance is a thought experiment Rawls developed to consider whether most people would prefer more egalitarian societies if they had the choice. When arguing from behind a Rawlsian 'veil of ignorance' people are asked to consider if they would condone practices like slavery if it is impossible for them to ever know whether they or their children would ever be enslaved or not.

Downs defined 'rational ignorance' as the tendency *not* to obtain new information when the cost of educating oneself about a new issue exceeds the advantages that the knowledge would confer. Downs' definition is influential in some circles of political science, but it's also a deeply problematic way to understand ignorance because it implies that future costs or benefits can be known in advance.[38]

I propose a different definition of rational ignorance. I suggest we define it as recognition that ignorance is always greater than knowledge, at both the collective and individual level. This might seem like an obvious point, but it actually challenges the dominant post-Enlightenment view, encompassed, for example, by the US statesman James Madison, who suggested that 'Knowledge will forever govern ignorance.'[39] The enlightenment fallacy has long been K > I. Madison gets the order wrong and it's time for a reversal, not out of nihilism, but out of empirical accuracy. I'm with Socrates: what we don't know governs what we do know.

I also argue that human beings are *equal unknowers*. We are *all* unknowers in two important respects. First, in the noun sense of the word. Each of us is an unknower because, obviously, no one is omniscient. And secondly, in the verb sense of the word, we *all* equally unknow: our actions are enabled and rationalized through unceasing processes of ignoring, through a necessarily selective engagement with knowledge around us.

My emphasis on *equal* unknowers is important to my argument. At first glance, it might seem to contradict my point about power and ignorance – my suggestion that some people are better positioned to exploit their own and other peoples' ignorance. I *do* insist this is the case and I spend upcoming chapters making this argument. But, at the same time, no hierarchy of ignorance is unchanging. No one can maintain a permanent monopoly on the unknown. And most importantly, measuring what someone does not know is impossible.

Because of the impossibility of ranking human ignorance, it becomes equally impossible to ever permanently rank human beings. People will likely never stop trying to stratify human worth according to intelligence or knowledge. Today, a movement defending so-called race and gender 'realism' is gaining force. It's an effort which resuscitates 19th-century ideas about biological superiority to argue that some races are 'naturally' more intelligent than others, or that men are 'naturally' more rational than women.

The problem with the resurgence of 'race realism' theory isn't simply that we have enough historical knowledge about the ways intelligence tests can be manipulated to be extremely wary about using their findings in policy making. Or that the 'science' of human difference, such as 19th-century phrenology which linked intelligence to skull size, tends to be discredited as science advances, another reason not to use pseudoscience in policy making today.[40] But even more fundamentally, to extrapolate from studies of human difference to make claims about the inherent inequality of human beings, as some on the alt-right do, has no scientific or philosophical legitimacy.

Indeed, enlightenment ideas about the value of labour specialization and the ways that human difference generates reciprocal need are, essentially, epistemological arguments about the impossibility of human survival without a social contract and political system that respects human difference, and, importantly (a point made by Adam Smith) regulates economic processes in a manner that rebalances structural advantages enjoyed by some groups (typically wealthy groups, Smith emphasizes) at the expense of others.

Some individuals *do* have more specialist expertise than other people. But even the most enlightened people are fundamentally 'ignorant' at some level. Humans are united by their unknowing. This reality should be welcomed rather than denigrated by individuals who are committed to the principle of human equality.

The relevance of these points for understanding social change and social stagnation is under-acknowledged in the social sciences. The idea that we should view ignorance as 'greater' than knowledge still strikes many people as doubtful, alarming, cynical, defeatist or simply stupid. But recognition of the power of ignorance is anything but irrational. The utility of ignorance as a tool of power is that it is a tool of reason. Once this point is accepted, it opens up new channels of social scientific investigation, because 'ignorance' becomes easier to see.

CHAPTER 2

SEEING
IGNORANCE
DIFFERENTLY

Ignorance is often perceived with moral censure, as something that is purely bad. But there are good types of ignorance. One example is the long-standing belief in western systems of law that the law should adjudicate 'blindly,' in conditions of deliberately imposed ignorance about specific aspects of a person's life that are deemed immaterial to a legal case.

One person's use of 'ignorance' may be the means to their survival. Fomenting public ignorance about Anne Frank and her family's location helped to keep them safe for a period. But more powerful forms of strategic ignorance were at work, from Hitler's efforts to keep his imperialist ambitions secret from other world powers in the early 1930s, to his lies and demagoguery at home. His malevolent deployment of ignorance trumped the efforts of Frank's allies to hide her.

Below, I introduce new concepts that illuminate the many faces of useful ignorance in more depth.

USEFUL UNKNOWNS

The first is 'useful unknowns,' defined as gaps in human understanding which provide clear benefits for different individuals and groups, even in situations where the beneficiaries may not have knowingly manufactured the unknown to begin with.

I developed this term after carrying out interviews with pharmaceutical regulators – individuals working at the Food and Drug Administration (FDA) in the United States, and its UK equivalent, the Medicines and Healthcare Products Authority – to understand how employees within these two regulatory agencies tried to protect public safety when faced with persistent uncertainty over the risk–benefit profile of popular pharmaceutical drugs.

The concept builds on earlier studies from historians and public health scholars who have explored the way that science-intensive industries like big food and big pharma often benefit from deliberately compounding uncertainty over whether their own corporate actions were directly responsible for disease or damage to the environment. 'Doubt is our product,' tobacco company executives used to say: keep uncertainty percolating and feign astonishment whenever more evidence of the links between smoking and lung cancer is revealed. Coca-Cola is another example: the company is proven to have paid university researchers at Harvard University and elsewhere to carry out studies to try to refute the idea that excessive consumption of sugar is linked to growing obesity levels in children, deliberately creating more uncertainty – more unknowns – about just how bad sugary drinks are for children's diets.[1]

In other situations, scientific unknowns don't stem from the deliberate creation of uncertainty. Rather, a lot of ignorance is naturally produced through happenstance and accident. Ignorance can be 'innocent,' to borrow a phrase from philosophers – and it can also be a force for good, spurring groundbreaking scientific advances.

Former US Secretary of Defense Donald Rumsfeld pointed to the complexity of ignorance when he offered his now-infamous remark about the problem of 'unknown unknowns' nearly 20 years ago. Rumsfeld offered his much-quoted comment during a Department of Defense briefing in 2002, in response to being pressed about the existence of weapons of mass destruction in Iraq. 'As we know, there are known knowns; there are things we know we know,' he said. 'We also know there are known unknowns; that is to say we know there are some things we do not know. But there are also unknown unknowns – the ones we don't know we don't know.'[2]

He is right. The full realm of the unknown is quite literally unknowable, and we do not know exactly how much we do not know.

But Rumsfeld's take on ignorance is also a highly limited one. He doesn't mention 'useful unknowns' – uncertainty which isn't necessarily generated by any one, identifiable stakeholder, but which is still beneficial for different stakeholders, often at the expense of a wider public. Just look at the near-collapse of the global finance and banking sectors over

2007–2008, where despite evidence of fraud, bank executives are generally seen as having gotten off remarkably lightly. While many companies faced stiff fines, the US chose not to jail executives whose activities were proven to be fraudulent. In other countries like Iceland, bankers who broke the law did serve time, but in the US fraudsters generally got off scot-free. Useful unknowns were mobilized opportunistically by various traders, bank executives and regulators in at least three key ways.

First, as *Financial Times* journalist Gillian Tett points out, some traders deliberately failed to raise the alarm on early warning signs surrounding the likelihood of mass homeowner defaults on subprime mortgages because feigning ignorance benefited their own trading positions. It was more profitable to say nothing, fuelling 'social silence' over perceivable financial risks. This earlier silence then helped the same traders to later avoid convictions for fraud because widespread 'social silence' in the years leading up to 2008 made it seem plausible that 'no one knew' a collapse was imminent. The fact that very few insiders publicly raised the alarm generated a useful defence in avoiding criminal convictions, because prosecutors were able to argue successfully that it was unreasonable to hold individuals responsible for a problem 'nobody could see.'[3]

Second, social silence wasn't just personally useful for traders and investment brokers. It also gave regulators an excuse for their own inaction and the failure at the Securities and Exchange Commission (SEC) and Federal Reserve Board to act swiftly upon known concerns about the mispricing of different classes of derivatives. Both regulators and traders had a shared interest in professing ignorance both before and after the collapse.

Third, ignorance was mobilized in order to command a sort of financial ransom from the government. Faced with impending collapse, a third 'useful unknown' emerged (useful for banks at least, but not the general public): the unknown level of exposure of Wall Street investment banks to their own toxic assets, a 'problem' mobilized as a trump card in forcing the hand of the US government to come to the financial rescue. Investment banks were saved not because of blamelessness, but because their recklessness was on such a massive scale that measuring the full risk created by the banks' exposure to their own bad loans was impossible. As one insider put it:

> There's no limit to the risk in the market. A bank with a market capitalization of one billion dollars might have one trillion dollars' worth of credit default swaps outstanding. No one knows how many there are! And no one knows where they are![4]

A similar remark was made by the economist Anna Schwartz, co-author with Milton Friedman of *A Monetary History of the United States, 1867 to 1960*, a book that has been influential on regulatory policy in the United States over recent decades.

'The real problem was that because of the mysterious new instruments that investors had acquired, no one knew which firms were solvent or what assets were worth,' Schwartz writes in an editorial in the *New York Times* in 2009. 'Investors who loaded up their balance sheets with these securities were ignorant of the great risks of trying to sell assets that are difficult to price.'[5]

Schwartz goes on to blame Ben Bernanke, who became head of the US Federal Reserve officials in 2006, for failing to detect the problem. 'Ultimately,' she suggests, '[Bernanke] failed to convince the market that the Fed had a plan.'

Schwartz's editorial displays strategic ignorance on her part, entrenching the myth that 'no one knew' that new financial derivatives were posing a threat to global markets prior to 2007. This is not true. As early as 2002, investors such as Warren Buffett termed derivatives 'weapons of mass financial destruction' and called for tighter regulation. Mainstream economists and regulators, especially those influenced by Schwartz and Milton Friedman's school of monetary policy, pooh-poohed their warnings. The avalanche of mispriced derivatives that Schwartz berates did not materialize as recently as she implies. The derivatives boom gained momentum over the two decades prior, a period when Alan Greenspan, a strong adherent of Schwartz and Friedman's monetary ideas, was head of the Federal Reserve for 19 years.

If warnings from Buffett and others were acted upon, the financial crisis might not have reached the devastating proportions that it did. Lives, jobs and homes could have been saved, and the Wall Street executives who were ultimately responsible for the mispricing of assets might have faced more scrutiny before it was too late, as well as jail time after the crisis hit.

These Wall Street leaders are not simply a manifestation of homo ignorans, they are *the* supreme manifestation of homo ignorans: those so adept at harnessing the useful unknowns around them that no other actor is safely insulated from the repercussions of what bank executives either could not or chose not to know. Far from being all-knowing masters of the universe, the instigators of one of the largest financial crises in history were abetted by the capacity to seem as uninformed as possible.

IGNORANCE ALIBIS

I define 'ignorance alibis' as any mechanism that obscures one's involvement in causing harm to others, furnishing plausible deniability and making unawareness seem innocent rather than calculated.

The phrase 'plausible deniability' was coined in the mid-20th century, and it is a useful concept for understanding why leaders might avoid or at least seem to avoid information that could be politically damaging to admit knowing.

But plausible deniability is also a much larger social phenomenon than simply leaders 'knowing what not to know.'[6] Denial is intertwined with feelings of self-respect and moral righteousness at a deeply personal level, as people are taught the norms of conduct of their social surroundings at an early age and told, often well-meaningly, that it is impolite to speak aloud about distressing or hurtful things.

'If you can't say anything nice,' the old saying goes. It may be a cliché, but the pervasiveness of the sentiment has real effects, leading people to censor themselves and others in subtle ways that reinforce large-scale 'ignorance alibis' as people insist they could not have known about seemingly evident atrocities because no one ever spoke of it.

The concept of ignorance alibis builds on earlier criminological studies of 'states of denial,' the criminologist Stanley Cohen's term for rationalizations that allow people and groups of people to avoid confronting truths that feel psychologically and culturally impossible to accept. In his words:

> People react as if they do not know what they know. Or else the information is registered – there is no attempt to deny the facts – but its implications are ignored ... I became stuck with the term 'denial' to cover this whole range of phenomena. I have never been able to find an alternative word – even though its conceptual ambiguities are so gross.[7]

Denial is similar to the problem that Audre Lorde described as 'historical amnesia,' the wilful forgetting of past atrocities and their ongoing effect on the present age.[8] 'Free trade' and 'empire' are good examples. Many people will readily acknowledge that British imperialism was underpinned by industrial dominance during the 19th century, but the same scholars label the 19th century a time of 'free trade' – even though economic exchange compelled through military occupation is obviously not 'free.' Only by accepting and perpetuating the racist 19th-century illusion that China and India do not count as real nations can economic liberals today still point to the 19th century as a high period of 'free trade.'

Recall the British government's decision in the mid-20th century to create false files to replace evidence destroyed by colonial authorities. Is 'denial' really the right word for such systemic fabrication? Rather than denial, we should speak more about the ignorance fuelled through affirmation, and the way that official narratives often furnish an aura of completeness that is false.[9]

The 1920 decision by Canadian authorities to stop counting the number of indigenous children who died after being forcibly removed from their families illustrates the same problem. The Canadian government's actions make it hard to precisely know the full scale of abuse against children and their families. The success of past silencing efforts enables racially and economically dominant groups to cling to ignorance alibis in the present. The erasure of alternative histories within dominant discourses makes it easier to ignore histories that our forebears successfully eclipsed.[10]

Strategies of ignorance are most powerful when their machinations are least apparent. To prove the utility of ignorance, researchers must demonstrate that strategic ignorance has a material concreteness that undermines its own ontological status. Ironically, once ignorance is defined, it loses its very definition.[11]

'Many of the factors that shaped modern political life remain obscure to us,' the historian Sophia Rosenfeld writes. 'Some of these factors are now imperceptible because they were private, illegal, off-limits, or socially marginal.'[12]

She makes a very good point, but the lumping together of 'private' and 'socially marginal' is problematic, implying a false equivalence between those who have the financial means to choose privacy and those who were involuntarily silenced or ignored.

Take the example of the Grenfell fire in London in 2017. Immediately after the fire occurred, Kensington and Chelsea Council chose to ban media from some stakeholder discussions. The decision rightfully faced a torrent of criticism from resident groups and the media. But the more systematic ignoring of safety concerns before the fire hit doesn't always seem to elicit the same media outcry, perhaps because the dismissal of the views of residents of social housing projects is so routine that it is rarely deemed newsworthy.

Sociologists Akwugo Emejulu and Leah Bassel identify a similar sort of systematic ignoring in their study of policy attitudes toward minority women in Europe, and especially toward women who are seen as failing to situate their own persistent economic inequality in a policy lens that makes their hardship more palatable for mostly white policymakers. Those in power would take the economic immiseration of minority women seriously only when issues such as domestic violence were emphasized; in both France and England, minority women become 'visible and audible only as domestic violence victims or rendered invisible if they do not conform to this identity.'[13]

The systematic ignoring of marginalized voices has been studied at depth in postcolonial and feminist theory, but it's still not recognized enough in mainstream social science, despite ample examples of the ways that pathbreaking academic work by female scholars is effaced or ignored in practice. Take the example of Anna Schwartz, who I mentioned co-wrote *A Monetary History of the United States* with Milton Friedman.

Friedman was awarded a Nobel Prize in economics in 1976. Friedman himself acknowledged that Schwartz was an equal participant in the writing of their masterpiece, *A Monetary History*. Her name might come second on the book's jacket but alphabetical orderings are common in academia, and the very reliance on a neutral, alphabetical ordering is done to emphasize that a second author is not of secondary importance. And yet the Nobel committee deliberately ignored the fact that Friedman's *Monetary History* was not his book alone, glossing over the co-authorship with Schwartz even as they praised the book as the crowning zenith of Friedman's career. A press release from the Royal Swedish Academy in 1976 stated:

> His major work, *A Monetary History of the United States, 1867–1960*, is regarded as one of Friedman's most profound and also most distinguished achievements … The critics agree that this is a monumental scientific work which will long stimulate the re-examination of the course of events during this epoch.[14]

Schwartz's name does not appear once in the Swedish Academy's press release. Her contribution wasn't simply forgotten over time, it was wilfully ignored. This is not dissimilar to the historical erasure of Harriet Taylor's influence on Mill, although there are also important differences.

When *On Liberty* was first published in 1859, Mill dedicated the essay to Harriet, 'the inspirer,' he wrote, 'and in part the author, of all that is best in my writing.' But he still signed his name alone. For this reason, anyone who wants to continue seeing Mill as sole author has a legitimate reason for doing so – but there are also equally legitimate reasons to cite them both as co-authors today, particularly given Mill's insistence over many pages of his autobiography that she co-wrote every sentence of the essay *On Liberty* with him.[15]

In Schwartz's case, the historical censorship is even more clear-cut. There is no question that she co-wrote Friedman's 'monumental scientific achievement' with him. In this situa-tion, the Royal Swedish Academy's omission of Schwartz's name is clearly a deceptive action. By implying that Friedman alone wrote *A Monetary History*, the Academy is actively constructing an untruth – producing ignorance which later furnishes respectability for people who can claim in good faith that few great female economists have existed, because if they had, then esteemed organizations like the Nobel com-mittee would commemorate more of their names.

ORACULAR POWER

The Nobel example is a good illustration of what I term 'orac-ular power': the ability to shape social consensus about where the boundary between ignorance and knowledge lies. In the cases I've just described, powerful individuals and institu-tions were able to strategically displace Anna Schwartz and Harriet Taylor from the historical record, making it seem as if Mill and Friedman wrote their best work alone and not in collaborative partnerships with women, even though both Mill and Friedman insisted otherwise.

But 'oracular power' is a much bigger phenomenon than simply a few isolated examples of historical censorship. It's about different institutions and individuals being widely treated as possessing special enlightenment and almost mystical authority, even in secular societies.

I first started thinking about the notion of 'oracular power' a couple years ago as I was writing the first draft of this book. I thought of the concept in a purely metaphorical manner, as a way to illuminate the rarefied authority of different expert groups in modern western societies. I didn't actually think many social scientists actually believed in the divinity of policy advisors.

But recently, within some libertarian schools of thought, there are people who argue for the introduction of new, explicitly anti-democratic forms of decision making that draw on what proponents describe as the superior authority of 'simulated oracles' to determine the best course of economic or political action in any given situation.

Hannah Arendt used to refer to this type of rhetorical authority as 'pseudo-mysticism,' and I suggest the problem may be worsening today.

ORACULAR POWER IN HISTORICAL CONTEXT

The ancient Greeks saw an oracle as a person or entity imbued with an otherworldly ability to understand things that lesser mortals could not grasp and who could predict the future based on their powers as interpreters for the gods.[16]

Oracular predictions were often wrong, but this fallibility only strengthened their influence. To understand why one oracle's predictions turned out to be wrong, different oracles were routinely consulted. The market grew. There was money in oracles.

The ambiguity of oracular pronouncements also had an important social function: it reminded listeners of the unknowability of the gods. To see the oracles as omniscient would be an error. Oracles themselves were *not* gods, merely the earthly representatives of the gods. Their quasi-humanness made them vulnerable to occasional misunderstandings or unfulfilled predictions. However, they were not exactly the equals of other humans either, because their closeness to the gods tended to give their insights more heft than, say, a cousin insisting on the value of a new property venture.

All societies have hierarchies of ignorance, and in ancient Greece, oracles were positioned at the summit of the unknown. Indeed, it was the Oracle of Delphi who reminded Socrates of the limits of his own knowledge, helping him to understand that his wisdom lay in the ability to recognize his own ignorance.[17] Today, we can appreciate the sophistication of Socrates' insight into the importance of recognizing one's ignorance even if we don't accept that his wisdom came from divine revelation.[18]

Oracular power, in short, does not necessarily come from feigning certainty and insisting that a course of action is fool-proof. Rather, the power of oracles comes from the act of advising, something that furnished petitioners with demonstrable evidence that they had taken reasonable steps to consult the most appropriate authorities. Greek oracles were at the same time a source of personal consolation and a tool of public leverage, signalling to other people one's prudence in preparing for a major decision.

This leads to a question. Who are our modern oracles, the institutions and people seen as the most trusted authorities on the boundaries between knowledge and ignorance during an era of heightened anxiety over shifting geopolitical struggles? Or to put the question a little differently: which people are *upheld* as oracles, and why? I suggest three general categories of people come to mind. First, natural and social scientists and especially economists. Second, people who work with financial markets. And third, religious figureheads.

ORACULAR 'ENLIGHTENMENT'

Readers might balk at the analogy I'm drawing between scientists and oracles of the past. But I am not arguing that scientists do have mystical authority or that they should be treated as having special or super-human enlightenment. Indeed, the opposite should be the case. The reason their expertise should be esteemed is to act as a check on superstitious assumptions about social life. A scientist's expertise is hard-earned and often justly elite in nature – in the early 20th-century sense of 'elite' as someone with advanced knowledge or superior skills in any particular domain: whether that be elite sportsman, elite guitarist or elite debater.

Over the past 100 years, scientific experts have taken on increasingly visible roles as scientific advisors to politicians and government officials, and often, this advisory role is a praiseworthy one, giving hope to the belief that when political decisions are made in democratic nations, the interests of different constituencies are weighed through impartial means, rather than distorted by the demands of moneyed lobbyists or partisan cronies.

But problems arise when the separation between political lobbying and scientific expertise is distorted in practice, like Coca-Cola funding scientists who downplayed the health risks of sugar consumption. Taking money from a corporation while studying the safety of its products is a conflict of interest. It's the type of unethical behaviour that riled influential progressive leaders at the turn of the 20th century, like Louis Brandeis, an influential lawyer who argued there needs to be more checks on what he called the 'financial oligarchy': powerful groups whose use their wealth to secure special governmental privileges, undermining the rights of less powerful individuals.

Today, the problem of conflicts of interest at universities and think tanks appears to be getting worse. Certainly there are more private think tanks funded by wealthy individuals like Charles and David Koch around today than there were in Brandeis' day, leading to growing concern about 'dark money' and its influence on political, judicial and academic decision making.[19] The impartiality of scientific experts is facing challenge from citizens on the right and the left, a backlash that some people are a little too quick to dismiss as 'populist' resentment, as if citizens have no right to question expert authority or to ask whose payroll an academic is on. Mistrust of scientific experts is, in turn, producing another level of backlash, this time from experts resentful of the ways they are mistrusted by the general public.

This second level of backlash is my focus here. Rather than acknowledging the problem of 'dark money' is a serious and legitimate public concern, there's a worrying tendency among some social scientists and political theorists to insist that the public is simply too ignorant to grasp the superior wisdom of experts, and for this reason, they argue, there should be more limits on voting rights in western democracies.

One of them is Georgetown political theorist Jason Brennan, who wrote a recent book, *Against Democracy*, where he calls for the introduction of a new type of governance mechanism that he calls a 'simulated oracle.' It is a type of algorithm that determines a voter's 'best' interests by modelling her economic circumstances, and then forcing her to vote on the basis of the algorithm's choice rather than the voter's individual preference.

Brennan doesn't suggest 'simulated oracles' are divine, but he does believe the 'oracle' can process 'enlightened preferences' better than individuals can. For this reason, I argue that what Brennan is calling for is a type of mysticism, because his idea ascribes super-human capacities to 'simulated oracles' which treat individual judgement as inherently subordinate to collective wisdom. In Brennan's proposal, human judgement is deemed inferior to algorithmic group judgement – which somewhat ironically undermines his suggestion that it's a 'libertarian' idea, because in his model, an individual must bow to the algorithm. But there are other libertarians who point out the problems with his proposal, and I draw on their work below.

Economists and other scientists are not the only 'oracles' in western societies today. Another group of individuals who are credited with possessing exceptional insight are highly successful financial advisors. For example, the word 'oracle' is used a lot as shorthand in the financial media to describe savvy financial investors like Warren Buffett, the 'Oracle of Omaha.'

One could say it's just a catchy nickname for a highly talented financial investor – that few people actually think Warren Buffett has a special gift from God. But I'm not sure that assumption is as widely held as secular thinkers tend to assume. As the influential sociologist Max Weber suggests in his book *The Protestant Ethic and the Spirit of Capitalism* (1905), financial success was treated in some Calvinist religions circles in the 17th to 18th century as a sign of predestination: the belief that God had blessed wealthy individuals with their good fortune. His main point was that this powerful belief lingers even in eras where religion is less obviously influential in shaping norms of conduct.

Nation-states, too, have tended at the heights of their power to assume that their dominance is a sign of godly grace, a view prominent among English high society during the 18th and 19th centuries. In 1804, for example, Cambridge University introduced an annual award that invited undergraduates to compete for prizes for essays on topics such as

'The Probable Design of the Divine Providence in Subjecting So Large a Portion of Asia to the British Dominion.'[20] This tendency didn't die with the 20th century as is sometimes presumed. The Conservative MP Enoch Powell referred to the divine righteousness of British Empire in a speech in 1961, suggesting 'there was this deep, this providential difference between our empire and those others.'[21]

Over the 20th century, British imperialists reluctantly relinquished the baton of godly exceptionalism to the United States, where conservative Christians like Ronald Reagan peppered their speeches with chest-thumping praise for America's manifest destiny.

'We cannot escape our destiny, nor should we try to. The leadership of the free world was thrust upon us two centuries ago,' he suggested. 'We are indeed, and we are today, the last best hope of man on earth.'[22]

Reagan's providential allusions (greatness was 'thrust upon us') are, as Princeton sociologist Keeanga-Yamahtta Taylor points out, 'wholly contingent on the erasure or rewriting of three central themes in American history – genocide, slavery and the massive exploitation of waves of immigrant workers.' Reagan's market fundamentalism veiled the reality of 'massive government subsidies' that benefited white recipients more than other groups, hiding 'the state's role in the development of the American middle class.'[23]

Reagan's religious triumphalism hasn't died today. Military theorist Andrew Bacevich suggests that a problem facing the effort to rein in America's military expenditures and to force the nation's military elite to accept accountability for military failures in the Middle East is the fact that many citizens see the nation's global leadership as 'indispensable' and 'exceptional' and in all likelihood bequeathed by God. It's hard to say for certain how pervasive the belief is, or whether it's growing or not. Bacevich doesn't cite survey evidence. But whether or not the belief is shrinking or growing, it is clear that 19th-century manifest destiny theories of US power never entirely went away.

IGNORANCE UNSHARED

It's also clear that today different groups in many western nations are explicitly trying to undermine voting rights and other democratic principles in a manner that revives pro-authoritarian arguments from the 19th century and the 1920s and 1930s, and they call on the authority of different 'oracles' to make their arguments stronger. For analytical purposes, I have given a nickname to these different groups: I label them the autocratic *strongs* and the autocratic *smarts*.

This focus is quite abstract, but it is useful for two main reasons. First, it helps to explore the importance of 'oracular power' in practice: the ability to create or impose a consensus on where the boundary between the known and the unknown lies.

Second, the framework of *smarts* and *strongs* is directly related to my overarching focus on strategic ignorance. This is because both the *strongs* and the *smarts* camps deliberately mobilize and exploit the problem of ignorance and the 'unknown' as a rhetorical weapon in order to gain more power and legitimacy.

It is important to stress that it's not simply anti-democrats who draw on scientific 'oracles' to make their policy arguments stronger. Democratic policymakers also rely, and often rightly so, on scientific expertise. It's also true that democratic leaders sometimes invoke the will of God to placate their populaces during times of war and peace.

But what sets apart the *strongs* and the *smarts* camps is the strategic, oracular exploitation of ignorance to explicitly defend anti-democratic and anti-egalitarian policies. In democracies, the problem of ignorance is acknowledged to be a *shared* problem, whereas in autocratic societies, ignorance tends to be derided as a problem limited to the masses, one that elite rulers alone have the superior capacity to overcome.

One of the main arguments in this book is that it's a delusion to see ignorance in this way, as a problem solely or even mostly limited to poor or to uneducated voters, but it is also a very seductive delusion, especially at times when the electorate seems to make ill-informed decisions.

The *smarts* camp is my term for anti-democrat thinkers who advance the authoritarian idea of 'rule by knowers,' pointing to political surveys of 'voter ignorance' as a justification for stripping voting rights from men and women living in western democracies today.[24]

The *strongs*, on the other hand, often leverage ignorance in a more general way, exploiting the fact that the future is genuinely unknown (Rumsfeld's 'unknown unknowns') as a rationale for obtaining information in intrusive and violent ways, such as through torture, as Donald Trump has done.

But both camps also sometimes switch oracles. This happens, for example, when the *smarts* camp points to the 'mystery' of natural laws of the universe to defend extreme wealth concentration and growing wealth inequality. It also happens when representatives of the *strongs* camp point to the seeming reasonableness of social scientific evidence to defend a practice like torture.

A closer look at the 'oracular power' of the *smarts* and the *strongs* helps to make these points clearer.

I start with the example above: that of torture, which I turn to for a couple reasons. First, strange as it might initially seem, legal attempts to ban torture from taking place help show the functioning of 'good' ignorance in practice. Second, a focus on torture shows the ways that the rhetorical strategies of the *strongs* and the *smarts* are not necessarily opposed to each other in practice. Rather, these strategies are interspersed through both camps, with the *smarts* and the *strongs* often drawing on a mixture of smartmen oracles and strongmen oracles to legitimate different forms of economic exploitation and political violence.

TORTURE AND THE TESTIMONY OF EXPERTS

By 'good' ignorance, I mean types of deliberate unknowing that democratic communities collectively decide to uphold through formal prohibitions against obtaining knowledge in a manner that violates human rights.

One example is the Nuremberg Code. At the end of World War II, the scale of Nazi experimentation on living humans became apparent. The horror of the Nazi era was not simply the way that millions of Jewish individuals and other groups of people were heinously murdered, but also the way that many people were forced to live: subjected to endless, unthinkable cruelty in Nazi medical experiments.

Knowledge of this medical barbarism led to the Nuremberg Code, a set of ethical principles for medical experimentation on human beings, the first principle of which is that no human can be subject to medical experimentation without their consent. The Nuremberg Code is an affirmation of the moral importance of not knowing in some circumstances. If knowledge can only be obtained through non-consensual human harm, then no one has a right to that knowledge. Good ignorance occurs when limits to human experimentation are enforced by commendable human consensus, by a sacred will not to know.

The Nuremberg Code was just one set of global principles to emerge post WWII, including the Geneva Conventions of 1949, which helped to strengthen earlier prohibitions within international law against the inhumane treatment of prisoners of war. The Geneva Conventions expressly prohibit torture and all forms of cruel and inhumane treatment. But just as history often repeats itself, no human code is ever safe from violation. When George W. Bush was president, the US government extricated itself from the duty to adhere to the

Geneva Conventions through a variety of legal manipulations that enabled it to bypass provisions contained with a bill to which Bush's own party, the Republicans, had given full support a few years earlier through the 1996 War Crimes Act, which made it a federal crime to breach the Geneva Conventions.

The perceived weakness of the 1996 Act is that it made US soldiers more vulnerable, because it exposed them to the threat of US prosecution on domestic soil if they were found to have been complicit in torture, for example. To mitigate that possibility, Bush Jr's advisors counselled him to pass new protocols that introduced a new way of *describing* war prisoners. Instead of being classified as 'prisoners of war,' suspected terrorists or terrorist sympathizers would be termed 'illegal enemy combatants.' It was a legal fiction: a deliberate change in terminology which made inhumane breaches of the Geneva Conventions harder to punish under international law.[25]

It was not an unusual case: the moral principles underpinning the Nuremberg Code and Geneva Conventions are breached often, in unsettling and deeply inhumane ways.

For example, when asked about the ethicality of waterboarding during his first televised interview as US president, Donald Trump said, 'absolutely it works.' He added that he checked with his intelligence chiefs about whether torture was effective: 'The answer was yes, absolutely.'

Trump's harnessing of expert opinion to defend torture illustrates the way that different 'oracles' are used by powerful individuals to legitimate brutally violent policies. Trump's government, as well as earlier US administrations, has on the one hand used a classic strongman oracular tactic.

That oracular tactic is the purposeful conjuring of a threat through imagery that vilifies a particular group, like the Nazis' use of deformed images of Jewish individuals. Trump and his presidential predecessors exaggerate the threat of the black-masked Muslim or the 'dangerous' migrant in a similar way, vilifying targeted groups through deliberate lies and race-baiting. But he doesn't simply amplify fear by denigrating specific groups, he also draws on the social scientific knowledge of intelligence experts to insist that torture 'works.'

This intermingling of oracles is important to my general argument, which is that both the *strongs* camp and the *smarts* camp often tack between a range of rhetorical devices to rationalize the imposition of policies that disproportionately benefit powerful groups by making certain forms of profiteering and violence less visible to the general public. It is a sort of epistemological hedging of risk: when scientific rationalizations fail, the powerful group appeals to more atavistic defences explicitly rooted in ideological or supernatural justifications.

What is particularly notable about the torture example is that, somewhat unusually, this hedging isn't particularly successful; appeals to different 'oracles' fail to lend *convincing* support to the practice of torture. This is *not* because all defenders of torture have weak scientific credentials. Indeed, the opposite is the case: world-leading psychologists have been complicit in honing torture techniques employed by the US military.[26] Their scientific testimony falters because torture, by its very nature, has a transparently weak status as reliable knowledge. It has a methodology that can't be hidden.

It is plausible that some truthful information might emerge through torturing someone. But it is just as clear that torture victims, especially those without 'useful' information, will invent things – that, indeed, they are forced to invent things by the method itself. Innocents are forced to finger other innocents in order to make the pain cease.[27]

The limits of torture as a means for producing truthful knowledge are self-evident in a manner than can't be entirely obscured. You don't need 'expert' judgement to understand why torture will produce information of dubious quality: you only need to imagine the sound of the torturer removing a set of implements to understand the lie.

This transparency is, in many ways, something of an anomaly in today's democratic societies. Techniques of high-frequency financial trading that give large investment banks an unfair advantage over average investors and commercial laws that allow pharmaceutical companies to legally hide evidence of the safety risks of pharmaceutical drugs: these are just some of the limits to knowledge with which citizens must grapple. And the same authorities that citizens are asked to trust – government officials and commercially funded experts who position themselves as arbiters of certainty in a 'post-truth' age – are often responsible for these very barriers to information.

GOD AND WEALTH

The study of the economy, and especially the academic study of wealth inequalities, is another area where 'oracular power' is visible.

Mainstream economists, for example, typically point to long-standing economic theories, such as an academic theory known as the marginal productivity theory of income distribution, to defend gross wealth inequalities. It is an economic theory that was first formulated in the late 19th century, and as I argue, it has become a powerful oracular tool, legitimating the belief that excessive CEO salaries, for example, are fairly earned. And yet, when the evidence base behind marginal productivity theory is challenged, both investors and economists swing *away* from smartmen and smartwomen oracles toward the symbols typically more preferred by strongmen and strongwomen, such as divine authority.

In 2009 for example, Lloyd Blankfein, CEO of Goldman Sachs, was questioned about whether Goldman Sachs deserved government protections and bailout funding during the 2007–2008 financial crisis given how much the firm had profited during the crisis. Blankfein insisted his firm was 'doing God's work.' He added: 'We help companies to grow by helping them to raise capital. Companies that grow create wealth. This, in turn, allows people to have jobs that create more growth and more wealth. It's a virtuous cycle.'[28]

The second part of the sentiment is not surprising: the idea that financial investment and exchange generates a 'virtuous cycle' of wealth creation is a fundamental tenet of contemporary capitalism. But his reference to 'God's work' raised eyebrows – he was seen as invoking an outlandish rationale.

But his rhetoric may be a cannier move than it first seems. In invoking God, Blankfein was simply parroting how the founders of contemporary political economy saw market volatility in the past – as God's will.

Edmund Burke, for example, suggested the 'laws of commerce' are 'the laws of nature, and consequently the laws of God.'[29] The belief that divine design shaped and constrained economic 'laws' was widely shared among many late 18th-century scholars. Blankfein's reference to the divine is not an accidental gaffe but an entrenchment of the long-standing tendency to proclaim that wealth is a godly gift.[30]

The ability for *strongs* and *smarts* to switch registers easily, without losing too much reputational capital, is underpinned by the intellectual advantages that powerful people are assumed to possess. Wealthy and well-educated people are often presumed to *know* better, even when their empirical evidence base is weak, or when their rationalization for their good fortune, like that of Lloyd Blankfein, is patently absurd ('God made me great').

The next chapter focuses on this problem: the way powerful individuals often benefit from the phenomenon of *credibility excess*, to repeat the abovementioned term from philosopher Miranda Fricker. Specialist experts can be perceived as having more well-rounded knowledge than they actually do have, and this perception can lead them to assume disproportionate influence over policy making, especially when the ignorance of a lay public appears to be more glaring than that of the elite.

I suggested in this chapter that the belief that poorer voters are inevitably more 'ignorant' than elite voters is a dangerous myth, leading poor voters to be blamed for decisions that are often spearheaded by wealthy interest groups. Even well-meaning, conscientious academics sometimes underappreciate the problem of elite ignorance. The following chapter turns to this problem.

CHAPTER 3

ELITE AGNOTOLOGISTS

One evening in the early spring months of 1927, the famous industrialist Henry Ford decided to go for a spin in one of his cars – a Ford coupe. Not surprisingly, Ford was a man who loved to drive. As he grew older, his wife Clara became worried about his lone jaunts and the possibility of kidnapping, but at the age of 63 Ford wouldn't desist; he often went for solitary outings, setting off from his home in Dearborn, a small town close to Detroit. On this particular evening it seemed that Clara was right to worry. Claiming later that he was struck from behind, Ford's car veered off-road and he wound up in hospital.[1]

The car accident happened at a convenient time for him. Ford had been scheduled to appear in court after a lawsuit was launched by Aaron Shapiro, a lawyer who sued Ford for defamation of character after Ford had spent years presiding over the dissemination of anti-Semitic lies through his newspaper, *The Dearborn Independent.*

Throughout the early 1920s, the newspaper was responsible for bringing a Russian forgery to a mass American audience. Ford's editorial team at Dearborn based their 'news' on a document titled *The Protocols of the Elders of Zion*, purportedly exposing Jewish world conspiracy. As early as 1921, *The Times of London* newspaper had furnished proof that *The Protocols* had been the work of a Russian agent who had plagiarized it from a satirical fictional exchange. It was, in effect, an early example of 'fake news.'

Ford's editors then bundled op-eds from *Dearborn Independent* into a book, *The International Jew*, translated into dozens of languages. A visitor to Hitler's Munich headquarters in the mid-1920s could browse through numerous copies of *Der International Jude* available in the waiting area. Hitler referred to Ford as his 'inspiration,' a view shared by Hitler Youth who pointed to Ford's anti-Jewish stance as a reason for supporting Hitler in the first place. 'The younger generation looked with envy to the symbols of success and prosperity like Henry Ford,' commented a leader of the Nazi Students' Federation. 'And if Henry Ford said that the Jews were to blame, why, naturally we believed him.'[2]

Facing growing public outrage over his attacks on Jewish Americans, Ford quietly signed his name to a public apology for his newspaper's earlier coverage. Interest waned in his car 'accident,' and some historians now suggest that Ford staged the accident to avoid testifying in his libel trial.[3]

Most media responses praised Ford's public apology and took him at his word when he claimed ignorance of the contents of the *Dearborn Independent*'s editorials, despite former employee Edwin Pipp's insistence that the 'anti-Jewish policy of the publication, now repudiated by Ford's statement, was laid down by the manufacturer himself.'

At least one voice among the American mainstream was unconvinced by Ford's apology. William Allen White, a Pulitzer-winning author and liberal Republican (he would later praise FDR's New Deal policies even though he never voted for Roosevelt) offered this remark: 'It is a sad commentary on humanity that Ford's great wealth has not revealed his ignorance, his mental sloth, and his incapacity to think. Man is always inclined to feel that greatness in one field of activity presumes greatness in all activities.'[4]

Today, Ford is being claimed by the new far right as their icon: any Twitter search reveals noxious homages to his anti-Semitism. If this fact is surprising, it is only because Ford's bigotry has been largely forgotten. His story reveals the truth of William Allen White's observation: great wealth is still seen as evidence of great intelligence or moral worthiness, no matter how many times the assumption is proven wrong.

MISPERCEIVING THE IGNORANCE OF ELITES

Why is Ford remembered as a hero of industrialism rather than one of the most harmful propagandists of the 1920s? The answer to this puzzle is that we have an ignorance problem. Our own ignorance of ignorance has enabled enduring myths to flourish, and the most stubborn of these myths is the assumption that ignorance is a scourge of the poor and the uneducated, rather than a resource for the powerful.

Just look at two major voting outcomes over the last decade: the Brexit vote and the election of Donald Trump.

British citizens were derided when Google Trends reported that online searches for 'what is the EU' spiked on the evening of the Brexit vote, after polls closed. The belated Google searching was evidence of pervasive ignorance at best and sloth at worst, as if it was simply laziness that stopped citizens from bothering to educate themselves. In the US case, Trump's narrow victory also led to handwringing over the public's ignorance, but the directionality was a little different. Unlike in the UK, where the public was condemned for not knowing enough about the referendum's implications to vote as they did, in Trump's case the public was chastised for the opposite problem: knowing *too much*.

Despite having information about Trump's history of bigoted remarks against Mexicans, his lead role in the Birther movement that sought to oust Barack Obama, and his predatory treatment of women, the US people chose to put Trump in office. This decision was proof of a different form of ignorance that is, in a way, more objectionable than the lack of knowledge the UK leave voter was accused of. It is ignorance characterized by knowing an individual is capable of derogatory treatment towards other individuals based on their religion or skin colour and choosing to embrace that person regardless, either because of an affinity with that prejudice, or out of strategic blindness to the problem. In short, the willingness to support Trump no matter how many groups he attacks.

There's some truth in these widespread attitudes towards Trump and Brexit supporters, but also a great deal that is not true. In Trump's case, people were assumed to gravitate to him because he spoke to their economic insecurity, marrying blunt talk with coded language in a way that conjured a tolerant space for their own intolerance. Trump attracts 'rednecks,' the basest version of the story seemed to go, and that's how America got Trump.

'The white American underclass is in thrall to a vicious, selfish culture whose main products are misery and used heroin needles,' writes Kevin Williamson in the right-wing *National Review*. 'The truth about these dysfunctional, downscale communities is that they deserve to die. Economically, they are negative assets.'[5]

This vicious attack on Trump's 'core base' was wrong, not simply due to being morally abhorrent, but because it was factually incorrect as well. The assumption that the poor gravitated to Trump in greater proportions than the wealthy proved to be erroneous. About two-thirds of all American voters earn more than \$50,000 a year, and these voters favoured Trump over Clinton: 49 per cent in comparison to 47 per cent.[6]

Once actual voting patterns grew clearer, some pointed to partisan loyalty to understand the vote split. It wasn't that Trump was particularly popular among educated Republicans, the line goes, it's that he wasn't a Democrat, and that was enough for Republicans to grudgingly back him. But why are poor Americans deemed more likely to back Trump *because* he makes bigoted remarks, while his wealthy backers are seen as backing him *despite* this? Why do the rich get a pass?

This problem seems rooted in the 'notion that higher class means higher integrity,' as the journalist Sarah Smarsh has observed. She calls for more balanced reporting about the class origins of xenophobia and racism in the United States. 'Ivy-League-minted Republicans shepherded the rise of the alt-right,' she writes, adding that a 'steady finger ought be pointed at whites with economic leverage: social conservatives who donate to Trump's campaign while being too civilized to attend a political rally and yell what they really believe.'[7]

Her concerns square with a growing body of research which suggests that social mobility can lead individuals to defend their own group interests in a way that perpetuates racial inequalities.[8] It is hard to know for certain how widespread the tendency is, as attempts to measure racist attitudes are affected by social desirability bias, whereby someone being interviewed tells her interviewer what she thinks is socially appropriate rather than what she really feels. But one thing is clear: news outlets such as Breitbart are not bankrolled by the poor.

AFFLUENT RACISTS

We can draw from history if we want to nuance a flawed narrative that pits racism at the door of poorer Americans while the wealthy are let off the hook.

In the 1920s, F. Scott Fitzgerald, used his bestselling fiction to criticize the views of well-heeled white racists in his day. Born affluent himself, Fitzgerald *was* the establishment, at ease among the east coast bankers whose weekend migration to the rural perimeters of New York City helped create the new safe space of American suburbia.

But unlike many of his friends, he refused to embrace the biological pseudo-science of the day that white elites drew on to justify their economic and political advantages. In *The Great Gatsby*, Fitzgerald lampoons this type through the character of Tom Buchanan. Chicago-born and Yale-educated, Buchanan is a boorish, brutal-handed abuser of women (he breaks his mistress's nose in one scene). His inherited wealth frees him from the burden of ever holding a job. 'Civilization's going to pieces,' Buchanan whines near the start of the book. The 'white race will be – will be utterly submerged. It's all scientific stuff; it's been proved.' Buchanan's defining character trait is that he is too insulated by his own wealth to recognize his own ignorance: he has no knowledge of how much he does not know.

If we take a look around, we can recognize the Tom Buchanans and the Henry Fords of today. Take, for example, the big money support for right-wing publications like Breitbart and Fox News. Both in the past and now, it's figures such as Ford in the 1920s and people such as Robert Mercer and Rupert Murdoch today whose money is used to fuel racially charged hostility in towns and cities across America and Britain. Mercer is a computer scientist who made a fortune through a hedge fund and used his money to back alt-right media vehicles such as Breitbart. Whether or not

Mercer or Murdoch personally hold racist views is not certain: Mercer has strongly denied this. But just as Henry Ford disavowed anti-Semitism while his newspaper continued to propagate lies, both Mercer and Murdoch have financially backed news outlets that publish discriminatory views against minorities. They also defend notions of national supremacy and sovereignty while, somewhat ironically, meddling in foreign elections and referendums.

Investigative work by the British reporter Carole Cadwalladr unearthed the connections proving that Cambridge Analytica, a firm then partly owned by Mercer, provided ongoing assistance to Leave campaigners during Britain's EU referendum vote. 'In-kind' support provided by Cambridge Analytica should have been declared to UK regulators but was not. Cadwalladr made this point to Leave.eu co-founder Aaron Banks, whose reply was curt: 'I don't give a monkey's about the Electoral Commission.'[9]

Speaking to Cadwalladr, individual staff at the Electoral Commission expressed anger at their Commission's impotency when it came to punishing infringements of electoral rules: penalties permitted by law are so minor they 'offered no deterrent to political parties.' One of the academic experts Cadwalladr spoke with summarized the situation bluntly: 'online campaigning has changed everything and none of the existing laws cover it … There has to be a principle of transparency. The public needs to know where the money is coming from. And we don't.'

One unintended consequence of reports into hacking and foreign meddling over 2016 is the inadvertent implication that cronyism, corruption and fraud across national borders is something new, when it's not, a reality benefiting Trump's camp as they could legitimately call attention to government–corporate cronyism in earlier eras.

Stephen Bannon, for example, received funding from Mercer to set up a think tank called the Government Accountability Institute. Its anodyne title was likely helpful in accomplishing one of Bannon's successful tactics. He mobilized the investigative prowess of journalists at mainstream newspapers like *The New York Times* by feeding them uncomfortable but not false information about the lucrative links between the Clinton Foundation and foreign philanthropists and governments.

'We have a mantra,' Bannon said in an interview with journalist Joshua Green, 'Facts get shares, opinions get shrugs.' Bannon shares with Green his underlying mantra for amassing power, claiming that he learned the tactic when he was a banker with Goldman Sachs.

'One of the things Goldman teaches you is, don't be the first guy through the door because you're going to get all the arrows,' Bannon said. 'If it's junk bonds, let Michael Milken lead the way.' He added that one of Goldman's strongest principles is 'never lead in any product. Find a business partner.'[10]

It's a doctrine of deliberate anti-visibility: the strategic effort to make one's idea seem to have originated elsewhere to avoid the appearance of primary involvement. It's a tactic for camouflaging one's direct complicity through complex partnership structures. It's a way to manufacture ignorance alibis.

IS 'FAKE NEWS' THE MAIN
PROBLEM?

Bannon's range of tactics points to a neglected reality. We shouldn't presume that 'fake news' is only a problem when obvious lies are driving news stories. The opposite might in fact be the case. News stories that appear honestly reported but which omit important contextual information can be just as damaging if not more so than clear smear jobs, because there's less inclination to expose falsehoods that are not perceived as being deceptions. 'The most mischievous errors on record,' the 19th-century romantic poet Samuel Taylor Coleridge once wrote, are 'half-truths taken as the whole.'

In his study into the killing of 96 innocent fans of Liverpool Football Club at Hillsborough in 1989, criminologist Phil Scraton offers a damning assessment of the way that half-truths and lies can crystallize into presumptions of fact when enough authoritative figures parrot a deception as accurate. In the weeks after the Hillsborough tragedy, the media failed to probe deceptive statements made by the chief superintendent David Duckenfield, who falsely claimed that drunken fans pushed through a gate that he had earlier ordered to be opened. Rupert Murdoch's newspaper, the *Sun*, ran lurid and deceptive headlines reinforcing Duckenfield's lies: 'THE TRUTH,' it blared: 'SOME FANS URINATED ON THE BRAVE; SOME FANS BEAT UP PC GIVING KISS OF LIFE.' Even though some newspapers published refutations of the false claims, the intensity of the allegations were 'so powerful they gained widespread recognition as fact … untruths and half-truths became reality as columnists added their opinion.'[11]

Reporting on the Brexit vote was rife with such half-truths. Take a story from Google Trends which implied that many British voters did not know what the EU is. Google Trends first reported this 'fact' the day after the referendum vote. *The Daily Mail* and *Washington Post* quickly released follow-up stories (in the *Washington Post*'s retelling, the entire British people were 'frantically Googling what the EU is').

There's an archetypal figure called to mind by Google Trends – the layman at home in his living room on the evening after the vote, laptop nestled on his lap so his missus or children don't notice what he's Googling. He is the scapegoated culprit of Brexit – the ignorant voter pummelled in the press for being too clueless to even know what the EU is.

The only problem is: he doesn't exist – at least not in the numbers that Google Trends implied. Google Trends refused to report the absolute numbers, spurring speculation about how many actual searches took place. Politifact, a fact-checking website based in the United States, dug deeper into available evidence, and suggested it's likely that less than 1000 people searched 'what is the EU' on the evening after the vote. It's not a high number in a nation with a voting population of about 40 million and voter turn-out over 70 per cent.[12] And yet, this single 'fact' gave the impression most voters couldn't be bothered to read up on their options. The lay voter becomes the fall guy, which isn't that surprising: mythologized perpetrators of wrongs are often the scapegoat of choice.

'Think the north and the poor caused Brexit? Think again,' ran the headline of an article from *Guardian* journalist Zoe Williams, pointing to data showing high support for Brexit in wealthy rural areas. The chequered picture of which regions in the UK boasted the most 'leavers' versus 'remainers' should have led to more sobriety, and to an admission of how little we really know about the political and economic beliefs of voters. Instead, Williams writes, 'we've taken it as a kicking-off point that the Brexit vote was won by a council estate in Bolton.'[13]

This lasting myth – only the poor could be ignorant enough to vote leave – is particularly remarkable given the long history of lobbying for a British exit from the EU among the Tory party's Eurosceptic core. This powerful, wealthy core of the Tory party doesn't bear much resemblance to the low-income Bolton resident upheld as a characteristic leave voter. But wealthy Tories *should* be the archetypical face of Brexit, because it's they who lobbied the strongest for a referendum to take place, rallying wealthy international backers to support the Brexit campaign.[14]

NATIONAL FORGETTING

I have suggested we tend to overlook the ignorance of elites, often wrongly presuming poorer people are more ignorant than their affluent counterparts. But this tendency doesn't always hold, and Trump is the obvious example. His degree from Wharton Business School hasn't dented his ignorant belief in pseudo-science or his links to anti-vaccine conspiracy theorists, for example. For many, he is the embodiment of elite ignorance, and they're not wrong: Trump's attitude to climate change and his brutally harsh treatment of undocumented mothers, fathers and children is harming people daily.

But it is also too simple a story to tell about elite ignorance, propagating the 'Trump as anomaly' narrative – the idea that Trump is an aberration from earlier presidential incumbents because his ignorance is so glaring. Trump tends to be contrasted with his immediate predecessor, Barack Obama, with Obama praised for his learnedness and Trump scorned for his lack of the same. Even right-wing conservatives sometimes adopt this line: when author Ann Coulter quips she wants a president 'who reads,' Obama is included in that category whether she likes it or not.

But during his tenure, Obama also relied upon strategic ignorance. He insisted, for example, that death tolls from US drone strikes were far lower than many scholars of US military policies believe, stating in 2016 that between 64 and 116 civilians were killed by drone strikes during his tenure as president.

This claim is questionable on many counts. For one, as journalist Spencer Ackerman writes, the count is 'incomplete, leaving out the civilian toll from drone strikes in Afghanistan, Syria and Iraq. Nor did the administration go into detail about where the strikes occur.' Ackerman adds that many drone strikes were an 'anonymous method of killing' known as signature strikes. The strikes are 'anonymous' because the US military specifically targets people 'whose identities it does not know, for fitting into what it considers patterns of life associated with terrorism.'[15]

In some cases, a victim might be a combatant, but it's also certain that civilians are wrongly mislabelled as acceptable targets. There is no way of ever knowing precisely how many innocents died, because the CIA-led policy deliberately hinges on making that knowledge irrelevant to their airstrike strategy. The clustered approach presumes that one's physical presence in a region of terrorist activity is sufficient grounds to deem *any* individual collateral damage. Civilian death counts are little more than ceremonial posturing in such a situation; an effort to massage public tensions by making US military actions seem more defensible than they actually are. Obama can't say truthfully that no more than 116 civilians died by drone strikes when his administration's official policy was to kill targets without knowledge of their personal identity.

At the same time, Obama isn't quite lying in the traditional sense, because he also can't say with any degree of precision exactly how many *more* than 116 civilians were killed by drones during his incumbency. The governmental policy that he sanctioned furnishes him with the power to speak truthfully, even when the numbers he cites are deceptive.[16]

TAKING ELITE IGNORANCE SERIOUSLY

Holding up Trump rather than, say, Barack Obama or George W. Bush as poster representatives of elite ignorance trivializes the problem of useful ignorance.

The common position on Trump's ignorance is that he knows too little to be in charge, that his own imperviousness to understanding scientific facts endangers others. His wilful ignorance is a sign of obvious incompetence or stupidity.

But to view his wilful ignorance as a personal liability misses the most important feature of his ignorance: that his selective use of facts has been an effective strategy, helping him gain and maintain power. Indeed, his refusal to know – his strategic denial of inconvenient evidence – often puts him in an advantageous position when it comes to things like political campaigning, negotiations and appearing confident as to the truthfulness of his claims even when others point out he is lying. It may be immoral, but there's nothing unusual about Trump's willingness to lie or feign ignorance to protect himself and his wealth and political power.

Trump's willingness to lie to gain power also illustrates the chief problem with the concept of 'epistocracy' – the idea that 'rule by knowers' will lead to either more morally just or more knowledgeable forms of governance.

Advocates of epistocracy such as Jason Brennan have pointed to Trump's win as a sign that democracy is failing in America, and that restricting voting privileges to people who pass tests of 'voter knowledge' is one way to curb the influence of men like Trump on politics today.

But Trump's own background illuminates the problem with this argument. Trump gained his business degree from Wharton. Stephen Bannon got his MBA from Harvard. Both these men clearly benefitted from an 'elite' education. If they were tested on their political knowledge, there's a very good chance they would pass the test – but this doesn't mean that America would be better off with more Bannons in charge, especially if there's no way to vote them out, because democracy has been intentionally undermined.

VOTER IGNORANCE AND EPISTOCRACY

Brennan defends his anti-democracy stance by pointing to the problem of 'voter ignorance,' defined as an electorate's lack of knowledge about politics, such as how political parties across the left–right spectrum voted on particular policies in the past.

A witty example of voter ignorance comes from the *New Yorker* magazine, reporting that approximately a third of American voters believe that the Marxist slogan 'From each according to his ability to each according to his need' is written in the US Constitution.[17]

Whether the problem of voter ignorance has become worse or better over recent decades is disputed, because there is no agreement on the best way to measure the problem.

As Ilya Somin, a law professor at George Mason University who has studied voter ignorance in depth, points out, available evidence actually suggests the problem has been *improving* in America rather than worsening in recent decades, albeit slowly. It is commendable of Somin to emphasize this, because in a way it undermines the larger argument he wants to make – which is that 'voter ignorance' is still grave enough for policy-makers to consider ways to mitigate the problem.

Somin is one of a growing number of libertarian thinkers who argue that the problem of voter ignorance in today's societies require fresh and 'bold' solutions. Some like Somin have proposed moderate reforms, such as attempts to devolve power from the central government to local authorities. He does not think the vote should be stripped away from people – whereas Brennan does.

As mentioned above, Brennan introduces the notion of 'simulated oracle' to describe his proposal. Within this system, citizens would be forced to respond systematically to opinion polls and to take a test of 'basic political knowledge' whenever they vote. As part of their test, they would be also compelled to share their demographic information (undermining the principle of a secret ballot).

Brennan argues that once the information from opinion polls and voting preferences is collected, 'any statistician then could calculate the public's "enlightened preferences," that is, what a demographically identical voting population *would* support if only it were better informed. An epistocracy might then instantiate the public's enlightened preferences rather than their actual, unenlightened preferences.'[18]

This is a deeply worrying proposal for a number of reasons.

To start with, Brennan ignores that politics is as much about values as it is about facts. Any algorithm could be laden with a programmer's values in a way that remains non-transparent to a citizenry, but importantly, can also perpetuate cognitive errors that remain opaque to the programmer herself. Facing no external feedback loop or check on the accuracy of the oracle's 'preferences,' it becomes impossible for those outside the narrow group of so-called enlightened 'knowers' to convince the 'knowers' that the oracle could be wrong.

An even graver problem, as Somin points out, is that in any anti-democratic system, formal rules can be manipulated to serve partisan and often racist interest groups. Throughout US history, attacks on voting rights have long been a way for mostly white legislatures to 'exclude minorities despised by the majority, especially African Americans in the Jim Crow-era South.' Somin rightly suggests that the explicit advocacy of disenfranchisement efforts could lead to a revival of 'harshly oppressive policies that victimized what were for a long time politically powerless populations.'[19]

MORALITY AND EDUCATION

Currently, voter ID tactics are *already* leading to voter suppression in the US, which raises the question of what's new about Brennan's approach. What's different is the reputational clout of his university, Georgetown, and the fact his latest book, *Against Democracy*, was published by the venerable Princeton University Press, conferring legitimacy on his assault on democracy and voting rights that more explicitly far-right speakers don't tend to enjoy.

That's not to suggest that Brennan's arguments against democracy should be censored. I don't think that they should be.

The solution is not censorship, but reason-based refutation of the false premises underlying the seeming appeal of the concept. And the most reasonable response of all is that epistocracy ignores the Henry Ford problem. It ignores the fact that intelligence in one area is not evidence of moral righteousness in other realms.

Just because some people have more expert knowledge does not mean they make better government representatives or leaders. Throughout history, more 'educated' groups of people have often condoned reprehensible abuse against the less powerful, as the examples of slavery and Nazi atrocities both show.

THE IGNORANCE EXCUSE

Today, not all affluent equivalents to Ford hold prejudiced views. Indeed, billionaire philanthropy is often channelled to support commendable causes.

But even laudable philanthropic donations have an unintended negative effect, which is the tendency to assume that all philanthropic bequests, including the use of deep pockets to buy media outlets, is inherently positive for society.

'It's their money,' people tend to say, 'they can do what they like.' But even great wealth, indeed, *especially* great wealth, should not be free to spread gross misinformation.

People *can't* do whatever they like with their money. They can't attack the life and liberty of others, as Ford did through his newspaper's anti-Semitic lies. Too often, mega-philanthropy is treated as a morally laudable gesture that should be beyond censure, but Ford's 'philanthropy' shows that mega-giving can be used to stoke racially fuelled hatred and social unrest, a problem that needs to be regulated in a democratic, transparent way.

Ford largely avoided any personal repercussions for the propaganda he disseminated. In his apology letter, he pleaded ignorance of the content of his newspaper's editorials, and reputation-wise, the tactic paid off. Even if most of America and Nazi Germany were apparently familiar with the Dearborn's news content, Ford purportedly didn't know.

CEO strategic ignorance is an old ruse, and in the next chapter, a story hailing from one of the most influential media empires in history illuminates the value of strategic ignorance to powerful individuals who avoid legal liabilities even while their employees and the general public suffer as a result of policies over which they preside.

CHAPTER 4

THE MURDOCH STRATEGY

Much had been made of Rupert Murdoch's frailness. On the morning of July 19, 2011, the media baron appeared before the UK parliament to give testimony in one of the biggest scandals in the history of British news publishing. He had been summoned to address revelations that the *News of the World*, one of the tabloid newspapers in his British media empire, had spent years illegally intercepting the voice-mail of Britain's leading politicians and celebrities, as well as some of the nation's most vulnerable citizens, including soldiers killed in Afghanistan and Iraq. They were targeted so tabloid journalists could trawl through phone messages left by government and policing officials, or by desperate family members.

Until 2011, the story failed to gain wider traction. Journalists and victims who demanded wider criminal investigation were either ignored or denounced by the same bodies supposedly tasked with protecting the public interest, be this Scotland Yard or the Press Complaints Commission, a now defunct regulatory body set up to monitor breaches of ethical conduct in the news industry. On July 4, 2011, *Guardian* journalists published their most explosive story yet. *News of the World* reporters had intercepted the voicemail of Milly Dowler, a 13-year-old girl abducted and murdered when walking home from school in the Surrey town of Walton-upon-Thames in 2002.

The question was no longer whether illegal and widespread phone hacking had taken place. It was clear that hundreds of people had been targeted. The question was who knew what about the illegal hacking and when. On the morning of July 19, the public queued for eight hours for the chance to witness members of the House of Commons Culture, Media and Sport Committee try to tease an answer from the patriarch himself, his son James Murdoch, and Rebekah Brooks, former CEO of News International.

Those expecting the physique or mental agility of the media mogul to live up to his fearsome reputation were disappointed. Reporters issued a unanimous appraisal: when Murdoch walked into the hearing room, the great businessman seemed gaunt, stunted and enfeebled, palpably bowed by the scandal bearing down on his empire. Though he would never be arrested or charged in relation to 'Hackingate,' just two days earlier Rebekah Brooks had been arrested on suspicion of corruption allegations and conspiring to intercept communications. She was released on bail, and the nation's gaze was on her and Murdoch senior and junior.[1]

The committee's opening questions were met with long stretches of silence. Later in the hearing, perceptions of Murdoch Sr's debility were enhanced by a now-infamous incident involving a pie projectile, as a protestor wearing a plaid lumberjack shirt lurched towards Murdoch Sr, foam pie in hand, compelling Murdoch's then wife Wendi Deng to crowdsurf forward, leaping to land a blow. 'This is the most humble day of my life,' Murdoch said quietly, and that was before Deng slugged his attacker.

The parliamentary select committee's report, released a year later, suggested that Murdoch Sr had displayed 'wilful blindness to what was going on in his companies and his publications.' In scathing language, the report concluded that his failure to investigate obvious signs of criminality 'speaks volumes about the lack of effective corporate governance at News Corporation and News International. We conclude, therefore, that Rupert Murdoch is not a fit person to exercise the stewardship of a major international company.'[2]

The press response seemed unanimous. *The Atlantic* suggested Murdoch 'might not survive this latest episode in the UK tabloid hacking scandal.' The BBC thought it would offer ammunition to New Corps shareholders who felt the company was more like a family fiefdom than a public company. Indeed, a lawsuit was filed in March 2011 over Murdoch's decision to buy a company managed by his daughter, Elisabeth. The suit alleged that he treated News Corp like a 'family candy store' – and was later expanded to include allegations that the board had failed to investigate illegal hacking taking place within the company.[3]

'If you have presided over an organisation that has conducted criminal activities, either you gave the orders, or you gave permission, or you connived, but if you did none of these things, then you were neglectful,' wrote Andreas Whittam Smith, a former editor of the *Independent* newspaper. 'That is the trap, that is the box in which the directors of News International will find themselves.'[4]

VICTORY FOR MURDOCH

But the doomsday predictions – the assumption that Rupert Murdoch might be held liable for crimes at his company – never happened, and the rest of this chapter explores *why* nothing much happened. Was Murdoch's 'wilful ignorance' really as aberrant as some observers suggested, or is deliberate CEO blindness to organizational illegality more commonplace than people suspect? And if so, then why are courts hampered from penalizing people like Murdoch?

In June 2015, Rupert Murdoch announced he was formally handing over control of his business empire to his sons James and Lachlan. Murdoch would remain executive chairman of 21st Century Fox and News Corp – the two largest holdings in Murdoch's mosaic of intersecting business concerns – but his sons would now play a dominant role in day-to-day management. Rather than forced expulsion, this was more like a coronation.[5]

There were other smaller victories for Murdoch. In 2015, the US Department of Justice quietly announced it would not pursue a prosecution against News Corp in relation to the hacking scandal. Meanwhile, although a UK court sentenced Andy Coulson, former news editor at the *News of the World*, to 18 months in prison for his role in the phone hacking, Murdoch's closest ally fared better: Rebekah Brooks was acquitted of all charges.

When illegal actions take place, we often presume that the regulators or enforcement agencies which detect the irregularities will be rewarded for their diligence and encouraged to take further steps to stop the practice. But in the case of the hacking scandal, this didn't happen. Clear early evidence of illegality was ignored by the same parties who later claimed that they *couldn't* have acted differently because they didn't have enough information to act.

THE TRUTH WILL OUT?

News of the hacking controversy emerged in slow, incremental stages, pursued by a few lone journalists who for years battled bureaucratic silences and evasion tactics.

One man at the forefront of this struggle was Nick Davies, an investigative reporter who had earlier taken an interest in the different tactics that British tabloid and broadsheet newspapers used to illegally dig into the private lives of leading politicians and celebrities. Davies later recounted that, when publicizing an earlier book about these various tabloid tactics, he happened to find himself face-to-face with Stuart Kuttner, managing editor at *News of the World*.

This was in 2008. Davies had gathered some evidence but not a lot of conclusive data about the use of private investigators at tabloid newspapers. He had heard stories that occasionally editors would outsource illegal activities to these private investigators – and he mentioned the problem while appearing on BBC Radio 4's *Today* programme. His fellow discussant that day was Kuttner.

'If it happens, it shouldn't happen,' Kuttner replied curtly. 'It happened once at the *News of the World*. The reporter was fired; he went to prison. The editor resigned.'[6]

Kuttner was referring to Clive Goodman, royal editor at *News of the World*. The private investigator that Davies had alluded to was a man named Glenn Mulcaire – a name that would appear time and again over the next few years, as evidence from his notebooks was one of the pieces of data used to identify legions of hacking victims targeted by Murdoch's media teams.

Kuttner's indignant retort to Davies – his insistence that the use of a PI to carry out an illegal act only 'happened once' – proved to be a mistake on his part. The comment was over-heard by a well-placed source, who remains unidentified, who then contacted Davies with a cryptic message, asking him to meet in person so he could elaborate further: 'I think you will like what I have to say.'[7]

During a meeting a short while later at a hotel in central London, the source bluntly told Davies that Kuttner was lying. The phone hacking incident that led to Goodman's departure wasn't an aberration – it was part of a systematic strategy that enabled *News of the World* reporters to gain most of their scoops. The source explained the strategy in detail to Davies. Any reporter could easily replicate the trick used to access voice messages: once they had a target's phone number, they would wait for a time when the victim was thought to be indisposed and unlikely to answer the phone. The reporter would then ring the number and, when the answer message clicked on, be able to access the messages simply by pressing '9.' Davies notes that it was often easy to guess the victim's password from their birthdate – or to simply use the default security setting which many people hadn't taken the time to change. The more laborious task was obtaining privately held phone numbers in the first place, and this is where Mulcaire came in. A seasoned private eye, he was directed by *News of the World* to illegally procure the private phone numbers of different celebrity targets so reporters could hack their phones.

Davies' next break came in the form of leaked documents from an ongoing lawsuit that had been filed in the aftermath of Clive Goodman and Glenn Mulcaire's arrest and imprisonment. The lawsuit was filed by Gordon Taylor, the chief executive of the UK's Professional Footballers' Association. In 2005, *News of the World* staff had hired Mulcaire to intercept Taylor's voicemail and, after listening to messages from his mobile and transcribing them, wrongly presumed that Taylor was having an extramarital affair.

Taylor learned of the false allegations and quashed the rumour before it was published. But still it nagged at him: how had reporters at the paper reached the false conclusion in the first place? Back in 2005, the *News of the World* had confronted him with a few cobbled together facts about his purported philandering to try to tease out a confession. He was astonished when they presented him with details of his private life that no one outside his immediate family could have known. Two years later, he learned that Goodman and Mulcaire had been sent to jail for phone hacking. Realizing he had likely been a hacking victim as well, he filed a civil lawsuit against *News of the World* seeking damages.

This lawsuit led to evidence Davies could sift through, from two main sources: files held by Scotland Yard and files held by the Information Commissioner's Office (ICO), a government regulatory organization tasked with protecting the information privacy rights of UK citizens. Thanks to Taylor's lawsuit, the ICO was ordered to disclose material that it had collected as part of an earlier 2003 investigation, labelled 'Operation Motorman.'

To understand how many intersecting but different bodies are tasked with policing rogue actors who steal people's private data and sell it to the press, some words on the ICO will help. Headquartered in Wilmslow, on the outskirts of Manchester, the ICO is one of the many regulatory agencies that comprise the capillaries of the British state, filled with staff working doggedly at repetitive and often unrecognized tasks. Taken together, this diligent work should provide the public with some security in knowing that intimate data about personal lives does at least have a sentry. It is an agency tasked with policing not simply blatant crime such as identify theft, but also quieter abuses of power, such as insurance discrimination by providers emboldened by the caches of personal information at their disposal.

At least, this is the dream of the ICO. In reality, it is a goal scuppered by the practicalities of regulating corporations and government departments that in size, authority and influence tend to be far more powerful than the watchdog itself.

The ICO's job is to ensure that databases of personal information – landline and mobile records; medical records; personal information held by the Driver and Vehicle Licensing Agency – are not illegally breached by third parties such as marketing firms or the media. The agency is also responsible for monitoring the use of personal information by governmental bodies. To give just one example of the breadth of this enormous task, the ICO has the authority to scrutinize whether different organizations, including the police, are complying with freedom of information requests by citizens. It can fine government bodies that fail to comply either promptly or at all. The problem, of course, is that in any situation where one branch of the government is supposed in principle to act as a hammer against another branch, it matters when the nail looms larger than the hammer.

Operation Motorman was set up to investigate the problem of 'blagging': the use of surreptitious, underhanded tactics to solicit private information from public or commercial organizations. The ICO narrowed in on a man named Steve Whittamore, a private investigator living in New Milton, Hampshire and in 2003 staff obtained a warrant to search his Hampshire home. Inside, they found that Whittamore possessed colour-coded notebooks – different ledgers in red, yellow, blue and green – detailing his price list for providing different types of personal information.

Some services were cheap: it took just £17.50 for an 'occupancy' search to determine where a celebrity target lived. At the upper end, Whittamore charged £150–200 for a vehicle registration search. The mundanity of it – the low-budget operation in New Milton; DVLA staff spicing up their earnings with low-level information brokering – seems small-scale. But it wasn't. The breadth of penetrated organizations is astonishing, from telephone companies to the Police National Computer.

Two years after this raid, Whittamore pleaded guilty to breaches of the Data Protection Act and received a two-year conditional discharge. It struck many people as an absurdly small penalty – so small that a year later, in a public report issued by the ICO, the agency lambasted the legislative restrictions that made it difficult for courts to issue harsher punishments. The report, *What Price Privacy?*, calls for custodial sentences in order to deter illegal information searches from taking place in future.

As far as dry regulatory reports tend to go, it is remarkably scathing: 'The fact that prison is not currently an option for persons convicted of section 55 offences belittles the offence,' one section reads. 'Not only is the unlawful trade extremely lucrative, but those apprehended and convicted by the courts often face derisory penalties.'[8]

Without stiffer sentences, the ICO concluded, it was 'not in the public interest to proceed with the ICO's own prosecutions, nor could the Information Commissioner contemplate bringing prosecutions against the journalists or others to whom confidential information had been supplied.'[9]

BUREAUCRATIC QUAGMIRES

The ICO report details a frustrating but not unusual bureau-cratic episode of regulators striving to do their jobs effectively but being hindered by institutional barriers outside their jurisdiction or control.

But that isn't the full story. After the report was published, the senior investigator on Operation Motorman criticized the robustness of the report's analysis. This investigator, Alec Owens – a retired police officer who moved to the ICO after 30 years with the police – insists that his efforts to link Whittamore's actions to the journalists who illegally com-missioned the services were deliberately thwarted by ICO's senior management.

Once a veil is lifted on official reports, it becomes clear that official claims of righteousness can mask disconcert-ing patterns of internal silencing. The more Operation Motorman revealed the possibility of corruption at an ever-escalating number of news organizations, the more difficult it became for ICO investigators to follow the story where it was leading them, which was deep inside powerful Fleet Street news firms.

Owens has stated in written and oral evidence to the Leveson inquiry, a large-scale judicial investigation into the media industry spurred into being by the hacking scan-dal, that he was told by ICO superiors *not* to investigate or interview any journalists, even though it was supposedly his job to do so. The ICO denies this. Speaking to the BBC in 2010, David Smith, a deputy information commissioner at the ICO, claimed the agency did not have sufficient evidence that journalists knew beyond reasonable doubt that soliciting private information was illegal. Owens, however, argues this supposed lack of evidence wasn't accidental. Rather, it was a purposeful refusal to elicit troubling information that ICO higher-ups didn't want to face.

Owens was present when Whittamore's multi-coloured notebooks were seized and, a few days after the raid, Owens gave a briefing on their findings to colleagues, including ICO Commissioner Richard Thomas. At this meeting, he told his superiors that he could use examples from the paperwork seized to confirm that a 'paper chain' existed linking specific journalists to particular private detectives.

'We could also prove by way of the seized bills for pay-ment and numbered invoices settled by the newspaper groups exactly how much money had been paid for each transaction,' Owens states in written evidence.[10] A few weeks later, he received a new instruction from his supervi-sors: he was told not to make contact with newspapers, not to speak with journalists, and not to investigate journalists. Owens was dumbfounded.

'Despite our protests we were told this was the decision of Richard Thomas and that he would deal with the press involvement by way of the Press Complaints Council,' he writes. 'It was at this moment we knew no journalist could or ever would be prosecuted in relation to our investigation.' During oral testimony before the Leveson hearings, Owens was blunt. 'We were stopped from getting the evidence.'

Called to testify before Leveson, Richard Thomas denied ever adopting a policy of deliberately not investigating journalists or their editors: 'If there was a policy it was not one which I had a hand in, one which I knew about, which I made or which I was told about.'[11] Owens does not agree: 'The decision not to pursue any journalist was based solely on fear – fear of the power, wealth and influence of the press and the fear of the backlash that could follow if the press turned against ICO.'

UNDERSTANDING THE ANTI-CLIMAX

In November 2013, a year after the Leveson report was first published, one former news editor, Whittam Smith of the *Independent*, commemorated the one-year anniversary of the report with a reflection on what had changed since news of the hacking scandal first broke. His verdict: not much. He suggested that the four volumes of Leveson's report 'seem to have since been placed on high shelves and forgotten.' Certain mysteries surrounding the hacking controversy have never been resolved, he points out, such as the question of why three separate watchdogs each failed to carry out their jobs.

'Inexplicably,' he writes,

the Information Commissioner's Office (ICO) never got as far as even interviewing any journalist to see whether there was a case for bringing criminal charges

... After Scotland Yard had dealt with Mr Goodman and Mr Mulcaire, it lost interest. The Information Commissioner never got started. And the PCC had a go but missed the point.[12]

Whittam Smith's reaction is an understandable one. If an organization tasked with protecting the public fails to carry out its primary duties, the failure seems like an aberration rather than a rational act. However, viewing the ICO's wilful blindness as irrational misses an underlying logic. To understand why ICO employees may have been directed not to investigate journalists, it is useful to consider something I term 'anti-strategies': the tacit interests at root in any regulatory process, inquiry or hearing which work in practice to contradict the stated goals of the inquiry.[13]

In the ICO's case, the anti-strategy appears to have been resource- based: the ICO feared the litigious clout of the press, and the likelihood of becoming immersed in ongoing legal battles that would overwhelm the small agency's staff and operational capacity. Rather than being inexplicable or irrational, the ICO's inaction served an underlying institutional need. That doesn't make deliberate ignorance at the ICO defensible in a moral sense, but it does make self-imposed controls put in place against information seeking easier to understand.

The same strategic inaction took place at Scotland Yard. In 2006, as part of an operation named Caryatid, officers at Scotland Yard raided and seized over 11,000 pages of documents from Mulcaire. Despite the importance of this material, the police chose to close the operation. They left the files unexamined, stating later that the scale of resources needed to investigate the files was an unjustifiable use of public money. If the police *had* combed through the files in more detail in 2006, they would likely have learned at an earlier stage that individuals targeted by *News of the World* journalists worked at the highest echelons of government, including cabinet ministers.

This decision was later condemned by members of parliament and the press, and it wasn't without dire consequences for senior members of staff. The highest-ranking officers at Scotland Yard, Police Commissioner Sir Paul Stephenson and Assistant Commissioner John Yates, resigned in close succession in July 2011 once the scale of incompetency within the Metropolitan Police became clear. It would be a mistake, though, to see the inaction as merely due to the force's incompetence.

Incompetency suggests accidental mishaps – human fallibility or isolated misdemeanours that occur in a haphazard and uncoordinated way. But, in truth, the police seemed wary of uncovering firm evidence that might force them to act more aggressively – a wariness that was revealed during the later legal trial of Andy Coulson and Rebekah Brooks.

In 2014, during their trial at the Old Bailey, a revealing email was disclosed in court. It had been sent by a lawyer working for News International to Coulson and contained a summary of what, according to the lawyer, the police had told Rebekah Brooks about their ongoing investigation. The email suggests that an aim of the police had been to reassure Brooks about the limited scope of their inquiry, telling her that 'they are not widening the case to include other NoW [*News of the World*] people but would do so if they got direct evidence.' That email was sent on September 15, 2006. Scotland Yard's decision to close Caryatid was taken shortly after.[14]

When Scotland Yard's botched handling of Operation Caryatid was disclosed in 2014, news columnists and members of parliament berated senior officers for grossly underestimating the gravity of the information in their possession. This, though, misses the point. In all probability, the reality wasn't that senior Met officers failed to understand how incriminating the evidence might be – they grasped all too well how serious the material was. The decision to ignore stemmed from the fear of finding out too much – of unearthing evidence that would require them to act – rather than the assumption the material contained little of interest.

MURDOCH'S WORD

The people who queued for hours outside parliament in the summer of 2011 to watch Murdoch's testimony steadied themselves for a reckoning that never happened. When he appeared before parliament, he described the day as the 'humblest' of his life. Two years later, he was filmed at the office of the *Sun* with a less self-deprecating manner, telling his news staff: 'payments for news tips from cops: that's been going on a hundred years, absolutely. You didn't instigate it.' He pledged loyalty to any staff convicted, promising to do 'everything in my power to give you total support, even if you're convicted and get six months or whatever. I think it's just outrageous.'[15]

Later, in May 2015, Anthony France, a crime reporter at the *Sun*, was found guilty of paying an anti-terrorism police officer over £22,000 in bribes for news tips, though he later successfully appealed the verdict. The presiding judge at his sentencing hearing suggested that Murdoch's News UK should pay the costs of France's legal fees, but the company refused to do so. France's friends launched a crowdfunding appeal; France's conviction was overturned in 2016.[16]

Murdoch appears to have been truthful and untruthful when he was filmed in the *Sun* offices in 2013 – the claim about helping his lower-ranking staff with legal bills wasn't necessarily true, but the observation about bribes for news tips being commonplace probably isn't that far off the mark, even if different branches of government have generally known 'what not to know' when it comes to identifying and punishing practices happening in open sight.

In 2013, News Corp reached a settlement in the suit launched after Murdoch bought his daughter's company. Shine had been Elisabeth Murdoch's vehicle, and she had done well with it, producing UK television hits including *Masterchef*. But News Corp shareholders felt she didn't do quite well enough to deserve the massive monetary windfall she received in 2011. In that year, her father's company bought Shine for £415 million – £131 million of which went directly to Elisabeth, who owned 51 per cent of the company. Later it emerged that Shine was £85 million in debt, a larger sum than initially claimed, leading shareholders to suggest nepotism was behind the deal. They won their claim, and News Corp settled the suit for £91 million. And yet, thanks to indemnities, no member of the management team or executive board of directors faced any personal losses – News Corp recovered losses from its insurers. Elisabeth kept her payout entirely.[17]

Murdochgate and related scandals barely scratched the façade of a business empire that many people thought might crumble entirely.

BEHIND THE FAÇADE

It would be possible to treat the 'Murdochgate' scandal as a sordid but not entirely unusual tale of bureaucratic negligence and corporate corruption, driven by the deep anxiety of offending a powerful media mogul. But to dismiss the scandal this way would be to miss a chance to tease out the larger significance of the case.

It's a story that, a bit like a Russian doll, has layer upon layer of symbolic meaning. At one level, there's the way that the main head honcho – the 'MMIC,' as traders in the City of London used to refer to the guy with the widest pinstripes back when pinstripes were fashionable – walked away unscathed.[18]

At another level, there's the way that even when executives are found to have breached corporate governance duties indemnities protected them from any personal financial loss.

At an even deeper level, as the dolls shrink smaller from sight, there are taboo topics that become strangely harder to perceive or to discuss openly even when their negative social implications become more apparent, there is the question of Elisabeth's privilege, and the way that nepotistic links to her father, as the lawsuit alleged, helped to net her a considerable fortune.

By any account, Elisabeth is a talented media producer whose company came out with a lot of crowd-pleasers such as *Masterchef* (I was glued to it for a couple seasons). No doubt she *has* worked hard over her life, but she embodies a larger problem: the links between inherited wealth and worsening social mobility in countries such as the US and UK.

The problem of inherited wealth is a sort of known 'open secret'; the US Brookings Institute reported recently that approximate 40 per cent of all wealth in the US is thought to be inherited, and yet to acknowledge or to criticize this reality is to invite accusations of 'class envy.'[19]

Sociologist Rachel Sherman noticed this problem in her study of the cultural habits of New York's uber-wealthy elite. One of her interviewees admits over lunch at a New York restaurant, that she removes the price tags off food or clothes, like 'the label off our six-dollar bread,' to avoid her nanny seeing them. 'To hide the price tags is not to hide the privilege; the nanny is no doubt aware of the class gap whether or not she knows the price of her employer's bread,' Sherman suggests. 'Instead, such moves help wealthy people manage their discomfort with inequality, which in turn makes that inequality impossible to talk honestly about – or to change.'[20]

In isolation, acts of 'forgetting' appear trivial, but taken together they can create durable matrices of silence; powerful non-utterances that impede people from asking tough questions about wealth concentration and corporate power in today's capitalist economies. They speak to the necessity of understanding strategic ignorance as a tool of class domination and corporate power, rather than simply as individual acts of ignoring divorced from wider economic contexts.

AN ACADEMIC SCANDAL

It is partly taboos around admitting financial privilege that help to keep the myth of meritocracy as buoyant as it is, but family silence is not the only problem. It's also the fault of academic silos and the limits of social scientists who study the economy but who don't scrutinize enough the way that our models are implicated in obscuring corporate impunity happening in plain sight.

Murdochgate is the story of a corporate scandal, but it's more than that too; it's the story of an academic scandal – it's the legacy of a university system incentivized to court 'gifts' from billionaires and consultancy fees from big business rather than to study business practices in an impartial way.

The point has been made forcefully by Rakesh Khurana, professor at Harvard Business School, who has spoken bluntly about what he sees as the corporate capture of US business schools. Khurana argues that when business schools were first established in the early 20th century, management scholars saw their work in a moral light, questioning whether corporate governance practices were ethically defensible or not. He thinks this focus has waned since, and he worries that business scholars may have turned into the 'hired hands' of industry, lulled by profitable consulting contracts into ignoring bad behaviour.[21]

THE NARROWING OF THE ACADEMIC GAZE

At first glance, the chorus of management scholars who angrily criticized Murdoch for his claims of ignorance seems to prove Khurana's pessimism wrong. Management scholars were vocal about Murdoch's failings, including Roger Martin, a celebrated writer and former Dean of the Rotman School of Management at the University of Toronto.

'When superiors put substantial pressure on their subordinates to achieve aggressive goals, and don't check up on just how those subordinates accomplish those goals, something sinister can happen,' he suggested. 'News International should be seen as a rogue organization, not an organization with rogue reporters buried deep inside.'[22]

Suzanne Young, a management scholar at La Trobe University, agrees. Taking responsibility for underlings' actions is 'Corporate Governance 101,' she said. 'As anybody with a basic understanding of corporate governance will tell you, the buck ultimately stops with the chairman and chief executive.'[23]

And yet, by calling News Corp a rogue organization, the implication is that the system that surrounding it is *not* rogue, that it's this particular company that is dysfunctional and not the system itself. Martin and Young's criticism doesn't address a larger problem, which is the fact that CEOs such as Murdoch get away with plausible deniability excuses all the time.

Take a recent case involving Jérôme Kerviel, a former trader at Société Générale, one of Europe's largest investment banks. He lost billions of his employer's money and was sentenced to five years imprisonment. His superiors claimed he traded without their authorization, but as one law professor points out, 'the bank failed to investigate even known breaches by Kerviel of market risk limits.'[24]

A similar pattern can be seen in the collapse of Barings investment bank in the UK in the 1980s, when 27-year-old derivatives trader Nick Leeson lost the bank £860 million. 'In a sense,' sociologists Bridget Hutter and Michael Power write, 'the Barings Bank organization had all the information which might have alerted it to Leeson's unauthorized trading.' They decided not to act on this information.[25]

The usefulness of strategic ignorance in avoiding liability, especially for those at the top of corporate hierarchies, remains a little-understood problem. The following chapters explore why, by turning to the history of 18th- and 19th-century economic liberalism to understand the origins of our ignorance today.

I start with the ideas of Adam Smith, who did believe in the value of private enterprise, but who was a much stronger advocate of government regulation and progressive taxation than he is remembered for today.

The reason why Smith saw an important role for government regulation is simple. He didn't think that wealthy people should be above the law, nor permitted to manipulate the law for narrow individual gain, an attitude that links his 18th-century writing about joint-stock companies to contemporary debates over corporate impunity.

Smith writes about the problem of tiered systems of justice throughout *Wealth of Nations*. Under feudalism, he suggests, noble lords were too powerful for the monarchy to tax fairly, and so the burden of supporting the government fell on the poor and defenceless: 'the sovereign,' he writes, 'was obliged to content himself with taxing those who were too weak to refuse to pay taxes.'[26]

Gradually, the rule of law in European nations improved, enabling a more just system of taxation to develop, closer to Smith's ideal of 'perfect justice.' But Smith was adamant the system in his day still wasn't fair enough, because the merchant class – the class which he saw as benefiting *most* from government subsidies and expenditures – paid too little in tax.

Smith was born into a financially comfortable family (his father was a solicitor and his mother born to landed gentry), but he didn't see his own financial comfort as evidence of the universal righteousness of the political or economic order in his day.

The same was true of many of his enlightenment peers, including Edmund Burke, who argued that British East Indian Company traders who tortured and killed victims in India for personal financial gain should be named and shamed personally and forced to face justice in Britain.

Their ideas about economic fairness clearly weren't perfect. They reflected racist beliefs dominant at the time, a point I return to in the conclusion. As the pioneering feminist thinker and political philosopher Mary Wollstonecraft pointed out, Burke especially was blinded by his own class bias. Burke tended to be much more sympathetic towards Indian workers than British ones, a view resonating today with debates today about whether it's better show empathy towards the 'distant poor' or towards deeply struggling workers closer to home. Wollstonecraft saw this as a false conflict, insisting it's possible to do both.

FROM ELITE TO REVOLUTIONARY IGNORANCE

How does this relate to ignorance? Because over the years, mainstream economic theory has effaced the emphasis that enlightenment thinkers placed on economic fairness and accountability for corporate crime. I show how this ignoring has come about.

Has it been due to strategic ignorance or to unwitting ignorance?

To give away the punch line now, it's both. Strategic ignorance of Adam Smith's writing, for example, can be traced to a *deliberate* effort to obscure his call for regulations on deceptive, self-serving business practices. But other times, well-meaning scholars cite the 'wrong' Smith unwittingly.

Regardless of whether or not interpretations of Smith's work are deliberately or accidentally narrow, this narrowness helped to generate two separate, distinctive attitudes to government regulation that are both, I argue, equally wrong in their understanding of Smith and other early liberal economists.

On the one hand, a narrow reading of Smith and other early political economists led to a Pollyannish, *conflict-free* interpretation of the growth of individual and corporate fortunes, sometimes known as 'positive-sum' or 'shared prosperity' theory. Shared prosperity theory is the belief that 'enlightened self-interest' and the pursuit of profits inevitably leads to wider gains for a larger public, especially when government regulation is minimized.

On the other hand, in the middle of the 20th century, a 'rediscovery' of Smith's concern about profiteering led to the adoption of an opposite perspective: to a Hobbesian counter-response to earlier enlightened self-interest theories. This response, spearheaded by a varied group of scholars including the influential economists George Stigler and James Buchanan, generated a *total-conflict* stance which proclaimed that most government regulation is doomed to failure *because* of a truth that Smith first observed: that most people will exploit the government for private advantage if given the chance.

Both the conflict-free interpretation, on the one hand, and the total-conflict stance on the other hand, while different in important ways, have been equally powerful tools for the political right, used to attack regulations aimed at holding wealthy corporations and wealthy people accountable for harms to the public.

This problem is not intractable. I suggest that better understanding of the value that enlightenment thinkers placed on economic fairness and corporate regulation can help to battle the problem of corporate impunity today. So while I'm writing about the 18th century, I do so with an eye on the present, and in the final chapters, I look more closely at how anti-regulation attitudes are affecting the public right now – and how the problem can be fought.

CHAPTER 5

SUSPICIOUS ATTENTION

Born in Scotland in 1723 and dying in 1790, Adam Smith had a small but vibrant social circle, counting scholars like the philosopher David Hume among his best friends.

He never married, and many evenings, Smith's dinner was made for him by his mother – a fact that was pointed out recently in Swedish journalist Katrine Marçal's bestselling book *Who Made Adam Smith's Dinner?*, a wonderful and witty book which highlights important points about the way that contemporary economic theories tend to ignore the economic importance of domestic, unpaid labour, especially the labour of women.[1]

My focus is a little different. I agree that much academic theory ignores the role of unpaid labour in creating economic value. But there's also another problem surrounding the treatment of Smith's work today. His book, *The Wealth of Nations*, published in 1776, is widely viewed today as the most important modern economic text ever written. Smith is seen as the patron saint of the belief that economic self-interest will lead naturally to positive economic growth for all members of a community. Steven Pinker and others call this the 'positive-sum' or 'shared prosperity' thesis and they attribute it to Smith.

The reality is different. It is true that Smith believed the pursuit of economic self-interest could be a force for moral and economic good by fuelling economic growth. But only when self-interest is restrained by just laws and prudent government regulation. Time and again in *Wealth of Nations* he insists that self-interest and commercial greed jeopardized people's lives, leading him to call for state regulations on practices that harm the public.

For instance, he was highly critical of a laissez faire approach to loan-making. He argued that government limits on the interest that lenders could charge on loans was necessary to protect debtors and creditors both. In *Wealth of Nations*, he makes the governmental case for regulating interest rates by comparing this type of governmental intervention to the need for adequate fire safety regulations. It is worth looking at Smith's wording in detail:

> Such regulations may, no doubt, be considered as in some respects a violation of natural liberty. But those exertions of the natural liberty of a few individuals, which might endanger the security of the whole society, are, and ought to be, restrained by the laws of all governments, of the most free as well as of the most despotical. The obligation of building party walls, in order to prevent the communication of fire, is a violation of natural liberty

exactly of the same kind with the regulations of the banking trade which are here proposed.[2]

He also thought the government needed to prevent East India Company merchants from abusing the population in India. He is scathing about the British government's willingness to continually bail out companies that recklessly wasted capital and human life with impunity.

After first being published in 1776, Smith's *Wealth of Nations* was updated five times during his lifetime, and in editions published over the 1780s, he amplifies his criticism, pointing out in 1784 that the East India Company was 'in greater distress than ever; and, in order to prevent immediate bankruptcy, is once more reduced to supplicate the assistance of government.'[3] He condemns Britain's army for giving traders the means to wage war on the Indian peasantry with abandon, with disastrous implications for the region. 'How unjustly, how capriciously, how cruelly [East Indian traders treated the Indian peasantry] is too well known from recent experience.'[4]

Smith didn't think that state protections and subsidies were inherently wrong (he saw a need for them in some circumstances), but he had two main concerns. First, government gifts to the rich were doled out too arbitrarily: he wanted the science of subsidies to improve. And second, he thought the revenue generated from government subsidies wasn't shared fairly among the wider polity.

Smith's criticism of monopoly protections introduced a notion later described as 'rent-seeking' – the gaining of private benefits through disproportionate influence over government decision making.

Smith also introduced a second aspect of rentier privileges, one that relates to the economic concept of 'rent.' By this, economists don't mean the common meaning of rent; the eye-watering £2000 or so per month a two-bed flat in London costs to rent monthly (more in higher-end areas). Rent in Smith's terms is used to refer to unearned income which an owner can monopolize by virtue of having exclusive ownership rights, including land ownership.[5]

Smith and his fellow 18th-century friends worried a lot about excessive land rents, where families lived off the proceeds of inherited land, gaining income regardless of whether they exerted any effort towards cultivating or otherwise improving the land. Smith extends the notion to companies such as the East India Company, criticizing them for price-gouging practices which drove up the cost of consumer goods and rendered the 'wages of labour ... much less abundant than they otherwise would be.'[6] In doing so, he paved the way for fuller-blown theories of rentier exploitation emerging over the 19th century.

Smith makes a case for joint-stock companies to have time-limited monopoly rights, after which he suggests that even infrastructure funded by a company should be taken 'into the hands of government, their value to be paid to the company, and the trade to be laid open to all the subjects of the state.'[7]

Although Smith insisted the government should avoid 'perpetual monopoly,' it would be nearly another century before Britain fully abolished the East India Company's monopoly privileges. The 19th century – a purported high period of British free trade – was really a time of ongoing government-sanctioned trade monopolies.

And after the British government finally *did* nationalize the East Indian Company, the abuse of the Indian populace didn't dwindle as Smith hoped.

Well into the 20th century, Britain's subjugation of the Indian peasantry continued to deeply anger thinkers such as George Orwell, who criticized the political left and the right for turning a blind eye to the mistreatment of Indian peasants.

'One gets some idea of the real relationship of England and India when one reflects that the *per capita* annual income in England is something over £80, and in India about £7,' Orwell writes in 1939. 'It is quite common for an Indian coolie's leg to be thinner than the average Englishman's arm. And there is nothing racial in this, for well-fed members of the same races are of normal physique; it is due to simple starvation.'

Orwell bitterly adds that his friends tended to acknowledge the problem only when it was unlikely to change: 'This is the system which we all live on and which we denounce when there seems to be no danger of its being altered.'[8]

THE NEOCLASSICAL TURN

Orwell was hardly the first person to point out that the labour of oppressed groups was exploited by the powerful. Workers had long made the same point before him, including Maria

W. Stewart, an American black woman who went from being orphaned at five to lecturing in public about race and gender-based oppression. 'Like King Solomon, who put neither nail nor hammer to the temple, yet received the praise; so also have the white Americans gained themselves a name,' she said in a public speech in 1833, 'we have performed the labor, they have received the profits.'[9]

Orwell offered his similar remark about the exploitation of Indian labourers just over a century later. By then, something had fundamentally changed within the discipline of economics that made it harder for economists to perceive the unfair rentier advantages that Smith had first warned about in the late 18th century. Something known as the neoclassical turn in economics had become ingrained in mainstream economics research and teaching. The rise of this new, neoclassical theory led to the popularity of an entirely different theory of income distribution than in Adam Smith or Maria Stewart's era. It is known as the 'marginal productivity theory of income distribution.'

This new theory hails from the late 19th century, a time when a new, neoclassical theory of economics began to displace the ideas of earlier classical economists such as Adam Smith and David Ricardo.

The new generation of late 19th-century economists *was* strongly influenced by earlier scholars including Smith, but they differed from his theories in important ways, including when it comes to understanding how various goods and services obtain their value and their fluctuating price in any given market. Neoclassical theory had sweeping, world-changing effects. The biggest effect was the way that new, marginal theories helped to generate strategic ignorance surrounding the problem of rentier wealth gains. Marginal productivity theories deflected and obscured the criticism that Adam Smith and his peers directed at rentier profiteering and corporate abuses of power. My argument is that paying more attention to marginal productivity theories helps to create a plausible 'ignorance pathway' for understanding why 18th-century economic concerns about corporate rent-seeking were largely dropped as a major focus of mainstream economists over much of the 20th century.[10]

The new, marginal productivity theory of income distribution suggests that, under perfectly competitive markets, the remuneration that people receive from different economic activities tends to align naturally with the economic value that they have generated to society. Both in the mid-20th century and today, this new theory of income remuneration has been brandished to discount Orwell and others' concern about labour exploitation. Even though clearly a colonized market such as India is not a 'competitive' one, the popularity of the marginal turn in mainstream theory suggested that if Indian peasants are malnourished or have stunted growth, it's because the 'marginal product' of their labour is negligible and thus their wages commensurately low. Rather than seeing Indian starvation and malnutrition for what is really was, a direct result of labour exploitation, marginal productivity theories whitewash this exploitation to make it seem as if it resulted 'naturally' from impartial market forces rather than deliberate British colonial policy. Orwell could see the obfuscation taking place through the language of political economy, but his peers didn't want to be reminded of the problem.

Ever since it was introduced, marginal productivity theory has been widely derided by scholars working inside and outside the economics mainstream, but it is still taught as orthodoxy at most US universities.[11]

One of the leading proponents today of marginal productivity theories is Gregory Mankiw, an economist at Harvard who argues that increased global wealth concentration – the fact the richest 1 percent of the global population control nearly two-thirds of the world's resources – stems naturally from wealthy people making more valuable contributions to society than other people.

He acknowledges that what classical economists like Smith saw as 'rentier' activities still do exist in theory, but he insists that rent-seeking plays little or no role in producing current wealth inequalities in countries such as the US.

In his words (quotes taken from his article 'Defending the One Percent'): if 'a person's high income results from political rent-seeking rather than producing a valuable product, the outcome is likely to be both inefficient and widely viewed as inequitable.' But to his mind, this problem is exceedingly rare: 'My own reading of the evidence is that most of the very wealthy got that way by making substantial economic contributions, not by gaming the system or taking advantage of some market failure or the political process.'[12]

His critics see this as nonsense.

Within mainstream economics, support for marginal productivity theories of income distribution has been fraying as an increasing number of reputable economists call the theory an illusion – an unprovable hypothesis that thrives on the impossibility of empirically testing its presuppositions.[13]

Writing in the 1950s, left-wing Cambridge economist Joan Robinson criticized what she saw as the theory's irresolvable circularity. The idea that one's income represents a 'natural' measure of one's economic contribution is an unprovable as the hypothesis that one's good fortune is granted by God; both the providential theory and the marginal theory suffer from the difficulty of being falsified. She called the neoclassical theory of income distribution 'a powerful tool of miseducation.'[14]

A few years ago, I published an academic article on the history of marginal productivity theory after being struck by what I saw as an under-emphasized point: that it's not simply economists on the left who persistently raise concerns about its accuracy. Marginal productivity theories of income distribution were first developed in the 1890s by an American economist named John Bates Clark, and when he first formulated it, economists further to the right of him were most vocal about the theory's limitations.

George Stigler, a right-wing Chicago School economist who clearly didn't share Robinson's politics, acknowledged that Clark's theory was treated as 'naïve' for much of the early 20th-century, with scholars like Frank Knight pointing out in the 1920s that, far from being 'ethically just,' the 'paramount defect of the competitive system is that it distributes income largely on the basis of inheritance and luck.'[15]

The economist Paul Samuelson would later reiterate Knight's concern, remarking: 'To my astonishment I find that the arbitrariness of J.B. Clark's views on the deserving-ness of competitively determined rewards is not universally recognized.'[16] But Samuelson's comment is a little naïve too: he assumes his peers follow the evidence impartiality, but economists over the years are not as ideologically pristine as he supposes.

When right-wing economists like Frank Knight queried Bates Clark's theory in the 1920s and 1930s, they had an incentive do so. At the time, unions were growing more pow-erful. Centrist and right-wing thinkers feared that if unions managed to command an ever-ballooning share of national wealth for their own workers, they could point to J.B. Clark's theory to defend high wages as only 'natural.'

Knight's fears weren't realized in the end. Globalization and anti-worker laws in the US and the UK eroded the bar-gaining power of workers, and across western nations, labour's share of national income has strongly declined over the past 60 years.

Today, as the proceeds of economic growth are increas-ingly reaped by corporate executives, more and more economists are rethinking the soundness of neoclassical assumptions about wealth distribution.

In her recent bestseller book *The Value of Everything*, economist Mariana Mazzucato calls for university teach-ing and textbooks to evolve, for students to at least learn about well-evidenced doubt over marginal productiv-ity theory's real-world explanatory value, as well as to be taught the history of economists who argue that the theory obscures the role of luck and inheritance in creating wealth inequality. Joan Robinson made a similar suggestion in 1953, nearly three-quarters of a century ago.

Their criticism seems to be having an effect. In recent years, marginal productivity theory has come under the same staunch criticism that it faced over 50 years ago. The pendulum has started to swing *back* to a problem first raised by Smith: to the problem of rent-seeking and corporate impunity.

SHARED PROSPERITY?

Some intellectuals today, including Steven Pinker, continue to ignore this pendulum shift. Echoing Mankiw, Pinker insists in his recent bestseller, *Enlightenment Now*, that wealth inequality is irrelevant to both societal and individual welfare. What matters is poverty alleviation. If, overall, some people are less poor, the line goes, it doesn't matter if other people are spectacularly rich. According to Pinker, 'Economic inequality is not itself a dimension of well-being.'[17]

This opinion, artfully claimed as fact, *was* indeed a popular one among mainstream economists over the late 20th century, but for at least a decade it's been waning within the economics mainstream, and Pinker dismisses this important shift entirely in his bestselling book, *Enlightenment Now*.

Pinker's problem isn't simply that he dismisses the importance of economic equality for overall social wellbeing.

The even bigger problem is that he attributes the idea that inequality is *unimportant* to Adam Smith. In *Enlightenment Now*, Pinker generalizes from a few short passages from *Wealth of Nations* in a deeply misleading way.

Pinker sees Smith as the originator of positive-sum, shared prosperity theory. Smith realized, Pinker claims, that 'whatever tendency people have to care for their families and themselves can work to the good of all.' The founding fathers of America, Pinker suggests, 'designed the institutions of the young nation' to nurture Smith's ideas through 'voluntary exchange.'[18] Quoting a famous passage from *Wealth of Nations*, it 'is not from the benevolence of the of butcher, the brewer, or the baker that we expect our dinner, but from regard to their own interest,' Pinker complains that today Smith's message about the value of self-interest 'is obscured yet again by political debates within modern society on how wealth ought to be distributed.'[19]

Pinker's take may be pleasing to many people (Bill Gates called *Enlightenment Now* his 'favourite book of all time') but that doesn't make it accurate.

Smith's celebrated passage about the butcher and the baker *is* correct, but it's also a tiny sliver of Smith's overall argument. Smith certainly never advanced the cheery and quite naïve suggestion that 'whatever tendency people have to care for their families and themselves can work to the good of all.' Rather, he highlighted the problem of profiteering and called for government action to *make* markets fair by holding merchants accountable for fraud and pillaging. He was a fierce critic of unregulated profiteering, just as influential voices on the left and the right today, from Naomi Klein to Andrew Bacevich, raise questions over corporate profiteering in war zones and elsewhere.[20]

Readers may doubt this (Naomi Klein and Adam Smith in the same breath?) but Smith's argument is accessible to read in *Wealth of Nations*. Smith's call for better government regulation largely failed in his lifetime, but gradually checks on corporate entitlements and laws against monopoly privileges helped to rein in some aspects of rent-seeking behaviour that Smith identified.

Especially at the end of the 20th century, many of these checks were eroded, often at the behest of international lenders such as the IMF and World Bank, which, from the 1970s on, lobbied for developing countries to weaken labour protections and to dismantle national health services.

When worker protections are lost, health and equality gains are lost too. Just look at the last 60 years, a period when the global income gap has 'roughly tripled in size,' as political economist Jason Hickel points out in *The Divide*, a book that offers contrasting statistics to Pinker on the evenness and fairness of global growth today.[21]

SMITH: THE GOOD, THE BAD AND THE IGNORED

Not only did Smith recognize the problem of inherent economic conflict where market fundamentalists today speak of a natural harmony of economic interests, Smith prophesied the very mechanism through which the merchant class would manage to trick the other economic classes into sacrificing their interests for the merchants' advantage.

That trick is the merchant class's ability to create an erroneous *impression* of shared public interest. Here's where the story really gets interesting, because there's a deep irony – even something of a two-century-long academic hoax – at the heart of Smith's romanticized legacy. The irony is that so-called 'wealth-creators' are *still* getting away with the exact trick that Smith first warned governments to watch out for.

To understand this trick, it's helpful to understand the way that Smith categorized different economic classes in his day. He saw society as divided into three different classes, or 'orders' as he sometimes called them: the landowning class, the merchant class and the labourer class. But what really made his framework new is his insistence that different class positions weren't solely economic in nature. One's class position also had important implications for people's mental state and capacity to make sound political judgements.

Today, many people on both the left and the right dislike what they term 'identity politics' – defined as the attempt to gain political recognition or advantages on the basis of culture, class, ethnic or gender identity.

But 'identity politics' is a much older practice than people sometimes realize. Indeed, Smith was a student and to some extent a proponent of identity politics in his day, because he believed that legislators should bear in mind class circumstances and disadvantages, including a lack of access to education for workers, whenever making laws, intentionally seeing a problem from different perspectives in order to judge a matter as fairly as possible.

He wrote about the problem frequently: the tendency for a person's economic and social circumstances to cloud their judgement.

For example, the first order – wealthy, landed gentry in England who owned land and lived off land rents – were made stupid, Smith suggests, by their inherited wealth. In his words, they were 'not only ignorant, but incapable of that application of mind which is necessary in order to foresee and understand the consequences of any public regulation.'[22]

The second order – wage labourers – were also dulled by their occupation, but their problem was the strain of their work rather than too little of it:

> His condition leaves him no time to receive the necessary information, and his education and habits are commonly such as to render him unfit to judge even though he was fully informed. In the publick deliberations, therefore, his voice is little heard and less regarded, except upon some particular occasions, when his clamour is animated, set on, and supported by his employers, not for his, but their own particular purposes.[23]

'His employers,' Smith adds, 'constitute the third order, that of those who live by profit.' This third order, Smith describes, is made up of dealers and merchants who have the ability to think more clearly about their own self-interest than the other two main orders do, especially when it comes to their own specific, narrow branches of business. And it's because of this reality – the fact that merchants tend to know their own business thoroughly, but the affairs of wider society far less so – that Smith suggests that government legislators need to be wary of the demands of business merchants. The problem with merchants, he suggests, is that their thoughts tend to be focused more on 'their own particular branch of business, than about that of the society.'

And yet, even though merchants are mostly preoccupied with their own self-interest, and not the interests of the general public, Smith argues that merchants have a knack – sometimes dishonestly so and sometimes out of innocent error – for tricking other groups, including legislators, into believing that the merchants' interest is the same as the public interest. Smith advises his readers against falling for this error. 'The interests of the dealers, however, in any particular branch of trade and manufactures, is always in some respects different from, and even opposite to, that of the publick.'[24]

Smith follows this with a passage about economic regulation that, to put it mildly, doesn't get much ink in the *Wall Street Journal* today. Smith was not against state regulation, a point admitted by 20th-century economic liberals like Friedrich Hayek. What Hayek fails to add is that Smith called for exceptional scrutiny of the *third* order, *because* of the businessman's tendency to deceive. He was sceptical of laws and regulations proposed *by* the third order – the merchant winners in the new economy:

> any new law or regulation of commerce which comes from this order, ought always to be listened to with great

precaution, and ought never to be adopted till having been long and carefully examined, not only with the most scrupulous, but with the most suspicious attention. It comes from an order of men, whose interest is never exactly the same with that of the publick, who have generally an interest to deceive and even to oppress the publick, and who accordingly have, upon many occasions both deceived and oppressed it.[25]

Smith and not Karl Marx first noticed a truth about class conflict: that the dominant often prevail because the law unjustly advantages them:

The workmen desire to get as much, the master to give as little as possible … It is not, however, difficult to foresee which of the two parties must, upon all ordinary occasions, have the advantage in the debates, and force the other into compliance with their terms. The masters, being fewer in number, can combine much more easily; and the law, besides, authorises, or at least does not prohibit their combinations, while it prohibits that of the workmen. We have no acts of parliament against combining to lower the price of work; but many against combining to raise it.[26]

Smith here identifies a form of 'micro-ignorance,' a behavioural pattern discernible at the individual level that compounds societal-level macro-ignorance. In this case, his astute insight is to see that it's the large numbers of workers that renders their organizing more conspicuous, while merchants can rely on their smaller numbers to evade notice, even though their organizing exerts greater influence.

'Masters are always and every where in a sort of tacit, but constant and uniform combination, not to raise the wages of labour,' Smith adds. He saw that collusion among business-men is a truth that is both self-evident and ignored, a sort of 'useful unknown,' and he berates his peers for wrongly assuming that the absence of clear corruption is proof that no corruption has occurred.

Smith makes short work of this type of observation – the earnest but hapless scientist who mistakes a lack of evidence as evidence a phenomenon can't exist: 'We rarely hear, it has been said, of the combinations of masters; though fre-quently of those of workmen. But whoever imagines, upon this account, that masters rarely combine, is as ignorant of the world as of the subject.'[27]

THE VALUE OF 'SUSPICIOUS ATTENTION'

'Remember your psychology,' Pinker writes in *Enlightenment Now*, 'much of what we know isn't so, especially when our comrades know it too.' He's right on that point, just as he is flat-earth wrong to suggest Adam Smith is *uninterested* in wealth inequality or wealth distribution. It's a defining ele-ment of *Wealth of Nations*.

For example, Smith didn't use the term 'relative poverty,' but he introduces the notion through his 'linen shirt' example, where he points out that a workman's desire to have a fine linen shirt might strike the rich as a greedy luxury, but a workman without a fine shirt loses the respect of potential employers, threatening his job prospects – thus 'luxury' becomes necessity.[28]

This linen shirt example is a forgotten aspect of Smith's oeuvre, perhaps because it underscores Smith's pragmatic approach to class position. Smith was prone to rather sweeping generalizations when he suggests that everyone's mental outlook is shaped by their class status. It is an overly simplistic way to treat people's mental attitudes. But importantly, he doesn't see class position as fixed or unchangeable. Give a working man a decent shirt, he suggests, and his job opportunities change. Give a working man (as Marçal notes, he overlooks women) a decent education, and class prospects change.

'The establishment of perfect justice, of perfect liberty, and of perfect equality,' Smith insists, 'is the very simple secret which most effectively secures the highest degree of prosperity to all the three classes.'[29]

Make no mistake: Smith isn't worried about labourers' wages because he was a bleeding-heart softie. He insists wages should be sufficient to meet a worker's individual needs, to raise a family and live in some comfort, but he's also willing to tolerate fairly high inequalities created through inherited wealth. The connections Smith draws between monopoly protections and a labourer's low wages have to do more with government revenue than with a worker's livelihood. Monopoly power, he suggests, 'diminishes, instead of increasing, the ability of the great body of the people to pay tax.'[30]

He was an egalitarian because it made economic sense and not necessarily for moral reasons. But that's still a far cry from the idea that he thought wealth distribution was unimportant, as Pinker wrongly suggests.

In fairness to Pinker, he has a slightly different problem than accepting everything your friends think – the problem of not being able to see a truth because none of your friends recognize it either. And one reason might be the way *Wealth of Nations* has been marketed to the public over the years.

A KNOWLEDGE HEIST

Wealth of Nations is a gargantuan tome comprising five books. Most editions today are abridged versions. Editors over the decades have been free to include sections they see as most pertinent to readers and to jettison others when compiling shorter versions for mass audiences. With any book this editing process is thankless work, with considerable bickering over whether the 'right' sections are discarded or retained.

But even allowing for an editor's prerogative, though, the editing of *Wealth of Nations* during the 20th century must still surely stand out as one of the most brazen knowledge heists in modern scholarship, with certain editions willfully cutting out the entirety of Book 5. Titled 'The Revenue of the Sovereign of the Commonwealth,' it is in this book – the longest of all five books in *Wealth of Nations* – that Smith details his arguments about the appropriate role of government in a market economy. He writes at length about the East Indian Company's abuse of monopoly privileges and calls for specific taxes on merchants who benefit the most from state subsidies. He discusses the state's responsibility for maintaining public works. He calls on the state to provide public education to all children.

Kathryn Sutherland, Professor of Bibliography and Textual Criticism at the University of Oxford, points out these elisions in her eye-opening introduction to an abridged version first published by Oxford in 1993. She notes that the editor of a 1970 Penguin version expects that his readers will agree 'that the first two books contain the central part of Smith's work as a theoretical economist, and the real basis of a profoundly influential school of thought.' Another editor, of the Everyman version in 1991, suggests the first four books 'contain the whole of what Smith had to say in carrying out his aim, "An inquiry into the Nature and Causes of the Wealth of Nations."'[31]

Sutherland makes an important and neglected observation. To discount the centrality of Book 5 might seem like an arbitrary decision, but when multiple versions omit the same book, it amounts to a pattern of wilful omission. The deliberate cutting of sections where Smith writes at length about the necessity of government intervention is an example of what I mean by elite ignorance, because it proves that what people today *don't* know about Smith isn't simply accidental, but rather results from the biases of earlier scholars who are influential in shaping what future generations understand about the past. It is ignorance born from too much narrow knowledge rather than simply a lack of information. And also, importantly, this example shows that it tends to be out-siders who *lack* specialist knowledge about a topic who can spot anomalies with a historical record, a point emphasized to me by Sutherland during an email interview that I carried out with her.

'I saw the flaws in the presentation and celebration of Smith's argument as the founding document of the modern discipline of economics because I could not lay claim to the economist's narrow expertise,' Sutherland told me.

> If you read on, beyond Books One to Three of the *Wealth of Nations*, into those parts almost never represented in modern selected editions, it becomes clear that Smith foresaw negative consequences to unfettered economic growth; that for Smith the moral economy still mattered. Female economists, of whom there have been a few over the intervening centuries, often seem to grasp that point, but it has been widely ignored in a predominantly male specialism.[32]

It is a very good point, but while gender plays some role, it can't explain all. Writing in 1952, the British economist Lionel Robbins suggested that to call Adam Smith a laissez faire thinker 'is a sure sign of ignorance or malice.'[33]

In other words, women *have* been at the forefront of a more accurate understanding of Smith's writing. But a small but vocal minority of male economists within the mainstream also tried to challenge doctrinaire interpretations of Smith and yet still failed to dislodge conventional wisdom.

Oevr upcoming sections, I explore this problem further, suggesting an 'ignorance pathway' for understanding where the doctrinaire version comes from.

It's almost a cliché in the social sciences to point out, as the economist Joan Robinson put it, that 'ideas can become a material force.'

My emphasis is a little different: I want to understand how ideas veil material forces, making it possible for someone as smart as Pinker to see economic progress but never economic predation, to valorize 'shared' gains while denying in the same breath that economic equality is an important component of individual well-being.

Here's the rub: the suggestion that inequality is *not* important for understanding well-being is ironic and contradictory *because* of the insistence that economic exchange leads 'naturally' to universally shared prosperity. Quite literally, faith in 'positive-sum' or 'shared prosperity' thinking hinges on the assumption that economic gains are fairly distributed, because to 'share' is to determine equivalence. If Pinker wants to call himself a 'positive-sum' thinker then that makes him by definition a student of wealth distribution whether he likes it or not. Instead, he makes the bizarre claim that a rational understanding of inequality is 'obscured' today by debates over 'how wealth ought to be distributed.'

Occasionally, Pinker does acknowledge the value of laws that protect workers and reduce economic inequality: he hails the early 20th-century US labor movement for improving worker hours, for example. But this is precisely why Pinker's blinkered approach to wealth distribution is surprising – he commends long-ago labour battles, but when low-paid service workers call for fair pay today he mocks them disparagingly as 'social justice warriors.' It's an illogical double-standard – a double-standard that is similar to debates over economic inequality and economic justice that raged in the 18th and 19th centuries.

VOLTE-FACE

To suggest that late enlightenment thinkers were preoccupied with the problem of economic justice is *not* to suggest that they all had a uniform view on how to make the economy fair.

Take Edmund Burke, a man upheld today as a father of conservative political thought. He was unusual in many respects. He was a fierce defender of English aristocracy's right to maintain almost feudal dominance over British workers. But he was an anti-elitist too. Born in Ireland and living there as a child and adolescent, he never really lost the perspective of the underdog, nor what it was like to experience bigotry.

Burke's rivals often resorted to religious prejudice and bigotry to condemn his politics. Although Burke was raised as an Anglican, his detractors insisted that his Catholic heritage barred him from holding political office in the UK. This line of attack is not dissimilar to Donald Trump's racist Birtherist attacks on Barack Obama – Trump's use of fearmongering and lies to try to deny Obama's right to lead his country. But the tactic is an old one, and Burke's experiences of religious discrimination might have opened his eyes to the brutality of British oppression abroad.

Almost alone among British parliamentarians in his day, Burke objected to the East India Company's plunder of India. During the American War of Independence, he also supported American colonists in their fight against British oppression. But when the French Revolution succeeded in toppling the French monarchy in the late 1780s, Burke condemned the revolutionaries, demanding a restoration of aristocratic privilege and the protection of dynastic wealth. He derided the idea that workers in France could be the natural equals of their aristocratic rulers.[34]

His condemnation of the French Revolution led to swift and powerful rebukes from British democrats, including Mary Wollstonecraft, who wrote 'A Vindication of the Rights of Men' (1790), published a few months before Thomas Paine's more famous rebuttal to Burke in his essay 'Rights of Man' (1791).

Wollstonecraft seizes upon the law and its injustices to make her case for equal rights and equal justice. She points out that hunting and game laws in Britain render 'the life of a deer more sacred than that of a man,' and 'that the liberty of an honest mechanic – his all – is often sacrificed to secure the property of the rich.'

What's more, she knows Burke knows about such injustices but denies the problem; he sees the cards are stacked, but he still insists the game is fair. She addresses Burke directly: 'you seem to consider the poor as only the live stock of an estate … Gothic affability is the mode you think proper to adopt, the condescension of a Baron, not the civility of the liberal man.'[35]

Paine echoes Wollstonecraft's argument, suggesting that Burke's attitude was more feudal in nature than enlightened. Paine suggests that if only 'Mr. Burke possessed talents similar to the author "On the Wealth of Nations"' he might have realized that his disdain for French workers is illogical. But alas, Paine sighs, Burke is no Smith.[36]

Burke's volte-face strikes Wollstonecraft and Paine as a glaring double-standard, a departure from the enlightenment values he helped cultivate. His denunciation of workers' rights is 'sound reasoning,' Wollestonecraft writes sarcastically, 'in the mouth of the rich and the short-sighted.'[37]

WHAT'S IN A NAME?

Upon publication, the first edition of Wollstonecraft's *Rights of Men* essay was hugely popular, selling out in weeks. It was published anonymously.

The next edition carried the author's name on the pamphlet, and (surprise) approval for her argument soured.

'The *rights of man* asserted by a fair lady!' One periodical exclaimed, chiding her for being too dense to realize that 'the *rights of women* were the proper theme of the female sex.'[38]

That a woman had the guts to refute Burke's argument led, interestingly, to the conclusion that Burke must be right:

his supporters brandished this example as proof that British people needed to be insulated from the democratic spirit, because otherwise other women might be foolish enough to see themselves as equal to a man.

The speed of her fall from grace is telling: Wollstonecraft's ideas carried authority only when she concealed her identity. A pseudonym is a type of micro-ignorance that reveals larger truths about inequality in societies that value a woman's insights only when her identity is veiled.

In her rebuttal to Burke, she is one of the first modern writers to articulate the problem known today as confirmation bias, the favoring of facts that support earlier assumptions. 'When we read a book that supports our favourite opinions, how eagerly do we suck in the doctrines,' she writes, 'But when, on the contrary, we peruse a skilful writer, with whom we do not coincide in opinion, how attentive is the mind to detect fallacy.'[39] Everyone does it, she emphasizes, but Burke's problem is that he doesn't realize he does it.

Her originality is still neglected, her primacy ceded to men who made her same points after she did. The dulling of Wollstonecraft's legacy contributes to the devaluing of women more generally; even today, most university students are taught – wrongly – that the most original political thinkers of the enlightenment were all men.

Wollstonecraft *is* remembered today, but more for her path-breaking *Rights of Woman* essay published in 1792 and less for her equally path-breaking rebuttal to Burke.

History has accomplished what her critics wanted: they have limited her legacy to women's rights, which is only half-correct, obscuring the economic liberty that she wanted for women and men both.

The significance of this point is not simply that Wollstonecraft's life illustrates the effacement of women thinkers from history, but rather that her effacement raises larger truths about the way that narrow history and rigid academic theories makes it possible for erroneous theories about economic exchange to reign in the present.

A good example is the marginal productivity theory of income distribution discussed over this chapter. I argue that its entrenchment in undergraduate teaching has influential oracular effects, making it seem as if gross wealth inequalities reflect one's 'natural' contribution to society.

But what if the theory is wrong?

The issue doesn't seem to be that Knight, Samuelson, Robinson, Mazzucato and scores of others are all deluded about the theory's limits (cross-partisan insistence about a problem is usually the first sign an emperor is sitting naked in open sight) but that people are wary of admitting they are right. Entire subfields of macroeconomics would be affected if the theory was overturned, and the hassle seems to be putting people off.[40]

Mankiw is the author of a bestselling macroeconomics textbook, a staple of economics teaching at Harvard and elsewhere. In it, he espouses neoclassical marginal productivity theory as if it is self-evidently true. Although persistent unknowns over the theory's plausibility predate Mankiw's writing and clearly weren't only fabricated by Mankiw, they are still 'useful unknowns' in my sense, a form of active ignorance that often requires insider will to change, and thus remains entrenched because key stakeholders have little to gain from changing their perspective.[41]

The reluctance to investigate the limits of one's own ideology is a problem all humans share. The great 19th-century political philosophers John Stuart Mill and Harriet Taylor wrote about this very problem in the famous essay *On Liberty* – the way that people's worst errors often stem from unwitting ignorance, from the tyranny of social or intellectual conventions that we fail to recognize as constraints.

I turn to this problem next, and I can see the knives already: why the insistence that Taylor co-wrote Mill's greatest essay with him? But it's not me suggesting this, it's him. History has presented only one side of Mill's story. And as *On Liberty* suggests: when we know only one side of any case, we know little.

CHAPTER 6

KNOW-IT-ALL EPISTOCRATS

The enlightenment is often hailed as a time when knowledge 'triumphed' over ignorance.

But really, it was a time when human ignorance was first born. People living in earlier times of course acknowledged the problem of ignorance, attributing economic hardship or military blunders to human folly or a lack of learnedness. But the ultimate authority on which actions were foolish and which were wise was surrendered to a divine power. The new ignorance was different. What humans did not know became their burden alone, rather than a curse attributable to a deity. People squabbled over precisely what type of human this was, but one thing seemed clear: *he* was a *knower*.

The realization that ignorance was *merely* human led to false arrogance, to the presumption that ignorance is as mortal as humans themselves, to the belief that human ignorance could be vanquished as completely as a living enemy in battle. Having seen the birth of human ignorance, many scholars of the day assumed they would witness its death, and if not them personally, then their children or children's children.

By the middle years of the 19th century, utilitarianism had taken hold of the British political imagination. Jeremy Bentham's most famous pupil, J.S. Mill, voiced the spirit of the age when he suggested that Bentham's theories promised an end to human conflict and a beginning to new rules for living 'so firmly grounded in reason and the true exigencies of life that they shall not, like all former and present creeds, religious, ethical, and political, require to be periodically thrown and replaced by others.'[1]

But Mill's confidence in Bentham did not last. Even as a young adult in his early twenties, he began to doubt the comprehensiveness of his early education, sensing he had learned only 'one side of the truth.' Mill realized that the capacity of humans to eclipse ignorance was a sort of false hubris unwittingly propagated by his own closest mentors, including Bentham. Mill vowed in his twenties to flout utilitarian orthodoxy and let wider scholarship shape his judgement rather than rely on the received wisdom of his peers. Or so he thought.

Some of Mill's ideas did succeed in challenging Victorian platitudes, including his championing of women's equality to men.[2]

But Mill's defence of human equality was not extended to all people. He thought that Indians and the Chinese were inferior to Europeans and incapable of their own self-rule. And although he disliked the 'coolie trade' in indentured servants, and had, in private correspondence, compared it to slavery, he didn't publicly criticize Britain's violent role in perpetuating the coolie trade, an omission which I argue continues to compound public ignorance today of the injustice of indentured contracts in his time – and in our own era.[3]

Mill was a casualty of an insight he helped develop: his perception of the ways that one's personal allegiances – to family, to political party, to nation – blind people to inconvenient facts. He recognized a problem he couldn't escape, but at least he saw the problem.

FROM KNOWERS TO UNKNOWERS

The difference between Bentham and Mill is this: Bentham was a *knower*, convinced that better evidence leads inevitably to better governance. Mill refused to accept this, gradually realizing that whether or not a system of governance is just or not depends on *whose* evidence is consulted. In short, over the years, he shifted from a *knower* to an *unknower*. Like Socrates, his wisdom came from realizing how much he did not know.

Today, Mill is sometimes enlisted by political theorists to support the anti-democratic notion of 'epistocracy' which I criticized in Chapter 3. And to be fair to those who do so, some of Mill's writing could indeed be fairly read this way. Mill was in favour of limiting the vote to people with education qualifications, for example. But this was at a time when the franchise was far more restricted than it is today. And it is also clear that Mill had a deep appreciation of the *limits* of human knowledge and thus, in turn, more appreciation of the inalienable nature of human ignorance.

For this reason, even if Mill himself might have supported the idea of epistocracy, this chapter suggests that the political theory that he and Taylor developed deals a number of fatal blows to the perceived merits of this type of authoritarian rule. And so does Mill's life story. Because Mill recognized that people who tend to be dismissed as 'ignorant' according to prevalent social customs can actually be sources of unexpected originality – an idea so offensive to his fellow liberals that they found ways to make sure that future generations wouldn't be tarnished by Mill's love-struck flight from reason.

CAN A MAN IN LOVE SPEAK THE TRUTH?

Many of J.S. Mill's ideas led to controversy during his lifetime, but only one of his ideas was seen as so outrageous that his 'liberal' friends insisted on censoring it: his suggestion that his wife Harriet and his stepdaughter Helen co-wrote his books.

Mill married Harriet in 1851, after the death of her first husband. Harriet died just seven years later, leaving a daughter, Helen Taylor, who was in her late 20s when Harriet died, and who continued to care for Mill until his death 15 years later. In his *Autobiography*, Mill sought to pay tribute to the influence of both his wife and his stepdaughter on his writing, but this effort enraged his peer group, leading them to pressure his stepdaughter to remove sections where she is mentioned in editions published after Mill's death.[4]

Mill drafted much of his biography over the 1850s, but it was not published until 1873, the same year that he died. He devotes particular attention to Harriet's influence on his political ideas, suggesting that while many of his readers might assume that Harriet influenced his belief in female equality rather than his ideas about philosophy and political economy, in reality the opposite is the case. He insists that he already believed in female equality long before they met (adding that for Harriet, it was likely 'the originating cause of the interest she felt in me').[5]

The two essays *most* influenced by Harriet were *Principles of Political Economy* and *On Liberty*. When it comes to *Principles*, Mill states that Harriet particularly influenced his ideas on the value of socialism. Regarding *On Liberty*, an essay which is widely seen today as one of the most important documents in the history of political liberalism, Mill claimed that Harriet was an equal participant in the writing of it:

> there was not a sentence of it which was not several times gone through by us together ... it is difficult to identify any particular part or element as being more hers than all the rest. The whole mode of thinking, of which the book was the expression, was emphatically hers.[6]

LIBERAL CENSORSHIP

By consulting later editions of his *Autobiography* published throughout the 20th century it is still possible to glean a sense of the anger that Mill's words elicited upon publication.

This is because this anger has never entirely faded, and so later editions feature a succession of good liberals venting their outrage at Mill's candour. Take comments from Asa Briggs, a left-leaning British historian who furnishes the preface to a 1964 copy of Mill's *Autobiography*.

Briggs writes that Mill's peers rightly agreed that Mill had 'outraged all reasonable credulity in describing her [Harriet's] matchless genius, without being able to supply any corroborating evidence.' Briggs then turns for evidentiary reinforcement to the figure of George Mill, one of John Stuart's brothers who Briggs admits became estranged from Mill after he chose to marry Harriet. Briggs upholds George's assessment of Harriet's intelligence as evidence of J.S.'s delusion. In George's view, Harriet was a 'clever and remarkable women, but nothing like what John took her to be.'[7]

Of course, nothing beats an estranged sibling when it comes to unbiased appraisal. The unvoiced reason why Briggs is uncomfortable with Mill's insistence that Harriet co-wrote his most important work is probably closer to the problem Kathryn Sutherland perceives in the reception of Smith's arguments. In both cases, it's impossible to prove exactly *how* large a role gender plays but to deny it plays any role is equally implausible. If Mill insisted that an intimate male relation shaped his best ideas I doubt Briggs' outrage would have been as palpable. I also think that Briggs might have seen that the editorial decisions he praises in his preface should be denounced, for they involve the deliberate censorship of Mill's writing.

Briggs points out approvingly, for example, that the philosopher Alexander Bain, a friend of Mill's, 'persuaded

Helen Taylor to leave out of the published draft of the *Autobiography* in 1873 certain passages which stretched credulity beyond all limits.' These excisions pertain to Mill's descriptions of his stepdaughter's influence on his ideas, and in the 1964 edition that Briggs introduces, the excisions are still there, marked with asterisks – little classical liberal snowflakes – signalling the places where Mill's thoughts about Helen and Harriet were erased because his friends can't bear for readers to see his uncensored views.

One of Mill's more arresting phrases from his *Autobiography* is this: 'Whoever, either now or hereafter … think of me or the work I have done, must never forget that it is the product not of one intellect and conscience, but of three.'

Unfortunately for him, pretty much everyone forgets this today, thanks to editors who intentionally excised the knowledge of his debt to his wife and his stepdaughter from his autobiography.

BLINDSPOTS

It is hypocritical of Mill's fellow liberals to censor his thought, but it's not particularly surprising, for reasons that Mill recognized while he was alive – the problem of elite ignorance. His appreciation of this problem grew from his work with the East India Company, and particularly his realization that the tendency of British intellectuals to deliberately exclude Indian perspectives that cast doubt on the robustness of British knowledge of India. He makes this point at the end of his essay *Considerations on Representative Government*. This essay is well-known and justly criticized today because of Mill's derogatory statements about British colonies and the racist division he makes between 'European' colonies and non-European ones.

But the essay is also noteworthy for a commendable insight: Mill's admission of how little English authorities actually knew about India. He makes his remark on the last page of the essay, where he expresses concern over the East India Company's actions in India, and calls for a 'much more profound study of Indian experience, and of the conditions of Indian government, than either English politicians, or those who supply the English public with opinions, have hitherto shown any willingness to undertake.'[8]

This statement is remarkable for a number of reasons, not least the fact that the foremost authority on India for much of Mill's life was his father James, who published a history of India in 1817 that was widely hailed as the definitive history of the continent, and which secured James a position as a senior manager in the East India Company. James wrote the book without ever visiting India or knowing any native dialects, something he was proud of because he thought he could write more sensibly about the country if he wasn't biased by an understanding of local customs. It took 40 years, but John saw the epistemological errors in his father's attitude.

Mill's unease over the robustness of European perspectives about colonized peoples has implications today for political theory, and particularly to the growing call among libertarian and liberal thinkers to embrace 'epistocracy.'

His gradual realization of the incompleteness of his own understanding of India is pertinent to the question I've been asking throughout this book: exactly *whose* ignorance is most damaging for different groups in society?

Today, for example, many public intellectuals insist on blaming the public for making electoral decisions that strike elites as uninformed. Take an article written by the journalist James Traub in *Foreign Policy* after the Trump and Brexit votes. Traub suggests that 'it's time for the elites to rise up against the ignorant masses,' which is a remarkable statement considering the Leave vote and Trump's win were engineered by some of the wealthiest men and women in Britain and the United States.

It is also remarkable for illustrating that little has changed since Mill's time. Back then and today, 'educated' individuals often assume that people who know the least about society must be the poor or the illiterate. But Mill disagrees, realizing the sharpest minds in his day had no 'willingness' to study a country they assumed they already knew. Their ignorance about India came from misplaced faith in the robustness of their own education.

THE SPELL OF PLATO

From an early age, Mill doubted a widely held truism in his time: the belief that wealthy individuals possess a superior moral compass. His scepticism even fuelled his earliest polemical essay, composed at the age of 16 'on what

I regarded as the aristocratic prejudice that the rich were, or were likely to be, superior in moral qualities to the poor.'[9]

The prejudice Mill observed has not faded today – just look at the assumption that Trump's strongest support comes from the 'white working class' rather than his wealthy Republican backers.[10] The assumption is doubly ignorant, first for perpetuating the impression that the US working class is exclusively white, and second, for ignoring Trump's support base among wealthy, upper-class racists.

Today, misconceptions about 'voter ignorance' are fuelling calls to strip votes from people because of their presumed inferiority as 'knowers.' Setting aside the fact that such proposals for epistocracy are inherently inegalitarian, they also suffer from fatal epistemological flaws, because they are rooted in a fundamental error: the presumption that 'rule by knowers' will lead to more knowledgeable rule.[11]

In reality, in the same way that the quality of British knowledge about India actually degenerated rather than improved over the 19th century because scholars based their assumptions on James Mill's errors, 'rule by knowers' leads to a contraction of knowledge rather than an expansion of knowledge because elite rulers face no checks on the spread of their own ignorance.

I mentioned that J.S. Mill wasn't alone in recognizing this problem. Wollstonecraft and, in our times, from the end of WWII onward, the philosophers Charles Mills, Audre Lorde and John Gray do as well. I want to emphasize one other figure: the Austrian philosopher of science Karl Popper, a critic of authoritarianism who suggested that blind, naïve faith that society is inevitably progressing to a more positive future can lead even the most educated people to have a bias towards optimism when analysing the social and the natural world.

Worried by anti-democratic fascism on the right and totalitarian Stalinism on left, he called on his peers to avoid the 'spell of Plato': the deluded belief that an unelected set of wise noblemen are more knowledgeable than democratic representatives of the people. Popper suggests that Plato's vision of elite rule leads to the development of a 'caste state' where freedom of thought is spurned and knowledge degenerates, starved of the oxygen supplied by a diverse constituency of both knowers *and* unknowers – people who sense flaws within an existent paradigm and are able to convince 'knowers' of the illusion of their certainties.[12]

Today, Popper is sometimes seen as a critic of government interventionism by his admirers on the political right. This is justified in some ways because he was a fierce critic of Marx, and his criticism of 'caste states' invoke similar criticisms to George Orwell's denouncement of socialist tyranny in Animal Farm. Popper was also a close friend of the anti-socialist economist Friedrich Hayek whose *Road to Serfdom*, published in 1944, came out just a year before Popper's *Open Society*, and then and today, their work is seen in a similar light. In a 2005 edition of *Open Society* published by Routledge, the blurb on the book's jacket praises Popper for 'exposing the dangers inherent in centrally planned political systems.'

But this was not what Popper was trying to do. He was not a socialist but neither was he a free-marketer. With realistic pragmatism, he thought that a mixed economy functions best.

Ideologically, his main commitment was to democracy, insisting that anything less, any political systems that prevented the right to depose a leader through a majority vote by the people was a barbaric society, returning people to the status of enslaved beasts rather than human beings – a peril he was convinced was worth dying to prevent. 'We can return to beasts,' he writes in *Open Society*,

> but if we wish to remain human, then there is only one way, the way into the open society. We must go on into the unknown, the uncertain and insecure, using what reason we may have to plan as well as we can for both security *and* freedom.[13]

Inside my 2005 copy of *Open Society*, there's a review quote from *The Economist* praising Popper's ideas as the best ever democratic defence against 'know-it-all totalitarianism.'

The *Economist* is right, and the magazine is still right if we substitute a word popular with today's anti-democrats: Popper's arguments for democracy remain the best ever defence against know-it-all epistocracy.

CHALLENGING THE KNOW-IT-ALLS TODAY

In this and the preceding chapter, I drew on epistemological theories developed in the 18th and 19th centuries to criticize the ideas of two different groups of thinkers who are becoming increasingly influential today: first, a group that I describe as 'status quo populists' because they dogmatically insist the world is 'better than ever,' ignoring counter-evidence that suggests otherwise. And second, a group that calls themselves the 'epistocrats.' These two groups share a common belief: the presumption that the main thing wrong with politics today is the problem of uneducated or 'ignorant' voters.

Challenging this assumption, I have pointed out that elite ignorance can be just as worrisome as so-called 'lay' ignorance, and might even be a considerably worse problem, because, as Mill and Taylor stress throughout the essay *On Liberty*, entrenched ideologies lead people to be less alert to their own mistaken assumptions.

Take, for example, the notion of 'progress.' Does anyone seriously doubt there's been social progress since the 18th century? That you're even willing to read these words knowing they're written by a woman is proof that my gender is no longer a sign of my obvious inferiority as it was for Wollstonecraft. Or is it?

In truth, I can't know the answer – I can't read your mind – and you may not know it either. You may hope you're free enough of prejudice to judge my words impartially, or you may think that I'm the deluded one – to use the language of the alt-right today, that I'm a 'gender irrealist,' denying my innate inferiority, and if you do, you're in plenty of good historical company.

'I detest women who write,' Alexis de Tocqueville remarks in his *Recollections*, describing a dinner where he was forced to sit next to the French female author George Sand, 'especially those who make a system of disguising the weaknesses of their sex instead of interesting us by having us see them in their true character.'[14] To his credit, at least he didn't compare her to a lobster.[15]

It's an undeniable banality to point out there's been 'progress' since the late 1700s. The real debate is over which factors have enabled some groups to prosper while many other groups lag behind: anti-trust laws or regressive tax policies? Conquest or consensual trade?

It's an open debate because there are few simple answers, and we should be sceptical of those who suggest otherwise. It's an open debate because both in the 18th century and today, there is widespread conflict among intelligent people over the level of government regulation needed to make sure the wealth of nations is fairly shared. It's an open debate until anti-democrats and status quo populists force the debate closed.

Why, for example, is Smith's writing about 'perfect equality' relatively unknown today? Can the problem be blamed on the so-called 'ignorant' masses as epistocrats suggest? Or as I suggest, are scholars to blame?

Over the years, a handful of influential thinkers *have* tried to spur more attention to the problem of ignorance in economics and political affairs. The economist John Maynard Keynes was right to point out 'the ideas of economists and political philosophers, both when they are right and when they are wrong, are more powerful than is commonly understood.'[16]

But he didn't detail the mechanism of ignorance transmission in any systematic fashion. Libraries are filled with studies of knowledge production, but the study of ignorance production is in its infancy.

Frédéric Bastiat, a 19th-century thinker and classical economic liberal, wrote about the problem of the 'unseen' in political economy. He was inspired particularly by Rousseau, who, as Bastiat put it, 'never spoke more truly than when he said: It takes a great deal of scientific insight to discern the facts that are closest to us.'[17]

George Orwell reiterated the point when he famously observed, 'To see what is in front of one's nose needs a constant struggle.'

These are compelling but also obvious points in a way: we know that people struggle to accept inconvenient facts, and we also have a good idea of why (Upton Sinclair's adage applies: 'it is difficult to get a man to understand something, when his salary depends on his not understanding it').

What we don't really know is *how*. How do some people 'get away' with sustained ignorance when others on lower rungs of a social ladder are treated as more ignorant than the elite?

We need to better understand ignorance pathways: plausible accounts of how micro-ignorance contributes to larger unknowns, and the next chapters introduce such a pathway by exploring how the language of 19th-century theorists of political economy made it seem as if economic exchange in the 19th century marked a clear break from earlier forms of state-facilitated violent appropriation, even though many mercantile forms of corporate privilege did not end.

Language plays a role in veiling economic privileges and economic exploitation through words that seem innocent but imply an erroneous impression of a historical era, like the claim that America's founding statesmen designed the nation to foster 'voluntary exchange' (Pinker's phrase) when the nation was really founded on practices of economic enslavement, legitimated through spurious systems of scientific classification that bolstered white supremacy. This reality is both known and unknown, admitted openly but tacitly dismissed by those who favour Pinker's Panglossian US origins myth.

It's not simply the deliberate misrepresentation of history that leads to macro-ignorance. Academics sometimes contribute unintentionally to misunderstanding about major historical change (or about the continuance of practices assumed to have disappeared when they haven't, like ongoing reliance on coerced labour in the post-slavery era). Compelled to find the right language to explain a historical transformation, social scientists christen a period 'new' in a way that veils the continuance of old practices that unfold in plain sight but jar with the new characterization, and thus tend to be ignored.

This seems to have happened when Smith wrote about the 'conclusion of the mercantile system' in *Wealth of Nations*. This was Smith's 'own goal,' allowing his followers to take him at his word.

Smith *wanted* to believe the era of mercantilism was fading, that the emerging system of 'free' enterprise replaced earlier forms of protectionism favouring the wealthy classes. But no matter how many believers a theory has, that doesn't necessarily make it an accurate reflection of reality. Keynes said as much when he suggested the main flaw with mainstream economic theory was that 'its tacit assumptions are seldom or never satisfied, with the result that it cannot solve the economics problems of the actual world.'[18] That's a pretty big problem, and as Keynes suggested, ignoring it doesn't make it go away.

CHAPTER 7

CONFLICT
BLINDNESS

Today, an explicitly mercantilist age seems to be re-emerging, and this worries people for the wrong reasons: not because it's new, but because people deny the ways that it is old.[1]

'Trump's trade policy is stuck in the '80s – the 1680s,' writes *Washington Post* columnist Catherine Rampell, reporting that Trump's trade tactics threaten to undo three centuries of free trade that ensued ever since a 'dude named Adam Smith waltzed into the scene.'[2]

She may be right about academic theories of global trade over recent centuries but she is not right about actual trade policy. 'The dispatching of mercantilist doctrine is one of the foundation stones of modern economics,' the *Economist* put it recently, but 'its defeat has been less total than an introductory economics course might suggest.'[3]

The magazine is using characteristic British understatement, but when it points out that the defeat of economic mercantilism – the death of economic nationalism – is 'less total than an introductory economics course might suggest,' that's British for a lot of textbooks are full of nonsense. And yet the textbook 'evidence,' even though deeply flawed, carries an epistemic authority more powerful than truth. Keynes tried with *his* typical British restraint to make this point clear: 'The difficulty lies not in the new ideas, but in escaping from the old ones.'[4]

Much like Smith, Keynes was not opposed to private property or capital accumulation, but he thought government regulation was necessary for ensuring that plunder and profiteering were restrained and punished. Writing in the early 1930s, he raises reservations about the doctrine of free trade that he and his fellow economists inherited from the 19th century. He acknowledged that to question the doctrine's righteousness was tantamount to questioning God's existence in earlier eras, but sometimes sacrilege is warranted. Was 'free trade' really as 'free' or as universally beneficial as presumed? Like Voltaire or Descartes wrestling with God, Keynes has his doubts.

'What did the nineteenth-century free traders, who were among the most idealistic and disinterested of men, believe that they were accomplishing?' Keynes asked in 1933. He answers his own question. They believed

> they were serving, not merely the survival of the economically fittest, but the great cause of liberty … that they were the friends and assurers of peace and international concord and economic justice between nations and the diffusers of the benefits of progress.[5]

Keynes isn't so sure. Let's start with peace, he writes. Can we be so certain 'free' trade has brought unrivalled peace? (It's sobering to emphasize this was 1933.) It is the inability to regulate cronyism and profiteering that worries him: 'The divorce between ownership and the real responsibility of management is serious within a country ... But when the same principle is applied internationally, it is, in times of stress, intolerable ... remoteness between ownership and operation is an evil in the relations among men.' The problem with 'free' trade for Keynes is that women and men can profit from corporate exploitation and mismanagement while shifting the blame to others.

Keynes' insights from the 1930s are valuable, but he was not the first to stress that unregulated profiteering can threaten human life and individual liberty. Enlightenment radicals over a century before him saw this problem too, and today, their ideas matter in an age when the 'wealth of nations' is not being shared; when more eyes are opening to the way that old patterns of wealth concentration and economic exploitation have long been with us and may be getting worse, not better.

Today, there is a growing assault on enlightenment principles of economic fairness, egalitarianism and democracy hailing from both the *strongs* and the *smarts*.

From the political right, there is white supremacy married to plutocratic law-making, forging a fresh vision of legal protections for the rich and the gifting of new entitlements to corporations while the rights of individuals are curbed. I introduce examples of the problem of tiered justice systems in Chapter 9. But equally, among epistocrats from the technocratic centre and also from many on the political left, there's a rise in anti-democratic proposals to restrict voting rights.

Democracy is threatened by bigotry of race and bigotry of education, by those working now to disenfranchise others based on their race or on what they are perceived to know. The most important shared trait of these two camps – the *strongs* and the *smarts* – is the *least* recognized aspect of their power; both camps amplify perceptions of the ignorance of the people while obscuring the ignorance of elites. Both the *strongs* and the *smarts* imply that either their education or their wealth confers on them special entitlement to govern, but the opposite is true: claims of special enlightenment are not 'special' but rather prosaic, rooted in centuries of anti-democratic strategies to defend inherited wealth and political favouritism.

Before the 18th century, God was conveniently drawn upon to rationalize the perpetuation of privilege. But enlightenment visionaries refuted this dogma. 'It is wrong to say God made Rich and Poor,' Thomas Paine wrote bluntly. Look instead to human laws that favour the rich, he insisted, and there you'll find the reason for inequality on earth.[6]

Today, the notion of 'economic justice' is treated like a dirty word by today's libertarians who claim to adopt a 'classical liberal' outlook, but their predecessors were far more open to different forms of wealth redistribution than is commonly understood today, even if they disagreed wildly, as Burke and Paine did, about how to make the economy more fair.

The glossing over today of their proposals for a more fair economy encapsulates a larger process of erasure: the glossing over of the reality of conflict between different economic classes and nations as a central, unavoidable problem of political economy.

This chapter and the next make suppressed conflicts more visible. First, by exploring Burke's failed effort to hold the East India Company accountable for the mistreatment of Indians, and second, by drawing on Paine's insights into elite ignorance to consider the significance of Burke's ultimately dashed effort.

My main point is this: by illuminating different enlightenment viewpoints about the obligations that a government owes to different generations and peoples, including foreign populations (Burke's point) and future populations (Paine), these chapters revive attention to a neglected enlightenment lesson: the recognition that economic conflict *is* inevitable, but that a prudent, representative and just government must and can strive to balance competing interests fairly.

A balanced, pragmatic approach to inevitable economic conflicts is very different from the attitude today, when people seem polarized by a Pollyannish attitude (Steven Pinker: globalization had made everything better) and a Hobbesian one (Stephen Bannon: globalization has made everything worse).

These chapters explore a plausible 'ignorance pathway' for understanding this polarization: the way that dominant theories of free trade crystallizing in the 19th century gave leading industrialists from Carnegie and Rockefeller onward a believable 'ignorance alibi' obscuring their own reliance on government protections and an exploited labour force.

UNACCOUNTABLE TRADE

At first, Burke championed the cause of the East India Company (EIC) traders. The wealth amassed by British merchants in the Far East led many 18th-century statesmen to discern godly sanction in the bounty brought to Britain's shores: 'I think there is something of divine providence in it,' Burke suggested.[7]

But over the 1770s, his opinion changed after a series of stock market crashes destabilized the UK's banking sector. Mushrooming reports of the harsh treatment of Indian peasants also raised concern among some, though certainly not the majority, of Britain's high society and intellectual elite. Not just Burke, but most scholars of the day followed the EIC's activity closely. 'Do these events affect your theory?' David Hume wrote to his close friend, Adam Smith, after a particularly sharp drop in the market.[8]

For enlightenment visionaries, the problem wasn't economic trade, but rather unaccountable trade, legitimated by the British government which preached the importance of separation of powers even as it allowed a company of businessmen to become tyrannically powerful, to the disadvantage of British consumers duped by EIC traders' fraud and price-gouging.

Since its founding in the 1600s, the Company had lobbied for and been granted various British Crown licenses, periodically renewed, which enabled Company traders to dominate the Indian market, aided by a private army of soldiers who used high taxation and the flogging, torture and murder of Indian tradesmen and peasants to keep a steady of flow of imports bolstering the company's share value.

Much like many multinational companies today, the East India Company was a public–private hybrid: it had a degree of legal autonomy from the government that protected its monopoly privileges, but it also depended on the government for military aid in India. Its hybrid status – neither fully private, nor fully public – was convenient for the company.

'When it suited, the EIC made much of its legal separation from the government,' British historian William Dalrymple writes, 'even though the government had spent a massive sum on naval and military operations protecting the EIC's Indian acquisitions.'[9]

Dalrymple is one of a handful of British historians who insist that even today, the Company's activities continue to be glorified in troubling ways, idealizing the history of a company that should be seen in harsher light than it often is.

The website of Britain's National Army Museum praises Robert Clive, one of the EIC's most influential Major-Generals, as a 'Heaven-Born General,' quoting praise from Prime Minister Pitt the Elder. Yet, Dalrymple and others are rather more circumspect about Clive's tactics.

Clive was instrumental in many military successes that enabled the company to gradually assume territorial control of large sections of India, including a military defeat in 1765 that forced Shah Alam, an unpopular Mughal emperor, to sign a document that surrendered tax collection privileges to East India Company traders in Bengal, Orissa and Bihar.

Protected by a large private army, the 'right' to collect taxes from the Indian peasantry enabled Clive and his friends to amass fortunes that made them Britain's wealthiest 'self-made' men. Their methods made even some of their most hardened peers in Britain blanch. Diaries from the time indicate that people were 'tortured to disclose their treasure; cities, towns and villages ransacked.' Dalrymple notes the looting did not require sophisticated execution: 'The entire contents of the Bengal treasury were simply loaded into 100 boats and punted down the Ganges from the Nawab of Bengal's palace to Fort William, the company's Calcutta headquarters.'[10]

Although the British later called the 1765 transfer of tax duties a 'treaty,' it was compelled by force, just as later treaties with China over the 19th century were 'negotiated' through military compulsion. Dalrymple identifies a sort of mutually reinforcing, corporate-state ignorance alibi: the EIC and British government would insist upon their distance from one other when it was convenient to ignore their integration and praise their connectedness when calling upon each other for favours.[11]

Dalrymple's research challenges a perception that remains widespread today about the East India Company's territorial dominance in India: the belief that Britain acquired control in India less through deliberate strategy than from a fit of 'absent-mindedness,' through parliamentarians back in London simply failing to notice as the firm expanded across Asia.

Even some of the world's most eminent scholars ever since perpetuate this misconception. In *Origins of Totalitarianism*, for example, Hannah Arendt suggests that until the late 19th century and the expansion of 'formal' imperialism, Britain's bourgeoisie were largely uninterested in affairs of parliament – as long as property rights were secure, 18th-century merchants were less interested in governing.

Her claim misses a practice that angered Burke a century earlier: the fact that many nabobs, a nickname for British traders in India, used their fortune to secure themselves seats in parliament. The link between commerce and parliament was as close in Burke's time as it was a century later. Even if they never travelled to India themselves, many MPs had an economic interest in the company's lucrative profits, and their stake may have coloured their decision-making.

Around the time when Clive assumed government control of tax collection in India, MPs voted on whether to retain the Company's legal distinctiveness from the Crown. Among those who voted on the decision, 'nearly a quarter of them held company stock, which would have plummeted in value had the Crown taken over.'[12]

It would be another century before the company was formally dissolved, in 1873, with handsome compensation paid by the government to the company's investors. The Prime Minister at the time, Benjamin Disraeli, helped secure Queen Victoria the title of Empress of India, and a new era of 'authorized' imperialism began. As George Trefgarne writes, 'the freebooting era of "informal empire" finally came to an end, and the short-lived period of "formal empire" replaced it.'

I'm not sure whether 80 more years of British domin-ion could be called short-lived, but Trefgarne's assessment is illustrative: even a conservative news magazine like *The Spectator* has difficulty refraining from a generous use of quo-tation marks when discussing the neck-jerking way the EIC's private directors and MPs in Britain would lob responsibil-ity for the company's atrocities back and forth like a spirited doubles match at Wimbledon. Paine called this sort of blame-shifting the 'rotary motion' of government, the way different branches 'cover each other until responsibility is lost.'[13]

That Burke tried to halt the rally mid-play is more unusual than the game's endurance for over three centuries, and he recognized how outrageous an effort it was.

As reports of brutality against Indians mounted, as it became obvious that returning nabobs' wealth stemmed from extortion rather than allegiance to British or Indian law, Burke worked for years to shift his party, the Whigs, away from their early defence of the East India Company's expansion.

Finally, with grudging Whig support, he eventually managed to introduce new legislation making the company beholden to parliamentary commissioners – but the effort was scuppered by George III. Monarchy and corporate tyr-anny had a way of working hand in hand.

Next, Burke turned to the courts and attempted to prosecute Warren Hastings, Governor-General of India from 1773 to 1786, for 'high crimes and misdemeanours.' The trial, launched in 1788, lasted seven years. Eventually Hastings was cleared by a House of Lords 'more interested in imperial acquisition,' his-torian Nick Robins writes, 'than points of principle.'[14]

Robins argues that Burke saw his effort to hold EIC traders accountable to British law as the most important action of his life. Burke failed, but even his failure is a type of triumph. He compelled his peers to reckon with their duties as parliamentarians in a manner that reverberates with women and men in office today everywhere – no matter where on the political spectrum they sit.

If Burke could trust until his death in the righteousness of his worst-ever flop as a politician, then why shouldn't others trust their conscience too?

If he almost alone was willing to become his generation's David, taking aim at the most powerful corporation of his day, then perhaps his example helps to reinforce the legitimacy of limiting corporate impunity today.

And yet, to his critics, and not undeservedly, his compassion towards Indians only highlighted the unfairness of his myopic unwillingness to see that French and British workers had a right to fight for *their* equal rights too.

What stands out about Burke's zeal in the case is not simply his insistence that parliamentary authority can and must outmuscle corporate clout ('To whom then would I make the East India Company accountable?' he asked. 'Why, to Parliament, to be sure'). Nor even his compassionate defence of the equal rights of Indians: 'I must do justice to the East,' he stated, 'for I assert that their morality is equal to ours.'[15]

Rather, it is that Burke's inability to convince his elite peers to support him didn't open his mind to the weaknesses of government by elites.

Burke issued his famous attack on the French Revolution at the exact time that he was prosecuting Hastings, and it's this seeming myopia on his part – his insistence that aristocrats and the nouveau riche were competent governors in England when their unlawful venality in India was at its most obvious – that baffles critics like Wollstonecraft and Paine.

In his plain-talking style, Paine wonders why Burke can't see that 'many things in the English government' are 'the reverse of what they ought to be, and of what they are said to be.'

The way the 'English parliament is constructed,' Paine goes on, is like a 'criminal sitting in judgement upon himself,' adding that 'a body of men holding themselves accountable to nobody, ought not to be trusted by any body.'[16]

Paine raises concerns about inherited privilege that apply today, a time when the US president has free rein to appoint his children to positions of power.

The problem with hereditary privilege, Paine insists, is that it puts men in power who not only 'trample' on the rights of others, but 'are taught and educated so to do,' whose 'ideas of *distributive justice* are corrupted at the very source.'[17]

His criticism of inherited power is summarized in a famous passage:

Every age and generation must be as free to act for itself, *in all cases*, as the ages and generations which preceded it. The vanity and presumption of governing beyond the grave, is the most ridiculous and insolent of all tyrannies. Man has no property in man; neither any generation a property in the generations which are to follow.[18]

They are stirring lines, but Burke's attitude to India also deserves remembrance. Another sentence of Paine's also gives me pause: 'It is the living, and not the dead, that are to be accommodated.'[19]

A prudent government must do both. Burke's insistence that the dead deserve justice too – that India's forgotten dead deserve a legacy – should not be dismissed either.

It might seem like a tall order to suggest the best of Paine should be combined with the best of Burke, but such idealism was what made the enlightenment what it was: the daringness to know differently, the presumption that new combinations were worthy of trialling, that experiments in governance could lead to the seemingly impossible: to honour the equal rights of all, to respect living and future generations both, to refuse to elevate the 'best' of any nation above the laws that make a nation great.

Today, for example, proposals for a basic income that guarantees a minimal level of livelihood to all individuals is gaining steam, and rightly so, but it's hardly a new idea (libertarians dislike hearing this, but basic income is essentially welfare by a new name).

Paine was among the first to raise such an idea. In one of his last and most ignored essays, 'Agrarian Justice,' he calls for the establishment of common wealth funds that could help a democratic nation to avoid the generational problems he outlines in *Rights of Man*, the fact that inherited private wealth immediately advantages some individuals over others at birth.

Paine recognizes the truth about the American and French Revolutions, that even supportive people dreaded their success: 'it is the hazard and not the principles of a revolution that retards their progress.'[20] His solution was to make 'society the treasurer' of a government programme that would rebalance inherited privileges by giving all women and men a lump sum in early adulthood and again in old age, financed through a tax on property and made appealing to the wealthy because it thwarted a bloodier threat: forced expropriation.

He saw the merits of establishing such programmes at the national level, so that a citizenry could vote on their management, and he was willing to pitch in even if he wasn't legally forced to do so.

'I have no property in France to become subject to the plan I propose,' he writes, 'But I will pay one hundred pounds sterling towards this fund in France ... and I will pay the same sum in England, whenever a similar establishment shall take place in that country.'[21]

UNFINISHED BUSINESS

Paine and Burke's separate proposals for economic justice illuminate the troubling reality of how little things have changed since, and in some ways might be worse. Certainly mainstream opinion is even *less* open to the moral and economic righteousness of distributive justice than it was in their day.

Many nations established welfare systems over the 20th century, but those systems have failed to protect human rights, including the right to adequate housing and the right to health. Rather than giving young men and women money in early adulthood as Paine suggested, England and America gouge students through high interest rates on student loans, a practice that persists despite government misgivings.[22]

The principle that Burke tried to establish – laws conferring extra-territorial liability for crimes carried out by a multinational company operating outside a home nation – is established under international law, but the law is breached with ease.

Canada, for example, is home to over half of the world's mining companies, many of which are implicated in human rights abuse. Although violations are often brought to light, justice is routinely hindered by two widely known problems. First, the difficulty in holding parent companies responsible for infractions carried out by subsidiaries, and second, by jurisdiction problems and debate over whether a lawsuit should be heard in a host state where a subsidiary operates, or in Canada where parent corporations are formally domiciled.[23]

Breaches of the Geneva Conventions are also common. Today, when American soldiers are ordered to commit crimes on foreign soil, the US government finds creative ways to limit their liability, even though if matters were reversed, and drones were bearing down on US soil, it is unlikely many Americans would want American citizens treated as cavalierly as the US's breaching of international law allows Americans to treat foreign populations.[24] This was Burke's point anyway ('I assert that their morality is equal to ours').

The attitude of late enlightenment thinkers towards economic justice invites sneers today, waved off as nonsense that good conservatives and 'classical liberals' should unite in opposing, lest politics become too charged. 'I believe that politics is way too intense. That's why I'm a libertarian,' the California investor and entrepreneur Peter Thiel proclaims.[25]

Thiel's simplistic attitude to political conflict is so widespread that people seem astonished to learn enlightenment thinkers didn't share it, especially Smith, who writes at length about the inevitability of conflict between classes and nations, necessitating prudent legislators to intervene in different ways. Smith thought that reducing trade tariffs, for example, would help nations to trade more peacefully, but he was practical enough to realize nations would still battle with each other. For this reason, he praises England's protectionist navigation acts. 'As defence,' he writes, 'is of much more importance than opulence, the act of navigation is perhaps the wisest of all the commercial regulations in England.'[26]

His attitude to national security is yet another thing ignored today. Below, I explore reasons for this neglect, starting with a brief summary of an important methodological difference between Smith and David Ricardo, an economist who, far more so than Smith, developed influential theories of free trade still dominant in political economy textbooks today.

FINE IN THEORY

Ricardo was born a generation after Smith, and much like Smith, he hoped that curbing trade monopolies would lead

England's wealth to be distributed more fairly. But he differed from Smith in important ways. His main innovation over Smith was to argue that even countries which had a *weaker* absolute advantage in trading terms could still benefit from lowering or removing trade protections, because the nations positioned themselves to exploit relative differences in labour and other costs of production, reducing the price of consumer goods.

He was able to show that his idea of comparative advantage 'holds' numerically through an idealized juxtaposition of 'England' and 'Portugal' that is based on a hypothetical comparison of labour costs in the two countries. His idea was elegant, but as many scholars since have pointed out, it has many problems.

'Ricardo's original numerical example strategically misdescribes in Panglossian liberal terms a deeply unequal trading relationship created through highly illiberal means,' British political economist Mathew Watson points out.[27] Lars Syll, a Swedish economist, agrees: 'Ricardo shunted the car of economic science on to the wrong track. Mainstream economics is still on that track. It's high time to get on the right track and make economics a realist and relevant science.'[28]

Cambridge University economist Ha-Joon Chang makes a similar point. As he puts it: 'Ricardo's theory is absolutely right—within its narrow confines ... Ricardo's theory is, thus, seen, for those who accept the *status quo* but not for those who want to change it.'[29] Chang's larger question is: *why* should countries accept their current technological state as a 'given' when doing so means acting as if all nations' relative power is itself an inalterable 'natural' fact, rather than a reality produced through earlier conquest and colonization.

The very wording of 'free trade' obscures the fact that no two nations start on the same footing. Probably the best real-world example is the US in the 19th century. Steel and oil tycoons like Rockefeller and Carnegie benefited from favourable protective tariffs, and they knew it – their support for the Republican Party over the Democrats was rooted in the GOP's protectionist policy stance in the 1870s to early 1900s. This is why it's untrue to claim that Trump's trade protections belong in the 1680s, because it wrongly suggests trade protections are new and not widely used throughout US history.

During the 19th century, economists working in the 'historical' tradition raised the same concerns that scholars like Watson and Chang raise today, insisting that universal 'laws' of economics are invalid because they ignore the cultural, economic and military might that makes every nation distinctive. Economic 'laws' might appear logical, but they fail when assumed to reflect the actual actions of nations and human beings.

An important representative of the historical economics school flourishing over the 19th century is Friedrich List, who was once seen as a visionary economist on a par with Ricardo and Smith, but whose ideas long ago fell from fashion.

List is probably the first great student of strategic ignorance in economics. He didn't use the word 'agnotology,' but he did accuse his predecessors of dangerous dogmatism that led them to ignore inconvenient facts, including Smith, who he thinks deliberately misconstrues the historical record, buffing his theory of free trade to make it shinier for others.

I think List is unfair because most of the buffing happened after Smith died. List misses an important split between Smith and his followers since, the fact that *Wealth of Nations* is a fact-based effort to understand market activity as it actually unfolds in practice, no matter how ugly, and it *was* ugly, so ugly, in fact that, Smith was under no illusions that his vision of fair trade could ever be realized perfectly.

Trade could never be *fully* equal *because* malfeasance is not always seen. But he wanted the state, the judiciary and the public to be vigilant towards the practices of businessmen. He wanted a sort of rights economy: a form of exchange that draws on governmental power to protect individual liberty – the liberty of the poor as well as the rich. To understand the distortion of Smith's greatest insights we need to understand the distortion of 19th and 20th-century history.

THE REAL WEALTH OF NATIONS

Friedrich List was born in Reutlingen, a small town in Germany, in 1789. In 1819 he helped establish an association of industrialists and tradesmen, and became active in a movement calling for internal custom duties to be removed in German states. This political activity was viewed as seditious and List was accused of treason and sentenced to ten months' compulsory labour. He escaped and travelled in England and France, before eventually returning to finish his sentence, moving to the United States shortly after.

There, he found an economic climate that would enable him to refine a theory he had started nurturing in Germany, his belief that countries should use *internal* custom duties sparingly, but not necessarily waive *national* custom controls. In the US, he stumbled happily on a national example that could prove his case: a muscular, highly interventionist government willing to flout European academic pieties about the value of free trade in order to steer its economy towards new heights.[30]

List took notes on the American example while studying the history of other nations, including England. He became convinced that Smith deliberately excluded evidence that didn't chime which his overarching theory. In List's opinion, Smith's most glaring omission within *The Wealth of Nations* was his failure to admit that a protective trade policy throughout the 18th century was key to England's growth as an economic powerhouse.

This charge is detailed in List's *National System of Economy*, published in 1841, where he examines England's mercantilist climb to economic superiority:

> The assertion that the English have attained to their present commercial eminence and power, not by means of their commercial policy, but in spite of it, appears to us to be one of the greatest falsehoods promulgated in the present century.[31]

In blunt language, he suggests Smith must have deliberately blinkered himself to avoid discovering unsettling truths:

for what reason could such a profound inquirer permit himself to abstain from an investigation at once so interesting and so fruitful in results? We can see no other reason than this – that it would have led to conclusions which would have tended but little to support his principle of absolute free trade ... These facts, it would appear, Adam Smith was not willing to know or to acknowledge; for indeed they belong to the category of ... inconvenient facts.[32]

It's a fair comment in many ways, pointing out that Britain's wealth came less from free trade than from explicit mercantile policies – but it also misses the thrust of Smith's criticism of government protections. Smith doesn't deny that England's protectionist policy helped to create considerable wealth in the nation. But he suggests the country could have done even better if it pursued a less protective approach. And his *biggest* problem was that the wealth wasn't fairly shared – monopoly privileges unfairly benefited merchants at the expense of labourers and consumers in both England and in the colonies.

Smith is particularly critical of the cost of Britain's military defence of the 13 American colonies, which he thinks placed too much of an economic military burden on Britain in exchange for profits that were captured by a small merchant class: 'To promote the little interest of one little order of men in one country, it [monopoly] hurts the interest of all other orders of men in that country, and of all the men in all other countries.'[33]

Smith asks: how did the short-sightedness of Britain's monopoly privileges come about? His reply: by letting a few 'shopkeepers' dictate policymaking:

> To found a great empire for the sole purpose of raising up a people of customers, may at first sight, appear a project fit only for a nation of shopkeepers. It is, however, a project altogether unfit for a nation of shopkeepers, but extremely fit for a nation whose government is influenced by shopkeepers.[34]

Today, this quip – a 'nation of shopkeepers' is attributed to Napoleon Bonaparte's sneering remarks towards England, with few realizing Smith used the phrase first, with no less disparagement. His point was simple: a nation that looks after its shopkeepers equally might not be too bad a thing. What's wrong is a nation whose government bows to monopolists.

And over the 19th century, as America grew, that's exactly what happened, leading to similar, spectacular economic growth that England experienced in the 18th century, but with the same sort of problems that Smith identified – the wealth wasn't fairly shared.

CHAPTER 8

MASTERS OF INDUSTRY, MASTERS OF IGNORANCE

The protectionist policies that Friedrich List admired so much in America in the 1830s were influenced by the farsighted writings of Alexander Hamilton, the first US secretary of the treasury – living the American dream these days in the Broadway hit *Hamilton: An American Musical*, first performed in the winter of 2015 and now touring globally.

Shortly after the popular musical launched, the US treasury announced plans to replace Hamilton's image on the US $10 bill. This did not fly. Lin-Manuel Miranda, the creator of the musical, was granted an audience with the current US treasury secretary, who assured him that he would help to protect Hamilton's legacy. Thanks in part to the popularity of the musical, there is growing recognition today that Hamilton's ideas chime well with left-wing thinkers today who champion the power of the state to fuel and fairly distribute economic revenue.

Hamilton proposed policies that look today like a prescient form of early Keynesianism. He proposed direct subsidies for domestic manufacturers; the establishment of a national bank partially funded by government; and widespread infrastructural development of roads, internal waterways and ports – policies outlined in a report now seen as a defining document of American protectionism, *The Report on the Subject of Manufactures*, presented to Congress in 1791. This report takes aim at laissez faire thinkers who suggest that 'Industry, if left to itself, will naturally find its way to the most useful and profitable employment.'[1] Hamilton insisted that for the US to compete fairly with Britain's economy, the US economy required 'the extraordinary aid and protection of government.'

IGNORED HISTORY

Derived from Hamilton's policies as the first secretary of the treasury, US policy throughout the nineteenth century had more in common with the protectionism practised by Britain over a century earlier – the period when Britain established its economic clout – than with classical economic liberalism as it's portrayed in textbooks.[2]

Eminent scholars like historian Colleen Dunlavy and sociologist Frank Dobbin and Timothy Dowd have forcefully challenged the assertion that a 'free market' ever spurred America's industrial growth. The common line, Dobbin and Dowd write, tends to go like this: 'Britain and the U.S. became economic giants by allowing free markets to build their respective economies and by embracing non-interventionist policies. Other nations have obtained – or will obtain – similar results by following the examples of Britain and the U.S.' But this belief is at 'odds with the reality that it describes.'[3]

Despite their efforts, a plethora of bestselling books continue to deny this reality, propagating erroneous assumptions about America's laissez faire past. In 1977, Alfred Chandler published an influential book, *The Visible Hand*, a history of the American corporation where he asserts that the US in the 1840s had become a 'believable illustration' of the unfettered market economy that Smith imagines in *The Wealth of Nations*. The book won the Pulitzer for history and is still assigned as core reading across many management and political science departments. Later, critics queried his ignoring of the state's role in 'large-scale public ventures such as the army, the military armory, government-chartered state and federal banks, and the postal system.'[4]

Over the years, many economic historians have called attention to the history of tariffs and other government inventions over US history, but these studies haven't really dented a popular imagining of America's history which romanticizes the country's laissez faire origins.

During the 1940s, thanks in part to pioneering research by a wife and husband team, Mary Handlin and Oscar Handlin, scholars were presented with evidence that should have 'collectively laid to rest the myth of laissez-faire during the antebellum period.'[5]

And yet, these studies also appeared just as New Deal social protections for the poor and the elderly were being widely rolled out. The establishment of new, highly visible welfare programmes over the 1930s and 1940s seemed to give both conservatives and liberals the impression of an unprecedentedly active state. A new spectre seemed to materialize, distinguishable from the unfettered market which Americans across the political divide imagined characterized the earlier century.

Really, all that changed in the 1930s and 1940s was that the *type* of private citizen entitled to government welfare now included more members of the worker classes rather than simply the wealthy. And even the New Deal policies largely favoured only white Americans and not black citizens.

Black Americans, as historian Howard Zinn points out, 'were ignored by New Deal programs ... as tenant farmers, as farm labourers, as migrants, as domestic workers, they didn't qualify for unemployment insurance, minimum wages, social security or farm subsidies.' Zinn adds that Franklin Roosevelt, to appease white politicians in the south, chose not to back a federal anti-lynching bill.[6]

It is not that commercial activity wasn't widespread in early America or that industrialists were not pioneering new methods; indeed, industries were mushrooming so quickly that Alexis de Tocqueville, visiting the country in the 1830s, grew concerned by the aristocratic propensity of the new industrialists. 'At the same time that industrial science constantly lowers the standing of the working class, it raises that of the masters,' he writes. 'What is this, if not an aristocracy?'[7]

The point is that these aristo-industrialists were so firmly ensconced in a web of protections that to speak of America as 'laissez faire' is to perpetuate a myth masquerading as reality.[8]

DEMOCRATIC WEAPONS OF FREEDOM

Tocqueville had surprisingly harsh words to say about the new kings of American industry, an aspect of his influential book, *Democracy in America*, that is almost as overlooked as Book 5 of *Wealth of Nations*.

Tocqueville's main point is that the growth of industry generates the need for greater government protection.

'The manufacturing classes do not become less dependent as they become more numerous,' Tocqueville writes, 'On the contrary, it would seem that they bring despotism along with them and that it naturally extends in proportion to their growth.'[9]

He saw that the integration of business and government risked compounding the 'rotary motion' Paine identified, the tendency for government to sit in judgement of itself in a 'dangerous and tyrannical fashion,' in Tocqueville's words.

But he doesn't think the problem can be fixed by a small or weak government – he insists upon the very opposite: 'It is both necessary and desirable that the central power of a democratic people should be both active and strong. One does not want to make it weak or casual, but only to prevent it from abusing its agility and force.'[10]

His solution was to make sure checks and balances were maintained, including checks on corporate influence over government decision-making.

Tocqueville *is* a free trader, but unlike today's free traders, he doesn't think free trade means immunity from government regulations.

Why? Because he saw that people are at risk of death and poor health if corporations are not regulated. In his words, private industry can

> … endanger the health, even the life, of those who make money out of it or who are employed therein. Therefore the industrial classes, more than other classes, need rules, supervision, and restraint, and it naturally follows that the functions of government multiply as they multiply.[11]

Like Smith and Wollstonecraft before him and Keynes after him, he was critical of corporate impunity – pointing out that individual businessmen tended to unite into all sorts of new industry associations ('new corporate bodies,' as he put it) that are 'stronger and more redoubtable than any private person could be and that they have less responsibility than the latter for their acts.'[12]

To Tocqueville's mind, this responsibility burden needed to be reversed. Rather than corporations being used as a shield enabling people to avoid personal responsibility for harms to others, he called for corporations to be granted 'less independence from the power of society than would be proper in the case of an individual.'[13]

And if they're not? If corporate power continued to trump individual freedom? In his view, the corporate threat to individual liberty was grave. He adds a last, rather chilling warning about the power of big business. It's a prescient warning in light of growing concerns about the erosion of democratic rights in America.

He suggests that as citizens either choose or are compelled to focus their energies on their private work, they might lose interest in the science of government: they might simply look away. And while they're not looking, a threat could gain force: the possibility of their government being either seized, or simply handed over willingly, to 'one irresponsible man or body of men. Of all the forms that democratic despotism might take, that would assuredly be the worst.'[14]

He viewed the rise and dominance of private industry as one of the roads a democratic people might walk towards their own 'servitude.' He *was* gloomy but he was a practical man too, and he suggested that two things can help to prevent this possibility. To keep their government free of corruption or complete tyranny, a democratic people have two aces up their sleeve: a free press and a free judiciary. Control over a people, he insists, cannot be 'complete if the press is free. The press is, par excellence, the democratic weapon of freedom. Something analogous may be said of judicial power.'[15]

Just like Smith, Tocqueville believed the government has a duty to protect human safety and elevate the well-being of workers (he expresses the wish that political and industry leaders would 'attach less importance to the work and more to the workman').[16] And just like with Smith, Tocqueville's call for active, prudent government regulation has been, to put it mildly, side-lined over the years.[17]

Closer scrutiny of the language of some of Tocqueville's peers shows why.

THE LANGUAGE TRICK

A good example is Frédéric Bastiat, an ardent free market advocate whose life circumstances exemplified a problem then and today: the question of whether gross differences in inherited wealth sit comfortably with the right to equal liberty.

He inherited his grandfather's estate at 24, leaving him well-off for life, at leisure to study and write about the merits of low taxation. He was an excellent writer, and like most good writers, he knew that language and rhetoric were key to propagating an ideological viewpoint. He thought economists needed to be more militant in disseminating laissez faire principles: 'It is above all in political economy,' he writes, 'that this hand-to-hand struggle, this ever reviving combat with popular error, has real practical value.'[18]

But, a little ironically, although he insisted the economist needed to attack competing theories like socialism with a warrior's militancy, he also suggested that the best way to convince people about 'free' trade was to minimize any association with war.

'Let us banish from political economy all expressions borrowed from the military vocabulary: *to fight on equal terms, conquer, crush, choke off, be defeated, invasion, tribute,*' he writes, 'such expressions are inimical to international cooperation, hinder the formation of a peaceful, ecumenical and indissoluble union of the peoples of the world, and retard the progress of mankind.'[19]

It's a sentiment that would not be out of place in bestselling books today from authors like Pinker praising the merits of free trade in achieving world peace – if only global trade was actually as peaceful as Bastiat claimed then or as status quo populists insist it is today (recall Keynes: it's never a good idea to pretend world peace has arrived; ignoring tensions doesn't make them go away).

Bastiat actively called for a sort of micro-ignorance, for a rhetorical strategy that obscured economic violence. To his credit, he didn't want opposing viewpoints subdued through brute force: he supported freedom of association and the press (he distributed pamphlets directly to French socialists during the workers' rebellion of 1848, trying to persuade rather than silence). But he also hoped that veiling conflicts through misleadingly bland language would help the academic theories he favoured to flourish, and he was right.

He might have been particularly forthcoming about the free trader's playbook – efface the language of conflict from theories of trade, then beat the public rhetorically with how peaceful free trade is – but his attitude wasn't unusual.

Many leading political economists of his day were convinced that mercantilism had ended and a new global trade based on consent rather than coercion had taken its place, even though the presence of European gun boats, a large territorial army in Asia, and reliance on slave and indentured labour in the US and elsewhere suggest otherwise.

Even J.S. Mill was guilty of romanticizing the peaceful nature of Britain's global dominance. 'In history, as in travelling, men usually see only what they already had in their own minds,' he writes in his influential essay *The Subjection of Women*, somewhat ironically, for in the same essay he praises England at length for stewarding a new modern era of free enterprise based on 'moral law' rather than 'force' – a debatable assertion made at the height of British empire, when a succession of 'heaven-born' generals imposed 'peace' through violent force.[20]

But I'm not making this point to attack Mill. My aim is the exact opposite. I'm trying to stress that Mill is right – we do tend to see what we want in history, and given that someone with Mill's brilliance and compassion was not spared this problem, his example serves as a warning today, when other smart people also make debatable assertions about the pervasiveness of peace in our day.

'War is illegal,' Bill Gates suggested recently, praising Pinker's book *Enlightenment Now*.[21] Gates' view on violence is not wrong in some ways: homicide rates in western nations, for example, have declined massively since the Middle Ages.

But it's also true that US-led warfare in the Middle East and elsewhere continues to cause death and suffering, often for financial profit, and naïve, self-pleasing statements like 'war is illegal' veil this fact.

As historian John Dower points out, the numbers of people forcibly displaced by war over the past 20 years is estimated by the UN to have risen by 75 per cent, from

37.3 million in 1996 to over 66 million today. The total number of displaced people today is greater than at the end of WWII.[22]

Many of these people have been directly displaced by US and UK-led invasions in the Middle East. Suggesting that it is irrational to worry about this problem isn't helpful – it certainly doesn't help policy-makers to generate political will and resources to find the type of lasting settlement solutions reached post WWII, or to hold the US and UK to account for their role in people's displacement. I asked a World Bank economist recently whether 'the world is wonderful' argument is helpful and his answer was blunt: a curt 'no.'

J.S. Mill had an obvious rhetorical aim when he praised England as a nation of peace-loving, enlightened people. He was flattering his audience to try to bring more people around to his argument for female equality. Today, Gates and Pinker seem driven by similar motives, hoping that the more good news there is, the more it will deter people from gravitating to political extremism and violence.

In ways, it's a commendable aim, but it's also an extremely blinkered strategy. In Mill's case, it led to the same sort of 'own goal' that Smith suffered: their writing gave unintentional cover to war profiteers and gilded-age industrialists who cited free trade theories to deter the very sort of worker-friendly regulations both Smith and Mill thought were necessary to ensure that wealth is fairly shared.

The fortunes of Carnegie and Rockefeller are a good example.

THE BIRTH OF THE CEO
IGNORANCE ALIBI

Both born in the 1830s, Carnegie and Rockefeller's industrial careers followed remarkably similar paths. Both commanded important roles in business at remarkably young ages. Both were committed to philanthropy throughout their lives and not, as is sometimes believed today, as reluctant benefactors who parted with their fortunes only at the end of their lives. But their commitment to philanthropy didn't stem from a commitment to the ideal of economic justice envisioned by earlier enlightenment thinkers. Robber baron charity was more reminiscent of feudal benevolence than the enlightenment ideal of 'perfect equality.'

Much like today's market fundamentalists, Carnegie and Rockefeller approved of government interventionism only when it aided their own interests. And similarly to Murdoch, they had a knack for 'knowing what not to know' when critics suggested their business affairs were anything other than pristine.

I argue that in distinctive but compatible ways, their attribution of their own business success to either evolutionary law or to godly grace helped to perpetuate the myth of America's laissez faire origins.

I look first at Carnegie's story, and then at Rockefeller, to make the same general point. While neither of them, to be sure, were the first 'self-made' industrialists in the US or Britain, there *was* something unique to their era that distinguished their fortunes.

For two centuries before them, the flourishing industrial economy conferred riches on new classes of men and women, and in important ways, this money was put to radical, world-altering good use. The clout of the new bourgeoisie was instrumental in breaking the grip of feudal, dynastic privilege in Europe. The birth of democracy is linked in no minor way to a demand for first property rights and then to universal voting rights.

But clearly it wasn't all good either, and until the early decades of the 19th century, when British slavery was abolished, the uglier side of business was obvious. The wealth of the new merchants was rooted in slavery, and laws everywhere were still stacked against free workers and slaves both, as Adam Smith observed.

The difference is, a century after Smith's death, gilded-age millionaires such as Carnegie and Rockefeller were the first 'self-made' men to benefit from the entrenchment of laissez faire theory in academic textbooks, furnishing respectability for their business practices that often eluded earlier merchants and industrialists whose wealth arose under more blatantly violent, explicitly mercantile economic conditions.

For this reason, I argue the gilded age was the era when the CEO ignorance alibi first emerged: the ability for a new generation to distance themselves from the sort of negative press attached to earlier men like Robert Clive, whose success in battle in India didn't save him from widespread criticism upon his return in England for his abusive methods. He experienced public shaming until his death, believed to be suicide.

No, they didn't lead military pursuits, but Rockefeller and Carnegie also benefited from the seamier aspects of 'free' trade that tended to be scrubbed from academic textbooks: from the use of coolie labour on railroads, from US settler colonization and its accompanying brutality, as well as tariff protections and government subsidies and low-interest loans to business to build the Union Pacific and Central Pacific railroads.[23]

Government subsidies and tariff protections *were* visible in plain sight – but when rich industrialists insisted their riches arose from the 'natural' laws of supply and demand, the press, influenced by the same academic philosophies of free trade as the industrialists, largely accepted their claims.

THE RIFLE DIET

In 1870, when Carnegie was 35 years old, the US Congress introduced a $28-per-ton tariff on imported steel, the goal being to break Britain's export dominance. Carnegie once claimed the tariff was 'the single most important event in prompting him to enter the steel business.'

High tariffs would stay in place until the late 1890s, when Carnegie and others, having established their competitive dominance, called for lowered import tariffs so that other, less powerful nations would follow suit, allowing US industrialists to access their raw materials more cheaply.

In his autobiography, Carnegie claimed to have never profited from trading and speculation in stocks, a practice he would castigate for fomenting price instability in the markets. This, however, was not true: for about 10 to 15 years from 1855 he engaged heavily in trading – 'buying and selling shares in companies whose assets he knew to be far less than the value of their stock,' historian David Nasaw describes.[24]

His lying was a habit: he relied on deception throughout his career to obscure public knowledge of business practices he sensed might seem unpalatable to the public, generating an ignorance alibi that made his claims of 'cooperation' with his workers seem more plausible.

Carnegie was perceived in the media as labour's friend, more sympathetic to their concerns than, say, Tom Scott, a friend of both Carnegie and Rockefeller who thought the 1877 railway strikers should be given a 'rifle diet for a few days and see how they like that kind of bread.'[25] Carnegie took an opposite stance in public, repeatedly telling media that he supported his workers' right to improve their pay and work conditions. 'Labor is all that the working man has to sell,' Carnegie suggested to media in 1885, 'and he cannot be expected to take kindly to reductions of wages, even when such are necessary in order that he may have any work at all.'[26]

Quietly, though, he suppressed all union organizing. One of his approaches, widely hailed in the media, was to introduce a 'sliding scale' system for his workforce, the idea being that pay would rise when the price of steel rose, and fall when it fell. In 1885–1886, steel prices rose by almost 40 per cent, and Carnegie proudly proclaimed he had increased his workers' remuneration by 10 per cent 'before they asked for it.' But only some workers accepted the rise, others fought on to

reduce working hours to eight hours – Carnegie had stealth-
ily squeezed through a rise to 12 hours during a price slump
the previous year. In 1888, workers at his Edgar Thomson
steel works plant were again asked to take a 10 per cent wage
reduction, as well as a return to a 12-hour day. They refused,
and a lockout ensued. Carnegie publicly proclaimed that he
would never permit substitute labour to replace his striking
workers, but behind the scenes he directed his managers to
hire replacements. He also must have at least tacitly approved
a decision to bring in the Pinkertons militia to break up the
strike.[27] The 1888 strike petered out, with a final concession
forced on the returning workers. Carnegie's management
declared they must sign an agreement barring them from
becoming members of a union.

What is most curious about the Edgar Thomson strike
of 1888, Nasaw suggests, is 'its virtual erasure' from history. Although a local labour newspaper published an article
declaring that Carnegie's true aim was to 'crush the union,'
adding that 'hypocritical protestations of love and regard for
his workmen will not stand when compared with the fact,' the
New York press failed to cover the more incendiary aspects
of the skirmish – and instead published fawning articles about
Carnegie's imaginative sliding scale concept.[28]

Partly because the press saw Carnegie as a man of the
people, the country was shocked and horrified by the bloody
battles that unfolded over 1892 at Homestead. Once again,
following the Homestead catastrophe, Carnegie would later
deny knowledge and support of his management's tactics.
And once again, that impression wasn't accurate.

Although Carnegie had managed to stamp out union membership from his Braddock mill, the Amalgamated Association of Iron and Steel Workers still had a solid standing at his Homestead plant, located across the Monongahela River. During the spring months of 1892, Homestead workers, enraged at the suggestion of a 35 per cent wage cut, voted to strike. Carnegie left for Europe in early April. Before leaving, he placed his business partner, Henry Clay Frick, in charge of quelling the simmering workers' rebellion; Frick was careful to keep Carnegie continually informed of his decisions by cables during Carnegie's stay abroad.

To the few determined members of the press corps who had sought Carnegie out in Europe for his views on the Homestead crisis, Carnegie professed shock and ignorance – telling one reporter in the early summer that he had long ago retired from active management, and had 'not attended to business for the past three years.' Later in the summer, pressed to reflect upon the catastrophe by a friend of his who worked as a journalist and news editor, Carnegie declared 'It would be absurd for me to write upon events which were as much news to me as to yourself.'[29]

But cables sent from Carnegie to Frick all summer prove he was lying. Not only was Carnegie aware that his management was willing to use the force of the Pinkertons to break the strikers in 1892, he also fired a predecessor of Frick's for settling with the Amalgamated workers during an earlier lockout rather than enlist the Pinkertons at that time; Carnegie had been furious that his underling capitulated, enabling the union to keep an upper hand longer than Carnegie was willing to tolerate.

Using tactics similar to Stephen Bannon's 'non-visibility' approach honed at Goldman Sachs, Carnegie's absence from the country gave him an ignorance alibi widely accepted in the media. His feigned ignorance helped him to maintain his public persona as a man of the people and, as Nasaw emphasizes, the mainstream media accepted this, believing him when he insisted that government tariffs were justified because he used his profits to pay his workers better. This wasn't true. Through the 1890s, for example, 'the value of goods shipped from the Carnegie mills increased by some 226 per cent in the seven years following the strike of 1892, the percentage paid out in wages *decreased* by 67 percent.'[30]

NEVER WRITE ANYTHING DOWN

Rockefeller was born four years after Carnegie. Hired as a bookkeeper for a partnership of produce shippers in Cleveland at the age of 16, he made chief bookkeeper at 17, and still dabbled on the side as a small-scale commodities trader – flour, pork and ham mostly.

In 1858, at the age of 18, he established a partnership of his own with Maurice Clark, a 28-year-old Englishman. Later they collaborated with another Brit, Samuel Andrews from Wiltshire. It was Clark and Andrews' friendship that sparked Rockefeller's involvement with oil. Andrews had founded the first oil-based kerosene developed in Cleveland, but needing capital to expand his new refining method, he approached Clark and Rockefeller. They offered $4000 towards the new venture, baptizing the company Andrews, Clark and Co. Rockefeller then bought out Clark's share in the oil refining venture two short years later, and by 25 he had majority control of the largest refinery in Cleveland.

When he was 28, Rockefeller colluded with Jay Gould and other insiders in a secret agreement that saw Rockefeller's firm receive a 75 per cent rebate on oil shipped on the Erie railroad system. Rockefeller's business promised rail operators steady shipments, something the rail bosses preferred to dealing with smaller operators. For Rockefeller, the benefits were obvious: a 75 per cent edge on his rivals, but for the smaller operators, Rockefeller's secretive rebate deals proved fatal to their ability to compete on fair and open terms. Rockefeller soon struck similar secret deals with the Pennsylvania Railroad.

As historian Ron Chernow describes, Rockefeller and Gould saw the rebates as a win–win deal, but both their rivals and the general public saw things different. Because rail charters stemmed from governmental prerogative, there was a public interest in ensuring that commercial operators did not abuse the privilege through anti-competitive, anti-consumer actions such as rebates, a theme that underpinned the business journalist and self-taught economist Henry George's massively popular criticisms of the rail industry.[31]

Rockefeller's private correspondence shows the aptness of Smith's point about the ways that industrialists are often able to collude with others in anti-competitive cronyism while publicly appearing to remain independent of each other. As Chernow points out, most rebate agreements were reached orally – they were rarely written down, a tactic allowing both parties to deny their existence if ever questioned publicly. 'Our people do not think it would be best for the Lake Shore Road, or us, to have a contract,' Rockefeller wrote in a letter to a railroad negotiator, 'but with good faith between us and desire to promote each other's interest, we can serve each other better by being able to say we have no contracts.'[32]

'Some of this derived from Rockefeller's humility,' Chernow suggests, 'but it also betrayed a lifelong habit of covering his tracks and pretending to be elsewhere when critical decisions were made.'[33]

During the late 1860s, falling oil prices threatened the profitability of Rockefeller's then fledging oil business. Explosive economic growth had lured more and more investors, speculators and manufacturers to the field. Consumers benefited from lower kerosene prices, but refiners such as Rockefeller were unnerved by plummeting profit margins. Rockefeller wanted to boost revenues, and his chance came when Tom Scott, president of the Pennsylvania Railroad, had the idea of establishing an alliance between three major railroad companies and a small handful of oil refineries, with Standard Oil one of the oil interests asked to take part. Scott's vision was to foster more streamlined economies of scale by reducing the number of players vying for rebates on shipping costs. Scott needed support from the Pennsylvania legislature and they gave it, awarding him a special state charter for the establishment of an entity with a euphemistically anodyne name – the South Improvement Company (SIC).

For many manufacturers, the cost of freight shipping had doubled over night, but the SIC collaborators were exempt from the sudden price hike. Thousands of protestors took to the streets, chanting 'down with the conspirators!' A local newspaper printed a daily list of the SIC members, featuring the names of SIC president Peter Watson, Rockefeller and others. It was a classic case of a select cartel of producers joining forces to try to corner the market. The state capitulated to public pressure. Pennsylvania's charter for SIC was cancelled before a single rebate could be collected.

Although the SIC was dissolved, Rockefeller would quietly allude to his ability to negotiate similar government charter rights in future to convince his rivals to surrender control to Standard Oil and receive some financial compensation rather than suffer eventual bankruptcy. Within less than two months – from February 1872, when news of the SIC surfaced – Rockefeller subsumed 22 of his 26 main competitors.

He was a master of strategic ignorance, recognizing early on in his career the value of appearing uninvolved in business that he secretly owned. In 1871 he bought Bostwick and Tilford, a firm that controlled a large New York refinery. Although Bostwick was really a subsidiary of Standard Oil, the company remained nominally independent, and was renamed J.A. Bostwick and Company. A pattern emerged: companies were 'instructed,' as Chernow puts it, 'to retain their original stationery, keep secret accounts, and not allude on paper to their Cleveland connection; internal correspondence with Standard Oil was often conducted in code or with fictitious names.'[34]

Through tactics like this, Rockefeller cultivated wider ignorance about his business concerns, a practice still popular today. Rex Tillerson, for example, the former CEO of Exxon Mobil, and for a brief spell Trump's Secretary of State, used the alias of 'Wayne Tracker' over a seven-year period at Exxon, in emails where he discusses concerns over climate change and its effect on the company.

WHO KNEW?

Sometimes an ignorance alibi is furnished by something as simple as physical absence. Carnegie's love of travel and regular summer stays in Europe made it seem plausible that he really was as little involved in union busting efforts as he claimed. But such alibis can take a more subtle form, for example in the way that Carnegie and Rockefeller mutually benefited from each other's self-pleasing understandings of economic development: their shared belief that they owed their wealth due to level economic playing fields, that their fortunes were the first truly 'self-made' success stories rooted in natural laws of competition rather than cronyism or government patronage.

Swayed by the dominance of academic theories of the value of unfettered trade, even industrialists who benefited from government protections failed to recognize them *as* protections. Was their ignorance real or feigned? It is a difficult question to answer conclusively. Rockefeller, at least, knew how much his business practices deviated from textbook conceptions of economic trade, and he even hoped that he might upend academic theories by demonstrating that his own business success proved that monopoly 'cooperation' and not competition was essential for a strong economy.

He tried to legitimize his cartel building by pioneering a theory of his own, one that he exalted as the 'new' principle of cooperation: 'The day of combination is here to stay. Individualism has gone, never to return.'[35] He 'tirelessly mocked those "academic enthusiasts" and "sentimentalists" who expected business to conform to their tidy competitive models.'[36]

Carnegie, too, praised 'cooperation' when it suited him, 'competition' when it didn't. 'Speaking of the present position of the workingman,' he suggested in 1885, 'I believe cooperation is his hope.'[37] But the reality of plummeting worker wages while his profits soared points to prescience of Adam Smith's point (Marx said something similar, but Smith said it first): there is an inherent conflict between workers and owners; it's in the interests of owners to pretend this conflict doesn't exist – and only the gullible take businesspeople at their word.

GLOSSING CONFLICT

Many people don't find it surprising that economics textbooks don't do a good job reflecting actual business practices.

But even though astute observers in Carnegie and Rockefeller's era and today disparage the unreality of economics textbooks, the wealthy continue to benefit from the ignorance alibi that misleading textbooks help to furnish, such as the way that Mankiw's bestselling *Macroeconomics*, now in its ninth edition, is upheld to defend wildly divergent ratios between CEO pay and average worker pay as only 'natural.'

Mankiw turns a blind eye to patronage and rent-seeking in the US economy today, just as professional academics averted their gaze in Carnegie and Rockefeller's day.

A recent article in a public health journal makes this point well. Its authors quote a compelling passage from *The Worldly Philosophers* by economic historian Robert Heilbroner. First published in the 1950s, Heilbroner's influential book explores the discipline of economics from Smith's era on. He frankly evaluates the reaction of gilded-age academic economists to the realities of the economy, and his point was blunt: they didn't react.

Heilbroner marvels at the emptiness of their language: 'The fantastic game of monetary cutthroat was described as the process of "thrift and accumulation"; the outright fraud as "enterprise"; the gilded extravagances of the age as colorless "consumption",' he writes. 'Indeed, the world was so scrubbed as to be unrecognizable.'[38]

The problem is, aside from Heilbroner whose work *did* reach a wide audience, the unreality of economic theory described in this chapter still doesn't get enough public notice today.

The excerpt I just quoted is taken from the *Journal of Epidemiology and Community Health*. The *New York Times* this isn't, which begs the question, why are public health scholars at the forefront of investigating the public toll of conflicts of interest in economics, science and medicine today? Why aren't the *Times* or the *Washington Post* doing a better job of scrutinizing the claims of scholars like Mankiw?

The fact that Rampell, a respected *Washington Post* columnist, is able to suggest Trump's trade policies break a 300-year pattern of free trade is only surprising for not being seen as the misleading claim that it is. Whether her aim is to mislead or not, she perpetuates a false impression of global history.

Zackery Carter, a journalist based at the *Huffington Post*, is one of the few mainstream journalists to point out the problem with Rampell's characterization. As he writes, 'Free trade rhetoric almost always serves a magical function: It erases ugly, violent political realities and replaces them with clean, natural progress.'[39]

Mainstream economic theories of trade and income distribution have an oracular power, conferring respectability on trade practices that in our day and in the past continue to veil the reality of ongoing global abuse towards workers, including unsafe working conditions for hundreds of millions of vulnerable labourers, many of whom endure early death and crippling illness while companies benefit from a global trade system that immunizes them from corporate liability for worker death – as well as liability from harm to the environment, to food systems and to pharmaceutical safety.

WORLD BANK DOUBLESPEAK

Status quo populists cherry-pick data in a way that blankets this reality. Bill Gates, for example, recently suggested that workplace death is reducing. He bases this on US data, which has dropped to around 5000 deaths a year, down from 20,000 in 1920.

'Today, we know better,' he writes, 'and we've engineered ways to build things without putting nearly as many lives at risk.'[40]

But globally the story is very different. Over 2.7 million people die from workplace accidents and work-related diseases each year. The vast majority of workers around the world don't have any accident or illness compensation and have no access to occupational health services.

The lofty insistence – 'we know better' – obscures the gravity of the problem globally. Gates also doesn't mention that workplace death in America has been rising in recent years. In 2017, the last year data is available, the US Bureau of Labour reported a steady climb in workplace death for every year over the preceding three years. It's certainly not at 1920 levels, but evidence suggests the problem is getting worse and not better.

In the US, it took decades of struggle by labour leaders, fought fiercely by industrialists at every step, for the status quo to shift, just as today wealthy individuals and powerful institutions continue to pit themselves against workers who try to improve conditions globally.

The World Bank, for example, has a 60-year-old history of encouraging countries to weaken labour regulations, enabling US corporations to benefit from cheap labour.

World Bank policies are also a major barrier to improving corporate accountability for poor labour conditions, which is a separate but related problem: the way that companies based in Canada, the US and the UK have for decades successfully argued that workplace deaths at their global subsidiaries are not their legal responsibility.

The Bank encourages poor labour standards through reports like *Doing Business*, first launched in 2003, which included 'Hiring and Firing Workers' indicators which gave highest scores to any country that has the lowest minimum wages protections and the highest worker hours.[41]

Why would the Bank routinely champion labour laws that undermine the health and safety of workers in the world's poorest nations? The answer is simple even though it bothers people to have it stated blunted: weak labour protections serve the interests of multinational corporations.

For over 40 years, every single World Bank president was either a Wall Street executive or a high-ranking US military leader or US diplomat (the Bank's presidents are always US citizens, legitimated by the fact that the US contributes the most funding to its operations): from Eugene Meyer, the former Chairman of the US Federal Reserve; to Eugene Black, a bank executive with Chase; to Lewis Preston, a former executive with J.P. Morgan.[42]

In 2012, the US government changed tack, appointing a global health specialist named Jim Yong Kim. Many people hoped that with his background in public health, Kim might initiate a new era of worker-friendly policies – especially given that, in 2013, a year after he took control, one of the Bank's own internal studies showed that weak labour laws have either no or little impact on employment levels. This study undermined the long-standing assumption that weak labour protections are necessary to ensure wider employment (the World Bank's position is identical to Carnegie's a century ago: that workers have no choice but to 'cooperate' with a manager's pay cuts in order to have work at all).

But Bank policies have stayed the same. In 2018, the Bank released a draft report calling yet again for developing countries to reduce minimum wage protections.

Carnegie's vision of 'cooperation' saw his workers lose 60 per cent of their pay despite soaring profitability, just like today, in the US, where the 1000 per cent growth in CEO pay relative to the lowest-paid US workers since the 1950s is legitimated through the belief that workers 'must' suffer more than the rich.

The question is: is a new sort of tradeoff possible, a tradeoff where the rich and not simply the poor bear a loss?

Because that's the irony of status quo tradeoffs, the fact that the rich are never asked to make the same concession.

We often hear uplifting – though much contested – statistics from the World Bank suggesting that more people than ever have been 'lifted' from poverty, but we hear less about the desperation of people's working lives: the 12-hour factory, field and mining jobs; the garment workers sewing 'help me' labels inside clothes shipped to the west, begging someone to notice and act. Hannah Arendt's reflections about British imperialists convinced of their beneficence in the 19th century applies to status quo thinkers today: 'They were monsters of conceit in their success and monsters of modesty in their failure.'[43]

Rather than more philanthropy or billionaire benevolence, development specialists suggest we need better mandatory measures like a global minimum wage, and their critics, in turn, deride such suggestions as ideologically motivated. These critics are not wrong.

Wage guarantees *do* have an ideological underpinning, rooted in socialist theories emerging over the 19th century. But so do 'free trade' theories – the difference is that one perspective seems obviously ideological, while free trade has the veneer of scientific naturalness, entrenched to such a degree that even well-meaning people like the economist Tim Harford can suggest in his article about agnotology that 'official data' from World Bank is needed to combat the problem of public ignorance.

Even sovereign governments don't have that level of perceived neutrality. The speeches of heads of state are rightly parsed for error and 'fake' facts, but Harford assumes that the World Bank is free of ideological leaning, a free pass that should change.

In 2018, for example, the Bank's chief economist, Paul Romer, acknowledged that his staff sometimes place a 'thumb on the scales' when it comes to the World Bank's *Doing Business* reports. He admitted that when Socialist Party leader Michelle Bachelet was president of Chile, the Bank used a methodology that led to worsening scores, but when conservative President Sebastián Piñera took power, the scores improved. Romer apologized to Bachelet – and then quickly vacated his role at the World Bank, seemingly facing backlash for his honesty.[44]

The World Bank does not deserve to be upheld as an antidote for the exact type of ignorance-production practices that it engages in itself.

MILESTONES

Sometimes concern over global labour exploitation draws enough public attention that everyday aloofness thaws, consensus opinions shift, new laws are passed or old ones enforced – and such a shift may be happening in Canadian courts today. Edmund Burke may still have his day in court, in Canada anyway.

Human rights activists have long suggested that Canadian courts should penalize Canadian companies when their subsidiaries breach either Canada's domestic laws or international law, including laws against slavery and torture, but so far, Canadian mining companies have successfully argued that crimes should be prosecuted in countries where a violation is alleged to have taken place rather than in Canada.

More and more, pioneering legal theorists, including Poonam Puri, a professor of law at the University of Toronto, are asking tougher questions about the corporate veil and the immunity it confers on corporate executives. Puri has stated:

My concern with the corporate veil is that it can be used inappropriately to insulate from liability, in particular in the context of parent companies that have foreign operations, and decide not to take responsibility on the basis that it's not the parent company that's involved in the misconduct, it's the subsidiary.[45]

The irony of the ease with which a parent company can pass on blame to a subsidiary is the fact that subsidiaries can be majority owned or fully owned by a parent company, thus extracting the bulk of profits from exploitative practices while assuming none of the responsibility for human rights abuse.

This situation should change, and it may well be.

One closely watched case involves Nevsun Resources, a Vancouver-based company which has a 60 per cent stake in Bisha Mining, based in Eritrea. Bisha Mining is accused of forcing conscripted military personnel to work against their consent.

If workers complained, they allegedly endured a form of torture known as the 'helicopter,' where people have their hands and legs tied and are left in the scorching sun for hours. 'I would never have worked in the conditions in which we worked, or for so little compensation, had I been free to refuse that employment,' an affidavit in the lawsuit quotes one military employee as saying.

Citing the risk that the Eritrean legal system would not offer a fair trial, lawyers on behalf of this worker and other plaintiffs argued that the case should be heard in Canada. With a 60 per cent stake in Bisha Mining, Vancouver's Nevsun Resources have a clear moral responsibility, in Burke's sense, even if legally Canada has typically failed to hear similar cases in the past. In this instance, a British Columbia Supreme Court judge ruled against Nevsun in favour of the Eritrean plaintiffs, and while the case is still ongoing, it's already seen a milestone case in international law.

SEE NO EVIL

The problem is: it's simply one lawsuit, and successful lawsuits like it are rare. Far more often, companies evade blame by offloading their liability to others even when their products lead to death.

Upcoming chapters explore this problem, coming back to a claim in the book's introduction.

I suggested at the outset that elite ignorance shouldn't be seen simply as the problem of powerful individuals being indifferent to the hardships of others. It *is* this at times, but it's also more than this. I defined it as the superior ability to manipulate the boundary between knowledge and ignorance for institutional or individual gain.

But, it's fair to ask of my argument, is it really possible to prove that the rich are 'better' at ignorance than the poor? Don't the poor ignore or lie about inconvenient evidence too?

They do. 'All human beings bend the truth and sometimes lie,' Pinker points out in *Enlightenment Now* – it's one of the good points in his book.[46]

The poor *do* engage in strategic ignorance, but the rich do it better, not because of innate superiority, but due to having more political and economic power to structure laws in their favour. The power of the powerful, to put it simply, is contingent on this very tactic: the attempt to dominate systems of law.

What this book adds is a new conceptual framework for understanding the role that strategic ignorance plays in age-old processes of political and economic domination through law-making.

Through new phrases developed in the book, from 'useful unknowns' to 'oracular power,' my aim has been to expand the language for understanding the social and political implications of the type of doublespeak that Orwell so evocatively warned about (here's one that Orwell might appreciate. Facing criticism, the World Bank promptly changed its 'Hiring and Firing Workers' index to the 'EWI,' the 'Employing Workers Indicator').

My empirical cases may seem like a scattered grouping, but they are chosen for their very eclecticism, to show the way that patterns of strategic ignorance can be seen in many different areas of social and economic life.

The ultimate aim of these varied cases is to demonstrate how the ignorance cycle that I pointed out – the way that micro-ignorance leads to larger macro-ignorance which in turn facilitates micro-ignorance – can be illustrated in practice.

Language tactics (a form of 'micro-ignorance') advocated by figures like Bastiat helped to generate wider unknowns ('macro-ignorance') about the interventionist nature of governments during the perceived high point of 'free trade' in the 19th century. Macro-ignorance perpetuated in textbooks then in turn leads to new micro-ignorance effects today, as a new cohort of policy-makers and academics draw on the oracular power of textbook theories to push for a hands-off approach to regulation where it's most needed, including pharmaceutical regulation.

Following chapters explore this reality. First, I introduce the way that ignorance doctrines in law can be manipulated to advantage the wealthy. After this, I explore the uses of strategic ignorance in pharmaceutical regulation. The points I make can be generalized elsewhere, because across most areas of social life, from the safety of food, to environmental regulation, to household debt (Smith's call for usury limits being non-grata today), the academic heirs of Bastiat are still waging hand-to-hand combat with the general public.

CHAPTER 9

THE OSTRICH INSTRUCTION

It can be legally useful to be as ignorant as possible. This fact often surprises people. But what's really surprising is that it surprises even lawyers who are not aware that a longstanding principle in western legal systems – the belief that 'ignorance of the law does not excuse' – has been waived over the years when it comes to white-collar crimes such as tax law and securities regulation.

USEFUL IGNORANCE IN LEGAL HISTORY

The legal usefulness of ignorance has figured into modern legal judgements since at least the 1860s, when 'wilful blindness' first started appearing in British courts.

One early case in 1861 centred on a defendant charged with illegally possessing military equipment. The aim of the prosecution was to prove that the defendant was *aware* that the goods belonged to the government, making his possession of them illegal. In quashing the conviction, the presiding judge stated that 'the jury have not found ... that [the defendant] wilfully abstained from acquiring that knowledge.'[1]

Although the conviction was quashed, the comment introduced the possibility that the court *could* have supported a conviction if the jury did believe that the defendant had deliberately blinded himself to available facts that could have made him aware that the goods were government property.

This case established a precedent: the belief that purposefully burying one's head, Ostrich-like, can be a criminal offence. Within two decades of this case, legal theorist Ira Robbins writes, 'willful blindness was firmly established as an alternative to actual knowledge in English law.'[2]

The language from 1861 is similar to an American description of 'wilful blindness' written nearly a century later:

> A court can properly find wilful blindness only where it can almost be said that the defendant actually knew. He suspected the fact; he realized its probability; but he refrained from obtaining the final confirmation because he wanted in the event to be able to deny knowledge. This, and this alone, is wilful blindness.[3]

The wording above is important. It makes it clear that western courts, and especially US courts, place particular importance on making very, very sure that a defendant really *did* deliberately blind herself to inconvenient knowledge. US courts, in short, insist that prosecutors have to prove that someone *knew* what not to know. The rationale for placing a high premium on *deliberate*, wilful ignoring is a sound one, because legal systems have made the problem of 'intent' a vital aspect in determining the level of punishment people should receive when they do break the law.

'Intent' features in the difference, for example, between a murder charge and a manslaughter charge.

With good reason, courts argue that someone who kills someone with calculated intent should get a harsher sentence than accidental killing. But this necessary and sound emphasis on proving intent is a real bugbear when it comes to wilful ignorance instructions. The challenge facing jurists is at once obvious to understand and yet frustratingly difficult to resolve in practice – and that is the challenge of determining whether an individual *deliberately* ignored evidence of wrongdoing or whether their ignorance is genuine.

There is a further complication to the problem. That is the fact that, on its own, wilful blindness is not usually treated as legal offence. Instead, the notion of wilful blindness can be used to satisfy *one* of the elements of a legal offence, which is to demonstrate that a person had ample means to inform herself or himself that her or his actions were illegal. The profound implications of this challenge are clear when you realize that, as I have discussed throughout this book, strategic ignorance is a tactic that is *most* successful when it is *least* detectable. The ability to hide the fact that people *did* have the means to inform themselves of illegality is what makes the tactic of strategic ignorance the powerful resource that it is.

Confused? If so, you're not alone.

Understanding the legal usefulness of different types of ignorance is one of the most complex and little understood problems in law and in politics more broadly.

Strategic ignorance can and does help to entrench legal impunity through a flurry of legal loopholes: a blizzard so dense that it's not an exaggeration to suggest the vast majority of legal professionals and scholars have left their snow-logged cars curb-side for decades.

It's true, for example, that the concept of 'wilful blindness' *has* been applied in western courts for over a century. But it's also true that until recently, wilful ignorance doctrines have not been a major preoccupation of legal theory. This inattention is started to change now. As one scholar puts it, the 'concept of Willful Blindness has gradually moved away from the fringes to the centre of the debate on how to determine intent when holding companies to account for criminal liabilities.'[4]

There's also been a push lately to make the legal concept 'wilful blindness' more understandable to a wide general audience. One good recent example is a book called *Wilful Blindness: Why We Ignore the Obvious at Our Peril,* by British businesswoman-turned-author Margaret Heffernan. Heffernan's book is an excellent study of wilful blindness in psychology, but her work doesn't probe at all the way that different legal juridictions treat the legal utility of ignorance differently. She also gives the impression that corporate executives are regularly penalized for their own 'willfull blindness,' but this is not the case. For example, Heffernan points to Enron as an example where wilful blindness does *not* pay. As she rightly describes, executives at the Texan oil giant were found guilty even though they insisted that they had no knowledge of illegal actions by subordinates. But Heffernan doesn't give a sense of the exceptionality of the Enron case. 'Outside of Enron,' legal theorist Justin O'Brian has pointed out, 'The government has had a mixed result in prosecuting white-collar crime.'[5]

Neither does Heffernan touch on a *different* ignorance doctrine than the 'wilful blindness' doctrine.

To understand the legal uses of ignorance, it is necessary to keep two closely related but also very different ignorance doctrines in mind. The first is the 'Ostrich instruction' or the wilful blindness doctrine. The second doctrine relates to an even longer-standing principle in law. Even schoolchildren know it. It is the principle that 'ignorance of the law does not excuse' – also known as the *ignorantia legis neminem excusat* principle.

A comedy sketch by Steve Martin focused on this second ignorance principle. If you're accused of a 'foul crime,' his defence is simple. Just say two words, 'I forgot.' And if someone replies – 'you forgot?' You say: 'Well. Excuuuse me.'

Martin is not saying: 'I didn't realize that my employee was selling cocaine to my clients and giving me a cut.' He's saying: 'I forgot it was illegal to sell cocaine.'

Now let me put this into legalese, relying on a legal expert and not a stand-up comic: Alexander Sarch, a leading legal scholar on wilful ignorance.

The important distinction between the two doctrines, as Sarch described to me during an email interview, is the distinction between questions of fact and questions of law. The willful ignorance doctrine blocks people from avoiding liability by preserving their own ignorance of the *facts* about what they were doing (e.g. that this substance is a narcotic) ... By contrast, 'ignorance of the law is no excuse' is the analogous doctrine for legal questions: it prevents people from avoiding liability by failing to learn what is or isn't legal.

Both principles, Sarch explains, can be seen as different 'applications of the same underlying idea – namely that ignorance generally does not excuse you insofar as you are responsible (or to blame) for your own ignorance.'

At face value, then, both principles *should* lead to the exact opposite conclusion to my claim that being ignorant can be legally beneficial.

The 'ignorance doesn't excuse' principle clearly states the opposite: that ignorance is *not* helpful. But increasingly, this principle has been selectively applied in a manner that makes white-collar crime harder to penalize – while street crimes do not enjoy the same leniency before the law.

I can't say exactly *how* severe the problem of blatantly unequal ignorance doctrines is today in US courts of law. No one can. But I do show evidence below that this problem exists, and I also point to legal scholars who suggest with good reason that it is getting worse.

There's a simple reason why I can't say how bad the problem is: empirical evidence on its severity doesn't exist. And that's my larger point, in a way. What's curious about this second problem – the relaxing of 'ignorance doesn't excuse' principles – is the fact that US legal scholars have almost entirely ignored the problem.

EQUAL CULPABILITY

To grasp the importance of ignorance in law, it's necessary to consider moral questions that underpin debates over the problem of 'intent' in law.

For good reasons, moral philosophers and legal scholars are genuinely uncertain about the question of whether or not it is morally or legally appropriate to presume that wilful ignorance can and should be treated as equivalent to possessing actual knowledge. As Sarch points out, there are legitimate reasons not to treat 'ignorance' as the same thing as having genuine, conclusive knowledge about something.[6] It's the murder–manslaughter problem. No, we shouldn't necessarily punish someone who kills in self-defence, for example, as severely as the person who does kill with premeditated intent.

The idea that deliberate ignorance and actual knowledge can and should be treated as equally blameworthy is known as the 'equal culpability' thesis. Sarch points out that scholars are very split on whether the 'equal culpability' doctrine should apply in all cases. The key challenge for jurists and scholars is, as he points out, the question of: 'Is wilful ignorance misconduct in all cases as culpable as knowing misconduct? Or is this true only in some cases of wilful ignorance?'[7]

Sarch is an American legal theorist who teaches in the School of Law at the University of Surrey. His path-breaking legal scholarship on the doctrine of wilful ignorance is pointing to new ways to understand the thorny problem of what could be called incentivized ignorance: where companies have an interest in *not* knowing about illegality carried out by subordinates.

Sarch makes clear the stakes of this problem by pointing to the case of Enron, where executives tried to blame their purported failure to detect criminality on auditors and vice versa.

Enron and their auditors' blame-shifting is good example of a long-acknowledged problem, which is that the companies are often incentivized *not* to disclose questionable or illegal actions to auditing firms or legal counsel, something that enables auditing firms to remain honestly unaware of criminality that has been hidden from them. Auditors, meanwhile, are rarely incentivized to unearth evidence of fraud, as it jeopardizes the harmony of their working relationship with the companies who pay for the service of being audited, and who are willing to pay extra handsomely for audits that reflect their activities in a favourable light.[8]

Sarch argues that when it comes to tackling crime, the doctrine of wilful ignorance is limited in worrying ways. The limits of the doctrine, in his view, mean certain serious crimes – like a company such as Enron purposely retaining auditing firms who couldn't 'see' illegality at the company – harder to prosecute than they plausibly should be. To combat this problem, Sarch has proposed new ways to expand the doctrine of wilful ignorance that could give the government more power to prosecute crimes of culpably ignorant actors in corporate settings – like the crimes that unfolded at Enron.

When it came to Enron, the auditor was Arthur Anderson. At one stage, Enron's VP, Sherron Watkins, told her boss, chairman Kenneth Lay, that she was worried that Arthur Anderson was helping Enron to devise illegal transactions that obscured the scale of Enron's indebtedness. In response, Lay asked Enron's traditional law firm to investigate the auditors – but he also 'instructed them not to look too closely,' as Sarch writes. 'Perhaps unsurprisingly,' Sarch adds, 'Vinson and Elkins eventually reported back that the transactions seemed fine, especially since the accountants signed off on them.'[9]

Sarch points out that there is no clear evidence Vinson & Elkins acted with the clear *purpose* of guarding their own ignorance. For this reason, the wilful ignorance doctrine, as currently understood, would allow Vinson & Elkins lawyers to 'escape conviction for crimes like aiding and abetting fraud – a troubling result, given their intuitive culpability.'[10]

To combat this problem, Sarch proposes the introduction of *reckless ignorance* provisions. His idea is that in cases where certain actors, such as auditors, have clearly remained ignorant beyond a reasonable degree, then courts should be committed to treating their reckless ignorance *as* wilful, even if it is not clear that they purposefully tried to shield themselves from inconvenient information. Such an approach would make Vinson & Elkins legally liable for their ignorance – but only if it could be shown that they had multiple opportunities to investigate worrying red flags but chose not to.

WHEN YOU'RE BIG ENOUGH, IGNORANCE DOES EXCUSE

Sarch's ideas are timely. Indeed, you could say they are pressingly urgent – and that is because of the existence of proposed new US legislation that could weaken a system that's already hamstrung when it comes to prosecuting privileged, white-collar offenders. The changes threaten to make the policing and punishment of white-collar crime – something that's already worryingly rare – even more difficult to address.

The legislation, termed the Mens Rea Reform Act, seeks to limit the scope of deliberate ignorance principles by proposing that for particularly complex and technical crimes, including financial crimes, the government must establish that one 'knew or should have known one's conduct was illegal.'[11]

Such a proposal would 'make it more difficult for federal authorities to pursue executive wrongdoing, from financial fraud to environmental pollution,' Zachary Carter writes in the *Huffington Post*. 'CEOs could be off the hook, even for gross negligence.' Robert Weissman, president of Public Citizen, pointed out that the legislation 'violates the basic precept that "ignorance of the law is no defense."'[12]

The proposed legislation was developed by a cross-partisan coalition of Democrats and Republicans. Once people realized the fact that the legislation could be used to let corporate executives almost completely avoid liability for federal crimes, the legislation was shelved for a bit. But with Trump in office, mens rea reform is back on the table.

Proposals for mens rea reforms are openly sponsored and championed by the Koch Industries, working in collaboration first with staff in the Obama administration, and now with the Trump team. The reason why Obama staffers jumped enthusiastically at the cross-partisan effort was the hope of passing other criminal justice reforms aimed at improving the problem of mass incarceration in America.

Cleverly, right-wing supporters couched their attempts to introduce new 'excusable ignorance' provisions in a language of human and civil rights, insisting that at a time of mass incarceration, legal reforms are needed to ensure fewer wrongful convictions occur and reduce the cost of maintaining large prison populations.

Critics of the Koch brothers, on the other hand, have pointed out the irony of the timing of the Kochs' sudden interest in the civil rights of black Americans.

For decades, the Koch family has staunchly supported political candidates who *oppose* criminal justice reform efforts aimed at improving harsh sentences that mostly affect people of colour. This point is made by legal justice specialist Lisa Graves, president of the board of Center for Media and Democracy. In the 1960s, as she describes, Charles Koch was a member and financial sponsor or the John Birch Society, which not so quietly tried to undermine Martin Luther King Jr's civil rights efforts. Today, Koch-backed groups have been at the forefront of voter suppression efforts which make it harder in practice for people from communities of colour to vote. 'It would seem prudent to view Koch support for criminal justice reform with a skeptical eye,' Graves suggests.[13]

THAT'S ILLEGAL?!

Why are the Koch brothers so interested all of a sudden in the problem of mass incarceration in America?

The holy grail they're after is something that could give them a sort of corporate 'get out of jail' free card in perpetuity for environmental crimes and work-related deaths. Their aim is to relax federal law that can penalize large corporations for cost-cutting measures that lead to severe environmental degradation and the death of workers even if companies don't intend to break the law. Currently, federal prosecutors don't need to prove intent. If a company directly pollutes waterways and federal wilderness reserves, as Graves describes, they can be held liable for doing so even if they didn't mean to. To hold their hands up and say, 'but we didn't mean to' or 'we didn't know we broke the law' – is not a permittable excuse.

The Koch brothers and their friends want this changed, and they're getting closer to passing mens rea reform bills that could make it happen.

Many Department of Justice staff are outraged at the effort, insisting that it would make 'it significantly harder to prosecute corporate polluters, producers of tainted food and other white-collar criminals,' as *New York Times* reporters Matt Apuzzo and Eric Lipton report. They quote Department of Justice spokeswoman Melanie Newman. 'Countless defendants who caused harm would escape criminal liability by arguing that they did not know their conduct was illegal,' Newman said.[14]

But so far, there's been little media discussion of an inconvenient truth, and that's one of the ways that 'ignorance of the law' principles are *already* regularly waived in US courts, in ways that appear to be systematically advantaging America's wealthy at the expense of the less powerful: men, women and adolescents who are increasingly treated as unequal before the law.

Law professor Sharon Davies was one of the first scholars to emphasize this problem, in a ground-breaking but neglected article published 20 years ago.[15]

She begins with a compelling summary of the rationale behind the 'ignorance doesn't excuse' principle:

> Citizens are compelled either to know the law or to proceed in ignorance at their own peril. While sometimes harsh, the gains secured by the maxim – a better educated and more law-abiding citizenry, and the avoidance of pervasive mistake of law claims – are thought to outweigh any individual injustice resulting from application.

Despite this belief, the principle has 'been seriously eroded over the last century,' as Davies writes.

Davies points out that in many areas of financial law – including tax reporting and federal anti-structuring provisions which make it illegal for companies to structure financial transactions in ways that deliberately allow companies to violate bank reporting obligations – the term 'wilfully' has been applied in way that makes it necessary for courts to prove that a defendant purposefully violated a 'known' legal obligation.

A lack of knowledge of the law is deemed to be a 'reasonable excuse' in these cases.

Davies adds that even though this shift is 'unprecedented in scope, the academy has yet to either confront the breadth of the trend or critically examine the rationales underlying it.'[16]

In other words, whether consciously or unconsciously, academics based in the world's leading departments of law have generally averted their gaze from the ramifications of changes to one of the most important principles in legal history. US courts' selective relaxing of the 'ignorance doesn't excuse' principle leads to an uncomfortable hypothesis.

It is not an exaggeration to suggest that different sections of America's power elite have been quietly introducing new legislation that enables them to legally benefit from what they either do not know or what they can persuasively claim not to know.

America's super-rich are increasingly positioning themselves to exploit a resource that is always self-replenishing and never out of reach: their own inexhaustible ignorance. Quite literally, the wealthy are striving to secure the right to remain wilfully and blissfully unaware. Ignorance really *is* bliss; depending, of course, on the crime.

So far, the full scale of the problem is still unknown, and that's because legal scholars, by and large, have ignored the implications of the practices to which Davies points.

I asked Sarch whether he felt that the wealthy either are or could be obtaining special privileges as a result of new proposed legislation and the earlier precedents that Davies discusses.

'It's an interesting hypothesis that must be investigated. It would take empirical study to determine whether the rich are deriving significantly larger benefits from the exceptions to the "ignorance of law is no excuse" rule than the poor do,' he replied. 'This may seem intuitively plausible, given that the poor are perhaps less likely to encounter complex regulatory regimes in their daily lives, but it would require systematic empirical research to conclude with certainty whether the hypothesis is true.'

We might not know how severe the problem is, but we do know that it's doubtful that proposed mens rea reforms will dramatically improve incarceration rates among populations that are currently disproportionately imprisoned in the United States.

This point has been stressed by the Lawyers' Committee for Civil Rights Under Law, an NGO lobbying for criminal reform of inequities which particularly affect African Americans and other ethnic and racial minority groups. They have suggested that mens rea reform legislation is 'not likely have an appreciable effect on "over-criminalization" or "mass incarceration" because their provisions will not likely impact drug and immigration offenses, which comprise the vast majority of federal prosecutions.'[17]

THE SNOWMOBILE FALLACY

One of the problems with proposed mens rea reforms is something that could be considered the 'snowmobile fallacy,' after a touchstone example used by corporate lobbyists who are trying to relax current federal legislation.

The case involves three-time Indy 500 winner Bobby Unser, who sought shelter in a snowstorm in 1997 and had to abandon his snowmobile in a federal wilderness area – a federal crime that exposed him to a fine and possible jail time, even though he didn't mean to break the law.

This 'snowmobile' precedent is brandished regularly by right-wing reform groups who insist that federal laws need changing so that more innocents like Unser don't suffer the same treatment.

But abandoned snowmobiles are hardly the main cause of widespread harm to public safety. By insisting that breaches of federal law can and should be deemed a criminal offence even if someone didn't mean to break the law, US legislators are trying to mitigate the type of large-scale harm caused by situations such as water poisoning in Flint, Michigan, or the ecological devastation caused by the Deepwater Horizon explosion in 2010, which led to the worst oil spill in US history. It is already hard to hold different stakeholders personally responsible for different corporate and governmental failures that can lead to large-scale public health and environmental crises. Weakening federal legislation would make it even harder.

It is true that Unser was exposed to severe legal penalties for an accidental breach of the law. But what if a nation-wide federation of snowmobile enthusiasts that had decided to hold a rally in a federal wilderness reserve, leaving a trail of litter and debris in their wake, also pleaded ignorance about the law?

Relaxing the same laws that treat Unser harshly doesn't simply mean that rare examples such as Unser's case are avoided; it means that larger, better connected organizations can flout the law without facing any serious deterrent. As Davies points out, 'While sometimes harsh, the gains secured by the maxim … are thought to outweigh any individual injustice resulting from application.'

VOTER IGNORANCE SEE-SAWS

There is something deeply ironic about efforts to exploit voter ignorance when it comes to mens rea reforms.

As earlier chapters pointed out, self-proclaimed 'epistocrats' are often quick to disparage average voters for their perceived 'ignorance' when it comes to electoral decisions. Deriding the average voters' knowledge about politics, epistocrats insist that it's reasonable to actively disenfranchise 'ignorant' voters. Indeed, Jason Brennan has suggested that any citizen deemed too ignorant to vote in the 'epistocratic' system that he proposes should 'get over it and study harder' if they're upset for being disenfranchised. When it comes to voting rights, the implication is that citizens should be striving for the same standard as, say, PhD-educated political theorists.[18]

But when it comes to mens rea reform, voter ignorance, almost magically, loses its association with lazy or uneducated citizens. What people don't know is no longer derided as a problem of personal incompetence; it's seen as the opposite, as a sign of collective, shared human fragility. When it comes to laws that disproportionately affect large corporations and not lone individuals, mens rea reformers insist that no one group – not even well-paid lawyers at large corporations – should be blamed for not knowing the law.

The see-saw moves up and down: sometimes ignorance is a sign of individual incapability; sometimes, it's a collective, shared problem.

Voter ignorance, inexcusable and punishable by disenfranchisement; legal ignorance, excusable (except for street drug or immigration crime).

GOOD TIMING

To make my point clear, the problem isn't simply that corporate groups are fighting hard to minimize their liability for corporate crimes. That effort has been going on for a long time. What's new right now is the fact that powerful groups are becoming much more *explicit* about their aim to relax 'ignorance does not excuse' principles. They have picked a convenient time to do so: the fact that there is understandable public support for ensuring that innocent people don't go to jail for wrongful convictions.

Rena Steinzor, a law professor at the University of Maryland, is frustrated by the timing of the focus. She has suggested that the Kochs and their allies are 'using people convicted of street crimes effectively as human shields.'[19]

As I discussed over Chapter 5, Adam Smith noticed a similar pattern over 200 years ago to the point that Steinzor makes. Recall the excerpt from *Wealth of Nations* quoted earlier, where Smith astutely observes that there tends to be convenient timing when it comes to the way that wealthy stakeholders will suddenly take loud notice of the plight of poorer groups.

As Smith pointed out, the needs of common labourers are typically 'little heard and less regarded' in political debates. Except, he added, at times when the 'third order' – the dealers and the merchants class – spies a new avenue for exploiting the interests of poor workers for their own gain. Upon such occasions, Smith writes, the 'clamour' of the worker is suddenly 'set on, and supported by his employers, not for his, but their own particular purposes.'[20]

At such a time, he adds, legislators need to be particularly 'suspicious' of the claim that a self-serving action will end up helping whoever it is purported to help. Smith might have said it first, but a song performed by Nina Simone says it even better: 'Same old game, same old thing.'

THE WILL TO IGNORE

Not all that long ago, large corporations *were* viewed with the 'suspicious attention' for which Smith called, not because of bitterness or 'wealth envy' – but because of a simple reality: unaccountable and unchecked corporate power was seen as threatening both democracy and equal rights.

During the mid-20th century, a University of Chicago school economist named Henry Simons made this point. 'The great enemy of democracy is monopoly, in all its forms,' he suggested, including the influence of 'gigantic corporations.'[21]

Simons was an admirer of the work of Friedrich Hayek. Although Simons died in 1946, his early championing of Hayek was instrumental in Hayek eventually coming to work at the University of Chicago in the 1950s. Simons never lived to see the way that Hayek's influence would steer Chicago economists away from an early appreciation of the problem of corporate abuses of power.

Over the 1950s, as Hayek and his colleagues took more and more money from large corporations and philanthropic foundations to carry out their investigations into market competition, their writing became less 'classically liberal' in tone and more and more illiberal.[22]

Today, a market fundamentalist attitude to pharmaceutical regulation and to government regulation more broadly – the insistence that regulation rarely works – is no longer seen as an extreme view.

Rather, an anti-regulation stance has become the standard position within mainstream economic theory over the past 40 years. Influenced by a diverse group of economists, including Chicago School economist George Stigler and Friedrich Hayek, and 'Virginia School' theorists such as James Buchanan, mainstream economics has adopted a perverse reading of Adam Smith which claims that because special interest groups can and do exert undue influence on regulators, it is better to have very little regulation in place than to have 'captured' regulation.[23]

Stigler was something of an outlier among major 20th-century economists because he *did* read and call attention to Smith's criticisms of business merchants. But he interpreted Smith's points about 'venal' traders in a way that ignored Smith's original meaning. The American economist Deirdre McCloskey once quipped of Stigler that he 'read a lot but was defective in paying attention,' and this applies to Stigler's reading of Smith.[24]

Stigler takes a point from Smith that I mentioned earlier – the claim that most people, if in the shoes of East India traders, would behave equally immorally – and perverts Smith's point to suggest that because humans tend to act, in Stigler's words, 'in predictable, and probably unchangeable, ways,' the effort to regulate or penalize misconduct is doomed to failure, because the urge to exploit one another for private gain leads individuals to rig regulatory structures in their favour.[25]

It's like saying that because some people might steal from your home, the only response is to give up trying to regulate intruders and to leave the front door wide open in order to prevent 'special interest' groups from charging a homeowner for shutting it.

The work of economists such as Stigler, Hayek and Buchanan, though different in important ways, collectively contributed to a new, *total-conflict* understanding of economic regulation that jarred with earlier attitudes to economic exchange.

This new, *total-conflict* perspective led to a spirt of regulatory defeatism that has distorted important enlightenment ideas about the relationship between private enterprise and public benefits. For example, the influential thinker Bernard Mandeville, an early 18th-century Dutch physician and philosopher, argued in his path-breaking essay *Fable of the Bees* that under well-regulated circumstances, private enterprise (or self-seeking 'vice' as he called it) could improve public welfare. But an important aspect of Mandeville's work is ignored today: his insistence that private enterprise is only beneficial 'When it's by Justice lopt and bound.'[26]

From the 1960s on, Hayek, Stigler and other economists' disdain for government regulation has won the ideological battle in mainstream economics theory, helping to entrench the bizarre prevalence across the political spectrum today of regulators who disdain the very idea of regulation, and who have lobbied to gut important watchdog agencies of much-needed public funding.[27]

As one economist put it, in 'deliberately creating a regulatory race to the bottom Stigler and the neoclassical economists created a self-fulfilling prophecy of regulatory failure.'[28]

The following chapters provide dispiriting glimpses of what happens when regulations are undermined – but also hopeful portraits too of regulatory heroes who are trying to construct new dams, who are trying to halt an anti-government deluge from entirely sweeping away democratic checks and balances achieved in the past.

CHAPTER 10

GOOD EXPERTS

It is the winter of 2005, in a low-rise building in Central London. Tim Kendall is dressed in full black – trousers, sports jacket, T-shirt. He looks young, but he's old enough for the Ford pickup truck of a job title – as co-director of the National Collaborating Centre for Mental Health, deputy director of the Royal College of Psychiatrists' research unit and a consultant psychiatrist in the Sheffield Care Trust, he divides his time between overlapping duties. Some of his days are spent in Sheffield, in the north of England, treating patients, other days he works down south, sifting through online evidence repositories and comparing the findings of published medical studies on the effectiveness and safety of different pharmaceutical drugs.

Britain's National Collaborating Centre is an organization that develops health standards, collating all the available evidence on treatments for different mental illnesses in order to develop guidelines for NHS staff. It is a job that was easier, or at least, for Kendall, it once felt easier, a couple of years earlier, when Kendall's team at the

National Collaborating Centre was asked to produce recommendations for the NHS for the treatment of depression
in children and adolescents.

'When we did the childhood depression guideline – in
fact, whenever we do any guideline – we wrote to all the
stakeholders, including the pharmaceutical companies, saying, "Do you have any additional data and in particular any
unpublished trials?" At that point in time, the answer was a
unanimous "No, there is no additional data,"' Kendall said to
me when I met him in London on a cold winter day in 2005.[1]

He assumed they were telling the truth. Then he was
handed something in secret: leaked information suggesting
that the companies had lied.

> I was passed a confidential internal memo regarding
> GlaxoSmithKline…The memo indicated that there were
> two trials which had not been published. It recommended
> that the company should not publish these trials as they
> showed paroxetine was not effective in treating children
> who were depressed.

Paroxetine is the technical name of an antidepressant SSRI drug
marketed as Paxil in the US and Seroxat in the UK. As an SSRI
drug, which stands for selective serotonin reuptake inhibitor,
Seroxat is in the same drug class as Prozac. Although Seroxat
was never formally approved for prescription to under-18s in
UK, it was widely given to them 'off-label,' whereby GPs prescribe treatment even if they haven't been formally approved.
Off-label prescribing is common, especially in paediatric care

where many drugs have not been formally tested on children. GPs are in a bind: they don't want to go 'off-label,' but if there's a treatment that works in adults and no alternative available, they often have to.

Around the same time he received the memo, Kendall was approached by the Medicines and Healthcare Products Regulatory Agency (MHRA), the UK's equivalent to the FDA.

Unlike Kendall's organization, the National Collaborating Centre for Medical Health, the MHRA is legally able to force pharmaceutical companies to disclose unpublished medical trials – data from medical experiments that were carried out but never actually published, usually because they show that a drug or other form of treatment did not achieve the positive result that the investigators were hoping for.

For the first time in its history, the MHRA told Kendall they were placing unpublished trial data from different pharmaceutical companies, including GlaxoSmithKline, on their website. They asked Kendall to take his unpublished evidence on the usefulness of SSRIs in children.

Kendall then did a comparison.

We decided to take the meta-analysed published data and say to the guideline group: 'If you had the published data only on the SSRIs, would you recommend these treatments on a balance of risks versus benefits?' The guideline group's response was that, although the evidence from the published data did not suggest that the SSRIs were fantastically effective, on a balance of risk versus benefit they would recommend them as treatments for childhood depression.

Kendall went on:

> We took the unpublished trials from the MHRA website … adding in the unpublished data, the apparent effectiveness that you saw with the published trials disappeared. Given that they weren't effective, and there was evidence in the trials of a significant increase in self-harming behaviour – roughly two and a half times that of placebo in most of the trials – the risks outweighed the benefits.

Kendall and his team published their findings in *The Lancet*, fuelling a furore and spurring civil society campaigns across Europe and North America for better access to clinical trial data.[2]

Concerned that the company had illegally withheld from regulators important medical trial data that showed their drug might be harming children, the MHRA launched a criminal investigation into GlaxoSmithKline that lasted four years. At the end of the investigation – the longest in the MHRA's history – the MHRA chose not to prosecute the company, claiming that limitations in the regulatory framework made a successful prosecution unlikely. In the US, meanwhile, GSK eventually pled guilty to the illegal promotion of its bestselling antidepressant and other popular drugs. The Department of Justice levied a $3 billion fine on the company, the largest ever in US history.[3]

British physicians have long called in vain for similar penalties in Britain, including Ben Goldacre, bestselling author of *Bad Pharma*: 'I can't see why the state doesn't impose crippling fines. I hope it's because politicians don't understand the scale of the harm.'[4]

SELF-FULFILLING REGULATORY FAILURE

This chapter and the next explore efforts at the MHRA and the FDA to determine whether a number of different bestselling pharmaceutical drugs are safe for use in children and adults, including SSRIs and Ketek, an antibiotic used to treat severe cases of pneumonia that was withdrawn from the US market after regulators at the FDA spent years trying to convince their bosses about the safety risks of the drug.

I am not suggesting that SSRIs are not useful for many people. The evidence on their efficacy is mixed, but especially in severe depression, they've been shown to be helpful treatments. I also don't want to imply that the effort to find new, safe antibiotics is not an important one. Far from it, antibiotic resistance is one of the gravest health dangers today, which makes it all the more important to find new antibiotic treatments.

At the same time, it is also clear from available medical evidence that both SSRIs and Ketek can lead to dangerous adverse reactions in a minority of users, and the public should be told about the known risks and benefits of different classes of drugs. Often that doesn't happen. These chapters show why, examining the way that different stakeholders, including companies and regulatory agencies, exploit strategic ignorance to avoid liability for bad behaviour.

PRUDENT REGULATION

Contrary to the defeatist insistence that good regulation is impossible, the history of pharmaceutical regulation provides ample illustration of the ways that prudent regulation *can* and does save lives and improve human welfare.

Take Thalidomide, a drug marketed by its German manufacturer, Grünenthal, as a mild sleeping pill and approved for over-the-counter use in many European countries over the 1950s and 1960s. Thalidomide was heavily marketed by Grünenthal and its UK licensee even after early signs of birth defects were apparent.[5]

In the United States, an FDA drug examiner named Frances Oldham Kelsey grew concerned by reports of birth defects in Europe and Australia. Supported by many of her colleagues and superiors, she refused to approve the drug. Her actions helped to avert American parents and their children from experiencing the tragedy unfolding in Europe, and also vindicated British health activists who had long campaigned for the UK to establish a system on par to the FDA in the US, a system that owed its existence to the influence of progressive American reformers at the turn of the 20th century.

Just over a century ago, neither the US nor the UK imposed rules on pharmaceutical companies to prove their products were safe. It wasn't illegal to make false claims about drug safety, something that shifted in the US in the early decades of the twentieth century, when a series of federal laws gradually strengthened federal drug and food regulation.

A turning point was the journalist Upton Sinclair's novel *The Jungle*. Published in 1905 and funded by an advance from a socialist weekly newspaper, Sinclair spent seven weeks living undercover around the stockyards of Packington, Chicago, observing the work and lives of meat-packers – labourers who hailed from diverse ethnic groups, were irregularly employed and paid next to nothing for working in gruelling conditions.[6]

Sinclair hoped to foster public sympathy for the conditions of immigrant meat-packers: his audience *was* outraged, but not on the behalf of immigrants: their reaction centred far more on the gross health violations he revealed in Chicago's meat plants. President Theodore Roosevelt tasked his Labor Commissioner to investigate sanitary conditions, and their findings supported Sinclair's observations.

The 1906 Food and Drugs Act was implemented only months after Sinclair's book incensed the US public. For the first time meat inspection and drug regulation came under the purview of federal authorities. But the Act was still relatively weak, and by the 1930s – the decade when a young pharmacologist named Frances Oldham (later Oldham Kelsey) arrived at Chicago to enrol on a PhD programme – FDA policymakers had long been calling for tougher rules prohibiting false claims about a new medicine's miraculous health effects. In 1937, they convinced Congress to pass new legislation after pointing to a disaster that led to 100 deaths within weeks of the approval of an antibacterial drug, Elixir Sulfanilamide. The tragedy spurred the establishment of the 1938 Federal, Drug and Cosmetic Act.[7]

But the system wasn't perfect. Too often, companies pressured regulators to expedite drug approval even when safety concerns were apparent, just as Merrell, an Ohio-based company with a licence to market Thalidomide in America, tried to do. The company hadn't bargained on Oldham Kelsey, whose life story, in a way, illustrates the importance of 'outsider' knowledge.

Born in Canada, in the province of British Columbia, she moved east to study pharmacology at McGill, and then, at the suggestion of one of her McGill advisors, she wrote to an eminent pharmacologist at the University of Chicago to apply for a PhD. Assuming 'Frances' was a man and addressing her as Mr. Oldham, he offered her a place. She wondered over her life 'if my name had been Elizabeth or Mary Jane, whether I would have gotten that first big step up.'[8]

In 1960 she moved to the FDA, taking up a position as a medical officer. Just a month into her new job, a new drug application was passed to her desk for Thalidomide, a sleeping pill highly popular among pregnant women in Europe for curbing nausea. She had been given the file as something of a safe bet – she suggested 'My supervisors decided, "Well, this is a very easy one. There will be no problems with sleeping pills."'[9]

But Kelsey realized that there was little evidence to prove the drug was safe to use, and she stipulated that Merrell need to supply safety data. When the company refused, she held the application for 18 months. In a 'useful unknown' tactic that would be replicated by the manufacturers of Vioxx, Ketek and Seroxat, Merrell insisted that European reports linking the drug to birth defects were 'inconclusive,' and that it was impossible to know whether the drug was a causal factor.

'I had the feeling,' Kelsey once wrote after meeting with Merrell staff, 'that they were at no time being wholly frank with me, and that this attitude has obtained in all our conferences, etc., regarding this drug.'[10]

The latest news from Europe came in: a mushrooming number of reports of babies born with stunted arms and legs. Grim images of half-formed infant bodies led to the acceptance of an irrefutable truth: the drug caused the malformation of limbs in infants. A *Washington Post* article in 1962 hailed Kelsey as the heroine of the FDA. Stricter regulatory laws were passed through Congress during the same year, expanding the FDA's remit.

The patterns from this incident, manufacturers sitting on inconvenient scientific evidence and trying to intimidate FDA staff, have not changed since. What's different is that tragedies on the scale of Thalidomide don't always have the same power to galvanize the US public in the same way they once did in the 1960s. Today, rather than seeing greater regulation as an effective way to police industry deceit, regulation is bemoaned as a cumbersome barrier to medical progress. When Donald Trump was first elected US President, to give just one recent example, Bill Gates hailed him for promising to 'get rid of regulatory barriers.'[11]

The entrenchment of an anti-regulation bias makes it hard for individual employees at the FDA and elsewhere to call for prudent regulation – to do so is to be branded 'anti' scientific innovation. If Kelsey was at the FDA today, could she have warded off the pressure to approve Thalidomide?

It's an impossible question to answer, but examples below suggest that an increasingly close relationship between regulators and industry has made it harder for the FDA to act as an independent check on corporate mal-feasance, a point emphasized to me when I spent time in Washington DC interviewing current and former FDA employees, including David Graham, a man applauded in the media as a national hero, but who was facing a far differ-ent reception inside the agency.

IGNORANCE BATTLES

In November 2009, I met Graham, a slightly built, grey haired, softly-spoken father of six in his FDA office in Silver Spring, on the outskirts of Washington DC.

Five years earlier, Graham had testified before the US Senate about the FDA response to the detection of lethal side-effects of Vioxx, an anti-inflammatory drug linked to heart failure in tens of thousands of users.

Manufactured by Merck, Vioxx was introduced in 1999 for the treatment of pain associated with osteoarthritis.

After the emergence of irrefutable evidence linking the drug to cardiovascular failure in some users, the drug was removed from the US market on September 30, 2004 – a day which Harvard University physician Jerry Avorn suggested is 'fast becoming a day of infamy for drug safety.'[12] Before its removal, nearly 107 million prescriptions had been dispensed in the US.[13] American cardiologist Eric Topol described the recall as the largest market withdrawal of a pharmaceutical drug in history.[14]

Merck was praised at first for recalling the drug voluntarily; the editor of The Lancet suggested, 'For Merck to act so promptly in the face of these most recent safety concerns is commendable and should serve as an example of responsible pharmaceutical practice.'[15]

A month later, though, the Lancet's editor retracted his comments, stating bluntly: 'our praise was premature.'[16] Leaked emails, published in The Wall Street Journal, indicated that Merck executive knew about the risks of the drug as early as 1997.

These emails revolved around the VIGOR study, a large-scale study carried out by Merck in 1999 comparing Vioxx to a drug called naproxen, a popular painkiller which was first licensed in the 1970s. Merck's aim was to expand Vioxx's FDA licence by demonstrating that Vioxx carried fewer gastrointestinal side-effects than naproxen. After an early safety analysis from this clinical trial, presented to Merck's safety board in 1999 revealed an 80 per cent greater risk of cardiovascular adverse reactions, including death, among participants who received Vioxx, the board chose to let the study continue. The final study did determine that Vioxx was effective in diminishing gastrointestinal events, but it also confirmed the increased risk of heart failure on Vioxx over naproxen, something Merck's chief scientist Edward Scolnick referred to in an email as 'a shame.'[17]

Because the VIGOR study was a comparison between two drugs – Vioxx and naproxen – Merck's scientists had a choice in how to interpret the results. They could either interpret the study as showing that Vioxx *increased* the risk of heart attacks, or they could suggest that naproxen was actually a protective agent – *decreasing* the risk. The company chose the latter option, publishing articles in reputable journals such as the *New England Journal of Medicine* and the *Annals of Internal Medicine* which argued that naproxen warded off the risk of heart failure – despite no evidence of this benefit in the decades that naproxen had been on the market.[18]

One public health scholar summed up the problem:

[I]t is hard to imagine that the company's scientists were deliberately promoting a drug they knew was unsafe. At the same time, it is hard to imagine they honestly thought naproxen reduced the risk of heart attack by 80 per cent.[19]

THE LEGAL FALLOUT

In the months and years following the withdrawal of Vioxx, over 30,000 legal claims were filed against Merck by users who suffered cardiovascular events or by the families of those who died while on the drug, including the family of David Ernst, an American Wal-Mart manager who ran marathons in his spare time. In 2001, at the age of 59, he died in his sleep of a fatal arrhythmia while taking Vioxx. In 2005, a Texas jury found Merck liable for Ernst's death, arguing that executives had deliberately hidden safety risk, awarding his widow $253.5 million in punitive damages.[20]

At first glance it's an enormous sum, and it led market analysts to suggest that Merck might collapse under the financial weight of legal liabilities. But much like in the case of the hacking scandal facing Murdoch's empire in the United Kingdom, doomsday predictions of crippling financial penalties or jail time for company executives at Merck never came about.

In November 2007, in a reversal of its earlier insistence that it would fight each individual civil case separately, Merck announced it would pay a settlement of $4.85 billion to cover the over 30,000 plaintiffs represented in various civil suits. This may seem like a lot of money, but it's far less than initial predictions of $30 billion.

Merck also pled guilty to a misdemeanour in a plea arrangement with the US Department of Justice in 2011, paying a nearly billion-dollar fine for illegal promotional activity. No executive was personally penalized.

FROM HERO TO PARIAH

David Graham first became concerned about the risks of Vioxx in 2000 following the publication of the VIGOR study.

His concerns led him to carry out a large epidemiological study observing over a million consumers who had taken either Vioxx or one of its competitors. Based on this data, Graham suggested to his colleagues that Vioxx might have been implicated in heart failure. He received a letter from the FDA's Office of New Drugs, who said that because the FDA was not considering a warning against the use of Vioxx, he should rethink his conclusions on the drug's risks. Graham was called to testify to a Senate committee looking into the FDA's handling of the Vioxx case, and he has harsh words for his employer, insisting that the Vioxx example was a part of the agency's systematic unwillingness to value epidemiological data that tracked the safety of drugs once they have already received an FDA licence.

His Senate testimony earned him widespread media accolades, even from unlikely sources such as *Forbes* magazine, a media outlet that tends to be friendlier to big business than to lone bureaucrats. But *Forbes* saluted Graham's courage. 'For his steadfast advocacy of drug safety and his willingness to blow the whistle on his bosses, we're naming David Graham our Face of the Year.' *Forbes* was also scathing about the FDA and big pharma, suggesting 'the withdrawal of Vioxx from the market looks like part of a systemic failure to properly weigh the risks and benefits of drugs' and adding that 'change would be good for regulators and drug companies.'[21]

When I interviewed Graham five years later, change hadn't arrived. He told me things were even worse, that it was harder for individual staff to raise valid concerns about the safety of different drugs, because the agency feared a revival of the reputational damage suffered over the early 2000s. Whistle-blowers might have been hailed publicly as heroes, but inside FDA walls they were often stonewalled and even vilified.

'I have no career progression really,' Graham said to me. 'I have a job title of associate director but that's really because people don't know what to do with me.'

Graham told me that his FDA superiors 'didn't like the fact that the recommendations I made contradicted official agency policy, which was that they declared the drug to be safe and effective and approved for us, so how could I say it's not safe and shouldn't be used?' He added: 'It's moronic when you think about it: as in, might the policy be wrong?'[22]

The reasons he was treated this way are complex, stemming from a mixture of financial and reputational pressures that chaff against a duty of care to the general public. In 1992, the FDA moved to a system that was more reliant on pharmaceutical companies paying fees to have their drugs licensed. Pharmaceutical companies insisted on a number of conditions in exchange for paying fees to the FDA, including that their money should be spent on expediting approvals and not on post-market safety studies, and that reviews of a new drug should be completed within six months. The closer reliance on industry may be compromising the FDA's ability to act as an impartial regulator of companies upon which it is financially dependent.[23]

Reputational concerns also play a role in undermining the robustness of regulatory decisions, a point stressed by Harvard political scientist Daniel Carpenter. In his words, 'it's perhaps audacious to claim, and certainly difficult to prove, that reputational incentives weaken the [FDA] Office of New Drugs' willingness to scrutinize drugs that have already been approved,' he writes. 'Yet characterizations to this effect have been with us for 50 years.'[24]

Another reason why the FDA has been shown to systematically ignore or downplay drug risks that appear once a drug has already been approved has to do with measurement challenges, a problem that illustrates the complexity of strategic ignorance in practice.

Difficulties in measuring a drug's risks can render strategic ignorance not simply a pernicious tactic, but rather a rational and even laudable response to the limits of scientific evidence.

SHOW ME THE EVIDENCE

Regulators and drug manufacturers rely on two main scientific methods for testing a drug's efficacy and safety. Each of these methods has its own strengths and weaknesses. The first is the randomized controlled trial (RCT), first used to test the benefits of medicines in the 1940s. Since then, RCTs have become a vital pillar in efforts to measure the risks and benefits of new medicines, seen as the 'gold standard' because the use of randomly allocated control groups helps to determine whether the drug itself or an external factor – such as the specific physiology of individual patients, or environmental factors – is directly responsible for a particular treatment effect.

The second method is an epidemiological study: a design which is able to measure drug effects among much larger populations than RCTs can usually capture. These studies have the advantage of size and historical perspective. They make it feasible to isolate different populations and geographical regions and to study a drug's safety once it is already on the market by tracking its use among millions of users rather than simply the smaller samples studies through RCT techniques.

In general, RCTs are seen as having the upper hand over epidemiological studies when it comes to determining causal effects, but like any scientific methodologies, RCTs have their weaknesses. The main problem is that RCTs can be too short in length (lasting a few months or a year) and have too few participants to reveal rare adverse risks that only become visible once the drug is on the market. As Carpenter puts it, their main drawbacks are that they are tested in 'homogenous patient populations ... and can often be too brief to allow analysts to detect whether the drug is inducing adverse events.'[25]

Despite widespread awareness that rare adverse drug risks are often only perceivable after a drug is licensed, the perception of RCTs as the ultimate 'gold standard' has led to a situation in which if a side-effect does not appear on a randomized trial, regulators tend to dismiss the side-effect as negligible and not worth worrying about.

The FDA invests substantial resources in post-market epidemiological studies intended to identify rare adverse effects. Typically, however, staff members at the Office for New Drugs, the office responsible for drug approvals, tend to dismiss epidemiological studies as less reliable than RCTs, and so considerable money and effort is spent on studies that are systemically ignored in practice.

Graham told me that many of his colleagues 'only believe – this has been said to me more than once by people from the Office of New Drugs, very high level people – they will only believe that an adverse effect is real when a controlled clinical trial has been done that shows an effect with a p value of less than 0.05.'[26]

Unless adverse effects are visible on RCT evidence, FDA reviewers have difficulty accepting that a drug's risks may be severe – even though staff members know that many RCTs are too short and have too few participants to reveal those very risks. Persistent faith in how regulation *should* work in theory – the hope that, ideally, regulators will pick up problems *before* a drug is licensed – leads to a sort of institutionally sanctioned strategic ignorance of problems that emerge *after* a drug is on the market. As Graham suggests, 'people can be blinded. They can believe so strongly in a product that they explain away things.'[27] He suggested that the FDA has adopted an 'asymmetric approach to safety' where the 'drug is effective until you prove to me [through RCT evidence] it's not. It's a very warped standard, one that doesn't protect the public.'

This warped approach to safety doesn't necessarily stem from deliberate negligence or clear collusion with fraudulent companies. Rather, it is, in some ways, a *rational* response to the widespread belief that RCTs are the best way to measure different phenomena. When adverse effects are not detectable on RCTs, many staff members believe in good faith that such risks *should* be ignored – it is considered one's professional duty to base decisions on only the most robust evidence. This leads to a form of rational but quite dangerous expert ignorance, because even though epidemiological evidence might be 'weaker' than RCT evidence, it is typically the only evidence that tracks large enough groups of people to capture rare, but often fatal, drug reactions.

The tendency to value RCTs' evidence over epidemiological studies has led to a paradoxical problem, which is that FDA insiders who have been *most* vocal about *known* concerns with RCTs have endured negative professional consequences inside the FDA for trying to deal with a known problem rather than simply continuing to ignore it.

EXPERTS AND EPISTOCRACY

The treatment of Graham, a 'good' expert who did his job conscientiously and correctly – and yet who was still treated internally at the FDA as a dangerous renegade – has implications for the belief that epistocracy will lead to more robust decisions.

Graham's experience underscores the way that sound regulatory decision-making requires people to examine a problem from multiple different angles – to understand the way that even the so-called 'best' evidence can be flawed – in order to make better decisions. And yet in practice there are often few incentives either professionally or institutionally to do so. Once an evidence base is established, it is difficult to convince people that 'anomalies,' as the philosopher of science Thomas Kuhn described them, might require an entirely new framing of a problem.

This problem is not limited to science. History and fiction abound with examples of a similar problem: the way that people will only change course when they experience a personal catastrophe so unsettling that it leads them to imagine their own world view or the suffering of others in a completely new light.

Mary Wollstonecraft, for example, is believed to have slept outside the door of her parents' bedroom, on the hallway landing, ready to intervene if her father started to beat her mother in a drunken rage, putting her body between them and taking the blows.

A woman who saw and felt such brutality as a child is understandably less willing to accept the righteousness of a society where women are widely regarded as the property of men. Political decision-making is, or at least should be, as much about expert knowledge as it is about the capacity to empathize with the perspectives of different groups of people – not simply because it is compassionate to do so, but because it leads to greater knowledge of social and economic realities that other people either can't see or refuse to perceive.

The novelist André Brink captures this reality – the personal danger of breaking societal or institutional expectations of complicity with unspoken things – in his novel *A Dry White Season*, set in South Africa in the 1960s. His protagonist, Ben du Toit, a white man, makes the 'unreasonable' decision to investigate the murder of a black colleague's son, a boy involved in anti-apartheid protests.

His actions have drastic consequences. His wife, the child of a member of parliament in the all-white government, and his daughter, married to a successful business man, gang up together on du Toit, trying to make him understand the 'insensitivity' of his dissent; to realize that his empathy is misdirected; to see that his insistence on questioning the system is, in their eyes, *more* immoral than perpetuating it. As he battles his family's misgivings, du Toit begins to see that 'my real problem is benevolence … Not open hostility: one can work out a strategy to counter that. But this, thick heavy porridge of good intentions on the part of people obstructing you "for your own good."'[28]

Wollstonecraft, too, was disparaged throughout her short life for living differently, for refusing to accept societal norms in her day as acceptable ways to treat women and children.

What these very different examples have in common is that the effort to expose strategic ignorance, to draw attention to palpable problems is, quite perversely, treated as the most inexcusable act. Exposing problems is often more personally dangerous than quietly perpetuating them.

I noticed this in my interviews with different FDA staff, and especially a man named David Ross who left the agency in 2006 after struggling for years to convince his bosses that the antibiotic Ketek was riskier than previously realized.

I met with Ross at a coffee shop in Washington DC the same month that I met with Graham. He told me that when Graham first appeared on numerous media outlets in the wake of Vioxx, Ross railed about him to his wife.

'I said, how dare he!' Ross admitted. It was only later, after his repeated attempts to flag safety concerns were dismissed by his superiors, that he began to realize that Graham's concerns about the FDA were accurate:

> I think part of it is: people don't want to hear that their framework for looking at the world isn't right. I really did [change my mind]. Partly because I ran into some bad behaviour. But also because I think that the regulatory decision-making tends to be very narrow and very focused. In a way it has to be, but I think that we're missing some important things.

IT'S EASIER AT THE TOP

Ketek is a noteworthy case, because unlike the Vioxx example, where Merck was at least forced to pay legal fines for concealing evidence even though no executives served jail time, Ketek's manufacturers, Aventis (later Sanofi-Aventis through a merger), was able to successfully deny legal responsibility for promoting an unsafe drug. Aventis avoided criminal changes despite at least one family practice doctor insisting that the company knew she was carrying out fraud and encouraged her to do so.

This doctor's name is Anne Kirkman-Campbell, and in 2004, she was sentenced to 57 months in a federal prison for mail fraud. Behind her imprisonment lies a story of ignored warnings and professional reprimands that caused at least two FDA medical officers to leave the agency over the FDA's refusal to listen to their concerns about Ketek's safety.

When Aventis first applied to the FDA for a licence for Ketek, reviewers discerned worrying side-effects, including a possible association with liver failure.

The FDA told the drug's manufacturer, Aventis, that the company needed to collect more data before the drug could be approved. Aventis launched Study 3014, which involved over 24,000 participants, carried out by more than 1,800 physicians across the US. To carry out this massive RCT, Aventis outsourced the data collection for Study 3014 to a subcontractor, an organization called Pharmaceutical Product Development Inc (PPD).

It was an observant staff member at PPD, Ann Marie Cisneros, who first noticed unusual behaviour at Kirkman-Campbell's lab and reported her concerns to both PPD and to Aventis.

Part of Cisneros' job at PPD was to monitor the quality control at Kirkman-Campbell's lab. Looking closely at Kirkman-Campbell's data, she found a number of irregularities, including the fact that Kirkman-Campbell had signed up 400 participants to take part in Study 3014. Another lab based in the same town had recruited only 12 participants. Kirkman-Campbell received $400 per patient whenever she enrolled a new participant, and this financial incentive seems to have encouraged an all-embracing recruitment style: most of the informed consent forms looked to have been initialled by a single hand; one form seemed to be obviously forged; one patient diagnosed with chronic bronchitis didn't have any history of that illness.[29]

Concerned, Cisneros emailed a summary of her findings to the head of quality assurance at PPD, copying Aventis staff into the email. She also took part in a teleconference call between PPD and Aventis where she discussed her concerns with Kirkman-Campbell's data.

EAR PAIN

The FDA, meanwhile, had learned about the suspected safety violations at Kirkman-Campbell's lab. Despite knowing about these safety violations, the FDA presented data to an advisory committee without mentioning that a criminal investigation into Kirkman-Campbell's actions was underway. Unaware of the criminal investigation, the committee voted 11 to 1 to recommend approval of Ketek. The FDA awarded a licence to Ketek in 2004.[30]

Between 2004 and 2006, over five million Ketek prescriptions were dispensed in the United States. Over a dozen people who took the drug died, including Ramiro Obrajero Pulquero, a 26-year-old construction worker with a wife and two daughters. He was prescribed Ketek when he went to his physician after coming down with a severe cold, and died three weeks later. The people who died while taking Ketek were otherwise healthy individuals, just as Pulquero was.[31]

David Ross told me that over 2005 and 2006, as reports of Ketek's side-effects grew more alarming, he repeatedly stressed to his supervisors that he was worried about the drug's safety. In June 2006, a number of FDA reviewers, including Ross, were summoned to a meeting with the then FDA Commissioner Andrew von Eschenbach. During this meeting, the Commissioner compared the FDA to a football team and told assembled staff members that if they publicly discussed problems with Ketek outside the agency, they would be 'traded from the team.'[32]

Feeling threatened with being fired, Ross chose to leave the FDA voluntarily. Also in 2006, Rosemary Johann-Liang, a former deputy division director in the Office of Surveillance and Epidemiology, wrote an internal memo suggesting that the FDA needed to at least warn parents about increasing knowledge of the risks of the drug, asking 'how does one justify balancing the risk of fatal liver failure against one day less of ear pain?' She also left the agency.[33]

RESTITUTION

Finally, in 2007, the FDA implemented label changes for Ketek, banning its use for two of its three previously approved indications (acute bacterial sinusitis and acute bacterial exacerbations of chronic bronchitis), and insisting on a black-box warning for the sole remaining indication, the treatment of community-acquired pneumonia.

The same year, the US House of Representatives' Committee on Energy and Commerce launched a hearing into whether different organizations, from the FDA to Sanofi-Aventis, knew about the adverse risks of Ketek before the drug was licensed in 2004 and wilfully ignored them.

These government hearings provide a rare glimpse into insider practices that are often veiled from public scrutiny. They show the way that strategic ignorance functions in practice.

Witnesses before the hearings included Ann Marie Cisneros, the PPD employee who first detected signs of fraud at Kirkman-Campbell's lab, and Douglas Loveland, an FDA criminal investigator assigned to investigate whether Aventis has complied with FDA regulations.

'Do you believe Aventis intentionally ignored evidence of fraud,' Cisneros and Loveland were asked, 'or is it a matter that their processes and procedures of verifying fraud were faulty and couldn't have detected it?'

Cisneros' reply was unequivocal. 'I personally believe they ignored evidence of fraud. You had to have your head stuck in the sand to have missed this.' She added that 'what brings me here today is my disbelief at Aventis's statement that it did not suspect fraud was being committed. Mr. Chairman, I knew, PPD knew it, Aventis knew it.'[34]

Kirkman-Campbell was adamant, too, that Aventis knew about her fraud. Kirkman-Campbell's credibility is clearly strained by her vigorous patient recruitment methods, and she deservedly served a jail sentence, but she perhaps didn't deserve this extra humiliation: she was ordered to pay $925,000 in restitution directly to Aventis. She appealed the restitution order, arguing that Aventis 'had been made aware of the fraud at my site by PPD. At NO TIME did they attempt to stop my participation.' Her motion was denied.[35]

To compare this to earlier examples, look at Aventis alongside Murdoch's News International, where senior executives allegedly knew too about illegal activity that was financially lucrative for executives even if senior management was legally exculpated. Murdoch may have reneged on helping with his staff's legal fees, but at least convicted employees didn't have to pay restitution to News International.

FDA investigator Douglas Loveland was also critical of Aventis. He insisted the company could have and should have known about the fraud. He called the company's risk-detection efforts a 'catastrophic failure.' But at the same time, he couldn't say for certain that Aventis definitely knew about the fraud, because the company took steps which, under the guise of seeking to examine Kirkland-Campbell's practices, enabled them to *avoid* perceiving her illegal actions:

> Mr. LOVELAND: When you get into a traffic accident, you call a traffic cop. These folks came in and they said, We have indicators of fraud, and they called a mathematician. A mathematician didn't know what fraud looked like, and he couldn't identify it. He looked at all the data, couldn't figure out a rule to apply to the data set, came back and said, I don't see fraud. They took that to convince themselves that two of the most serious allegations raised by Mrs. Cisneros and by other PPD folks weren't indicators of fraud.[36]

Through the guise of vigilance, Aventis managed to deflect the possibility of inconvenient findings, enabling them to remain convincingly ignorant of effects widely visible to others.

In this case, Aventis employed a statistician to investigate data where signals of fraud were *least* likely to be visible.

Early on during Study 3014, as Loveland states, Aventis and PPD 'detected protocol violations which were significant enough to potentially affect the integrity of data at a minimum of eleven sites.' Aventis then directed a statistician – the mathematician Loveland refers to – to perform an analysis of Kirkman-Campbell's lab data. The statistician concluded that data from Kirkman-Campbell's sites wasn't suspicious because it was no different than other high-enrolling lab sites.

But Loveland argued that the problem with the statistician's investigation is that statistical analyses are not capable of discerning mundane discrepancies, such as 'ink irregularities' – the reworking lab results written in different coloured ink after data are first recorded.

Such irregularities are warning flags to FDA investigators that evidence of a drug's adverse effects may have been manipulated or deliberately erased, and are visible only to those dealing with handwritten reports, not to statisticians working with computerized data sets.

The statistician's expertise is noteworthy here. Despite appearing to be, in hindsight, the *least* able to perceive fraud that had been erased from case notes by the time he examined the computerized data, his conclusions were privileged over PPD staff such as Cisneros. Once an expert statistician couldn't find a problem, it became more plausible for Aventis to assert there was nothing to find. His ignorance furnished an institutional alibi, helping higher-ups to maintain that a phenomenon was impossible to know, rather than simply unknowable by the unenlightened. The statistician's ignorance trumped the knowledge of experts lower down the totem pole.

Did Aventis deliberately try to avoid unsettling information, or was the statistician's finding of nothing simply convenient for them?

It is difficult to know for certain. Aventis' appointed statistician, working in all likelihood in good faith, nonetheless helped to shield the company from legal liability for fraud at Kirkman-Campbell's site.

Finding an expert who knew what not to know protected the company from blame. After the FDA banned the use of Ketek for treating sinusitis and bronchitis, a consortium of US health plans launched a suit against Sanofi-Aventis for racketeering, arguing that the company committed fraud by failing to disclose risks. The Second Circuit rejected the case against Aventis, claiming that deliberate fraud couldn't be proved, and that 'the ultimate decision regarding which drug will be prescribed to a patient rests entirely with the patient's doctor.'[37]

KNOWING WHAT NOT TO KNOW

Aventis' reliance on expert ignorance illustrates the way that 'useful unknowns' can have commercial value, helping companies to avoid legal liability and financial penalties even when a company has been informed many times about concerns over safety risks.

Government regulators also have an incentive for ignoring evidence of corporate crime, especially when they are financially dependent on organizations that they are meant to be regulating.

The following chapter expands on this point, returning to the example that opened this chapter: SSRI antidepressants such as Seroxat and Prozac.

The SSRI case illustrates a point that I made earlier: that it is not innate ability, but rather jurisdictional advantage that lets corporations avoid legal penalties in some countries while avoiding prosecution in others.

The UK has a much weaker record than the US when it comes to prosecuting companies for withholding clinical trial data from regulators that shows their products may be harming children and adults. Since the 1980s, the MHRA has been 100 per cent financially dependent on fees from pharmaceutical companies for the service of medicines licensing, and while it's hard to prove a causal relationship between this funding relationship and the MHRA's record of non-prosecution, it is possible that cosiness between regulators and the regulated leads to the 'rotary motion' problem that Thomas Paine pointed out.

As I describe further in the next chapter, I interviewed a representative of the MHRA, the agency's CEO at the time of our interview, about the UK agency's failure to prosecute pharmaceutical companies. He told me that prosecution is rarely needed because pharmaceutical companies have an interest in voluntarily complying with the law.

I suggest that the presumption that companies *want* to stay within the law is the ultimate corporate ignorance alibi. To understand where this ignorance alibi comes from, it is necessary to trace the ignorance pathway backward, to economic theories that emerged in the mid-20th century and that continue to influence policymaking today. To that end, my next chapter also explores the ideas of economists who have popularized misguided and historically inaccurate theories about the ability of government regulation to improve public welfare, leading to an erosion of checks and balances when it comes to corporate power in our time.

CHAPTER 11

THE PRETENCE
OF IGNORANCE

Prozac, the first ever patented SSRI, was licensed by the FDA in 1987. In the decades since, it's been a financial wonder drug, generated billions for Eli Lilly annually, accounting in some years for a full quarter of the company's total revenues. 'Prozac and its kin have been one of 20th-century medicine's great success stories,' *Fortune* magazine described in 2005, 'Perhaps one out of 20 adult Americans are on them now.'[1]

That was 15 years ago. Today the number has climbed to over one in ten; approximately 13 per cent of the American population are on antidepressants.

Despite their enormous popularity, reports of worrying side-effects from SSRIs were apparent as early as 1990, when Martin Teicher, a psychiatrist at Harvard University, published a study in the *American Journal of Psychiatry* detailing six cases where patients experienced suicidal thoughts while on Prozac.

His article chimed with an explosive number of patient reports of adverse effects filed by physicians across the

United States. By September 1991, the FDA had received 14,000 patient reports detailing unexpected side-effects from Prozac. The FDA convened its Psychopharmacological Drug Advisory Committee (PDAC) to investigate the possible link between Prozac and suicidality. Despite hearing oral reports from parents of children and other family members who harmed themselves or committed suicide while on Prozac – reports that came to 110 transcribed pages – the PDAC committee voted against the implementation of any label change that could advise physicians of the uncertainty over the drug's safety.[2]

The worry that SSRIs, a drug intended to treat depression, may be leading to suicidal reactions posed a particular problem given that it's very hard to know whether it is the underlying depression for which the drug is intended to treat, that leads a person to take his or her life.

But it's also where the unique strengths of RCTs are apparent. SSRIs are one of the most tested drugs in history. Because of the high number of participants enrolled on trials, even a rare adverse effect like suicide, could in theory show up on RCTs, making it possible to determine statistically whether or not the drugs themselves were directly causing this rare effect. That is, unless pharmaceutical companies deliberately withhold unpublished data showing negative effects, and unless regulators fail to carefully examine RCT evidence that they *do* have. Which is exactly what happened.

COMPROMISED EXPERTISE

The United States wasn't the only nation seeing a hike in patient reports of adverse effects while on antidepressants. The tipping point galvanizing British regulators into paying closer attention to self-reports from patients or their doctors was a 2002 televised exposé aired by the BBC's *Panorama,* a popular investigative TV programme which ran a series of documentaries on the subject. Over four million people tuned into *Panorama*'s first programme in the series, *Secrets of Seroxat.* The show drew a phenomenal response: the BBC received about 65,000 phone calls and 1,374 emails from viewers saying the programme had resonated with their own unexpected side-effects while on GlaxoSmithKline's Seroxat.[3]

In 2003, the MHRA convened its Committee on Safety of Medicines (CSM) to explore the question of SSRI safety. It wasn't the first time the British regulator addressed the question. Following Teicher's study in 1990, the CSM had first reviewed the issue, finding no evidence of a causal link between SSRIs and suicidal behaviour. Between 1998 and 2000, the MHRA again re-examined the data, and they did rule that the patient-information labels for SSRIs should reflect general clinical experience that suicidal behaviour could increase in the early stages of treatment. But they also concluded that there was no firm evidence to confirm an association between SSRIs and suicidal behaviour. Yet another review was carried out in 2001, and the same conclusion was reached.

During a 2003 review into SSRI safety, the MHRA's efforts were scuppered before it even got started: a news article in *The Guardian* reported a worrying conflict of interest – over half of the members of an expert working group established to lead the regulatory agency's inquiry held shares in SSRI manufacturers such as GlaxoSmithKline. The MHRA chose to dissolve this first working group entirely and set up a new one composed of practitioners who had fewer ties to industry.[4]

Perhaps to alleviate simmering public frustration over what was already seen as a lethargic reaction by the MHRA to antidepressant concerns, the agency took an unusual step with this second, hastily composed committee. For the first time in its history, the MHRA chose to include a lay member of the public among the scientific experts on its expert advisory panel. Richard Brook, the chief executive of Mind, one of Britain's largest mental health charities, was asked to serve as that non-scientific member.

Brook's relationship with other panel members soon grew acrimonious. After serving on the group for a year, he resigned in protest over what he called a cover-up by the agency of the finding that daily doses of SSRIs over 20mg were no more effective at treating depression, regardless of severity of depression, than doses at 20mg.[5]

The SSRI working group discovered this through a re-analysis of clinical trial data that had been in the possession of the MHRA for over ten years, overlooked during previous inquiries into the safety of the drugs. Despite the fact that the new finding had a bearing on the 17,000 individuals in Britain who were receiving daily doses of SSRIs at 30, 40 or 60 milligrams – increasing their risk of suffering serious adverse effects – the working group chose not to publicly disclose the new information.

When Brook voiced his dissatisfaction over the decision to withhold the information and insisted the information be made public, the CEO of the MHRA, Kent Woods, sent him a letter indicating he would be in breach of Section 118 of the Medicines Act if he revealed the data, and noting he had advised Brook's lawyer of this fact. Breaches of Section 118 then carried a maximum jail term of two years; the clause was later repealed in January 2005.

Feeling intimidated and fearful of arrest, Brook submitted his resignation from the CSM after receiving Woods' letter.

'Despite four major regulatory reviews during this period and considerable consumer reporting and disquiet, the Committee on Safety of Medicines failed either to identify or communicate these key facts,' he wrote in his resignation letter. 'As far as I am aware, the MHRA has not seen fit to acknowledge or address what in my view appears to be extreme negligence.'[6]

'At every meeting [of the working group],' Brook said to me during an interview a few years after his resignation,

> the chairman reads the riot act over the meeting reminding you if you say anything then you're going to be in trouble … from my observation, it was always predominantly driven by their fear of having a row with pharmaceutical companies over leaking commercial secrets.[7]

Over a year after meeting with Brook, I was granted an interview with MHRA CEO Kent Woods, visiting him at the MHRA's London headquarters in Vauxhall, just south of the Thames.

I raised Brook's concern with Woods: his feeling that a fear of offending the pharmaceutical industry may have contributed to the threat to prosecute him if he revealed his concerns about dosing levels. Woods denied that the threat *was* a threat.

'[Brook] asked me a question: would I give him my permission [to release data]? And I said no,' Woods said,

> to mention, in doing so, that he was going to be in breach of Section 118 was not exactly a threat of prosecution. We didn't have policemen standing outside his door. When I saw that matter presented by Mr. Brook in the media as though we had threatened him with a prosecution I thought that was a complete misstatement. He had asked for permission to break an undertaking of confidentiality, and I had declined that permission.[8]

Woods stressed to me an important point. Antidepressant drugs, like a lot of medicine, can be dangerous if stopped abruptly. It's true, as Woods suggested to me, that information needs to be carefully disseminated to the public in order to avoid public panics. But it's also true that unnecessarily high doses of drugs can lead to grave side-effects.

Brook, in my view, was in the right to publicize his concerns. And, yet, Woods wasn't wrong either to take the reality of public panic seriously. Also, to the credit of the agency under his watch, the MHRA *did* reach out to Tim Kendall to take a closer look at the unpublished evidence on SSRI use in children.

HIDDEN DATA IN PLAIN SIGHT

In the early 2000s, when Kendall first took on the job of Britain's National Collaborating Centre for Mental Health, few doctors or consumers realized just how serious the problem of unpublished pharmaceutical company data was. Certainly Kendall was surprised by what his team found out.

When he wrote in 2003 to various drug companies, requesting all unpublished and published clinical trials testing the safety and efficacy of SSRIs in children, he saw it as a standard request. He was writing on behalf of government policymakers, he never presumed at the time that companies would lie to him – but they did.

The line from the pharmaceutical companies, Kendall told me during our interview, was not 'no, we won't give it to you,' it was 'no, we haven't got any' – they insisted that any relevant data were already in the public domain. Then Kendall was contacted by MHRA. There *was* unpublished clinical data, and the MHRA wanted to share it with Kendall's team. This led to Kendall's *Lancet* article on SSRIs – and the following furore that I described in the last chapter, where suddenly physicians worldwide became more aware of the seriousness of a problem that was known about earlier but that tended to be dismissed: the fear that pharmaceutical companies were hiding scientific evidence that showed their products were directly harming people.

PRUDENCE OR NEGLIGENCE?

In the US, in 2003, an FDA safety officer named Andrew Mosholder was immersed in the same deep-dive into available data as Kendall's team, reexamining both published and unpublished SSRI data. After reviewing 22 clinical trials involving more than 4,100 children and eight different antidepressants, he reached the same finding as Kendall: that there was an increased risk of suicidal behaviour among children being treated for depression with SSRIs.

He raised his findings with superiors, suggesting that the FDA should publicly disclose the evidence of the increased suicide risk. Instead, as journalist Jeanne Lenzer reported in the *British Medical Journal*, Mosholder was barred from presenting his report at an FDA advisory meeting in February 2004 – despite the fact that his name was listed on the initial agenda. He was also told that if asked questions at the meeting, he must stick to a prepared script from his supervisors.[9]

Robert Temple, associate director for medical policy in the FDA's drug evaluation centre, insisted that the treatment of Mosholder was prudent. Raising similar concerns as Kent Woods' response to Richard Brook, Temple said he feared that publicizing the findings might kindle unwarranted public alarm – compelling parents to abruptly take their children off lifesaving treatments.

Others were more sceptical.

'The FDA … attempted to silence Dr Mosholder [but] repeatedly claimed to "support his concern" for the safety of children,' Jerome Hoffman, a professor of medicine at the University of California at Los Angeles, suggested to Lenzer. 'But this apparently didn't extend to supporting his desire to express that concern publicly. That may be the most dangerous aspect of this entire affair.'[10]

The FDA contracted experts at Columbia University to conduct a re-analysis of the RCTs data on SSRI use among children; their report confirmed Mosholder's findings, stating there was a two-fold higher risk of suicidal events on the anti-depressant arms of trials in comparison with the placebo arms.

The FDA then chose to hold a series of panels inviting family members and SSRI users to testify to their experiences with observing the drug's effects. After the public panels, facing pressure from Congress, the FDA chose in September 2004 to implement a black box label on SSRI use in children: the drugs could still be prescribed, but with the highest possible FDA warning against the possibility of serious and fatal side-effects.

DAUGHTERS

It is possible to lose sight of the tragedy at the heart of debates over drug safety, corporate malfeasance and regulatory failure. Glenn McIntosh and Linda Hurcombe do not have that luxury.

McIntosh is one of the dozens of parents who testified during FDA hearings over the years. Testifying in 2004, he held up a photo of his daughter to the panel so they could see an image of her face.

'I would like to introduce you to my daughter, Caitlin Elizabeth McIntosh,' he said. Caitlin was in grade six when she hung herself using shoelaces in the bathroom of her school. She had been taking Paxil – marketed as Seroxat in the UK – for two months.

'We were lied to,' McIntosh told the FDA panel. 'The pharmaceutical companies have known for years that these drugs could cause suicide in some patients. Why didn't we?'[11]

Linda Hurcombe's daughter was also named Caitlin. Her daughter died by suicide on April 6, 1998, at the age of 19. At the time of her death, she had been taking a therapeutic regime of fluoxetine hydrochloride – more commonly known as Prozac.

Five years after Caitlin's death, her mother, Linda, published *Losing a Child*, a guide for helping other parents experiencing the sudden death of a child. In the book, she describes the last few months of Caitlin's life. A 'normal, self-conscious, complicated teenager,' Caitlin told her mother she wanted to take Prozac after a difficult Christmas season left her feeling depressed and upset with herself for gaining weight. A few months later, during the last days of her life, Caitlin's behaviour became frighteningly erratic. In early April, slinging her childhood pony's lunge rope over a wooden beam in the family's guest bedroom, she hung herself.

Hurcombe is British. McIntosh is American. For information on a drug's risk, they are reliant on two different agencies, the FDA in the US, and the MHRA in the UK – and to this day, it's still hard to determine conclusively whether the FDA's and MHRA's actions were justifiable or not.

Many patients swear by the drugs. Looking at sales figures, it is clear that antidepressants have been one of the largest commercial successes in medical history. Praised in popular bestsellers such as Lauren Slater's *Prozac Diary*, a book charting her emergence from a debilitating depression thanks to the drug, for over three decades demand for antidepressants has skyrocketed.

But Hurcombe and McIntosh's daughters did not live through this medical miracle. And as McIntosh told an FDA panel in 2004, clutching the photo of his daughter, the pharmaceutical companies knew about the risk of suicide all along.

CROSSING THE LINE

When I met for an interview with Kent Woods in 2007, the MHRA's criminal investigation in GSK was still ongoing. Kendall and others were watching the case closely: it was the first time ever that Britain's drug regulator might end up going forward with a formal prosecution of a pharmaceutical company for shady behaviour that most people *assumed* was illegal – the withholding of relevant safety data from regulators.

Since new regulatory laws were established in Britain in the wake of Thalidomide, regulators were mandated to disclose pertinent safety and efficacy data to regulators. But the system had rarely been tested. No company had ever been criminally prosecuted in the UK for withholding unpublished medical data. I asked Woods his views why. He suggested the MHRA's record of non-prosecutions was evidence of the companies' good behaviour.

'Our first step to achieve compliance and prosecution is very much a long step,' He told me.

> And secondly, industry has a vested interest in not actually stepping over the line. The suppression of data would clearly be a very serious matter. And one on which we would be particularly willing and able to take enforcement action. It is not something which is in a company's best interest to do.[12]

A year later the MHRA announced the close of its four-year investigation in GSK's actions. The agency was closing the case. No prosecution would take place.

The regulatory agency was advised by the UK's Department of Justice that a prosecution was likely to be unsuccessful because of previously undetected limitations within the UK's 1968 Medicines Act. With slim chances of winning, a prosecution wasn't seen as feasible. There were two main, previously unnoticed loopholes in the law.

First, under the 1968 Medicines Act, pharma companies were only obligated to show regulators evidence of adverse effects detected 'in the normal conditions of use of the product.' Initially licensed for use in adults in the UK in 1990,

GSK's blockbuster drug had never been officially approved for those under the age of 18. Its widespread prescription for treating childhood depression was considered 'off-label' – a frowned-upon but common practice. GSK knew, of course, that thousands of children in Britain were taking the drug. But it wasn't required legally to *act* on that knowledge: it was legally free to keep regulators in the dark.

Second, because GlaxoSmithKline's Studies 377 and 329 were carried out outside the UK, there was no legal onus to report adverse effects to UK regulators. Companies were free to use positive results from trials outside the UK to gain marketing approval; but when the same trials flagged safety risks, companies could legally suppress them – even if it meant millions of people were exposed to unnecessary risks. The medicines legislation has since been amended, closing these two loopholes.[13]

The refusal to prosecute was as much a decision of the Department of Justice as it was of the MHRA, if not more so. Woods and the MHRA are not necessarily at fault for being too 'soft' on GSK. It is weak UK laws that deserve the most blame.

But Woods' presumption that companies have 'a vested interest in not actually stepping over the line' needs scrutiny too.

Back in 2007, I came away from my brief meeting with Woods convinced he was being entirely honest with me. He really didn't think any pharmaceutical companies had an incentive to lie to regulators or to withhold evidence from them.

This struck me as worse, in a way, or at least more perplexing, than if he had been lying.

This was in 2007. Three years earlier, even *Forbes* magazine (the *Socialist Worker* this isn't) acknowledged that corporate crime in the pharmaceutical industry was a problem when it called David Graham its 'Face of the Year' in 2004. It would have been obvious to any general news reader over the mid-2000s that pharmaceutical companies such as Merck and GlakoSmithKline had selectively hid scientific evidence that threatened the companies' own commercial prospects. But here was the chief executive of the British pharmaceutical regulatory agency claiming the exact opposite truth. Despite news story after news story exposing bad behaviour in the pharmaceutical sector, Woods was insistent that such behaviour was likely to be rare.

Excessive trust when it's *not* warranted is a type of strategic ignorance. Woods' role as the head of Britain's drug regulatory agency is to assume that drug companies need regulating.

Instead, he presumes their innocence, and it's this very presumption that helps to confer innocence upon them, helping to generate a spotless reputation of non-prosecution which he can then point to to legitimate *his* own presumption of their good behaviour. While this all might be legally legitimate, that doesn't make it right. Regulatory inaction is a type of bad faith born out of genuine goodwill. It's a regulatory position that doesn't so much as turn a blind eye to problematic behaviour, but does something even worse, in a way than secrecy or denial.

Bad faith, the existential French philosopher Jean-Paul Sartre once suggested, is not exactly lying to others. It is the problem of lying to oneself, which makes it much more insidious, much less perceptible, and much less challengeable than obvious cover-ups or clear efforts to deceive. 'The true problem of bad faith stems evidently from the fact that bad faith is *faith*. It can not be either a cynical lie or certainty,' Sartre writes. 'The essential problem of bad faith is a problem of belief.'[14]

Secrecy *hides*; strategic ignorance *creates*: constructing plausible rationales ('it's not in their interest') for why problems should not exist, and therefore do not require closer investigation or penalization.

Secrecy *veils*; strategic ignorance *unveils*: fomenting the impression of good behaviour rather than hiding bad behaviour. The inability or the refusal to prosecute a crime is the ultimate oracular power: it makes it credible that no criminality occurred. Like the Ketek mathematician's ignorance trumping the expertise of a lesser expert, it's hard to come across a more convenient ignorance alibi than the head of a national regulatory agency convinced there's no crime to halt.

ENTRENCHED BELIEFS

Many of the regulatory heroes I interviewed were not treated like heroes. Instead, people such as Brook, Ross and Graham were penalized for daring to pierce institutional ignorance alibis.

Their stories serve as cautionary tales for any system of governance which presumes so-called 'rule by knowers' leads to more robust decisions. This is not because the powerful are all corrupt, but because specialist experts, by virtue of their expertise, have a bias towards prioritizing their own knowledge and excluding alternative opinions – even when an 'unknower' ends up being right.

In 2003, serious problems with the MHRA's regulation of SSRIs were made public by an 'outsider,' Richard Brook, a lay person who *did* have a great deal of institutional power at his own organization – a major mental health charity – but who did not have the same pharmacological expertise as other expert advisors to the MHRA, nor the same close relationship with pharmaceutical companies.

He could 'see' in different ways than other experts could.

Much like Kathryn Sutherland's ability to perceive problems with Adam Smith's legacy that professional economists couldn't, Brook's knowledge was more robust, in many ways, than the knowledge of narrow 'knowers.'

This reality – the fact that different forms of evidence and expertise can't be ranked as easily as some experts assume, has far-reaching implications, extending far beyond the seemingly esoteric realm of drug regulation.

The challenge of ranking different types of knowledge is relevant to debates explored over this book, including the advantages of democracy as a system of government.

The realization that people can be blinded by their own narrow expertise, and also the flipside of this problem, the fact that people's individual experience can often lead to radical new ways to understand and to resolve different social or political problems, lie at the heart of ancient and modern debates over the value of democratic governments. The following section explores these links.

THE DEMOCRACY ADVANTAGE

The fact that knowledge and ignorance are not as easy to rank as they first appear – the realization that the 'ignorance' of an outsider can often lead to new understandings of the truth – is one of the many reasons why ancient Athenians supported the very notion of democracy – despite the limits that the concept of democracy seemed to carry at the time.

Clearly, Athenian democracy was not a rosy one for many groups. As political theorist Ellen Meikson Woods emphasizes, Greek democracy helped to entrench and increase the reliance on slavery. It also entrenched the marginalization of women, a group that had no political rights.

And yet, although democrats in ancient Greece were willing to tolerate and even to glorify practices no longer accepted today, in other ways, Meikson Woods suggests, their conception of the epistemic importance and value of democracy 'far exceeds our own.'

This is especially true when it comes to *isegoria*, a word for which there is no equivalent today in common western political vocabulary. *Isegoria* 'means not just freedom of speech in the sense we understand it in modern democracies but rather *equality* of public speech.'[15]

This belief in the *equality* of public speech was directed at anti-democrats such as Plato who thought that only people who were wealthy enough *not* to work themselves should be allowed to make political decisions.

Critics of democracy, including Plato, decried the idea that 'the labouring multitude, the *banausic* or menial classes, should have political rights.' Plato fiercely condemned the idea that 'such people are able to make political judgements.'[16] The word democracy itself may even have been invented 'as a term of abuse.' For these critics, the weakness of the notion was naked in the very term: democracy was maligned for being a type of 'class rule – rule by the poor.'

For defenders of democracy, the opposite belief was just as obvious to them. Of course people with varying degrees of economic status can make sound decisions. Indeed, proponents of democracy insisted that this capacity is what makes democracy the superior system that it is. The ancient Athenians saw that democracy's great value rested in its perpetual check on the knowledge of the powerful. It thwarted the entrenchment of power monopolies by people with an incentive *not* to learn about the weaknesses or errors of their own decision-making.

The epistemological strengths of democracy are one of the many reasons why Karl Popper would later criticize the philosophical assumptions underpinning Plato's attacks on democracy.

Democracy is a superior system of government not simply because it is more inherently just, but because it is epistemologically superior to other forms of governance. It is epistemologically superior, in Popper's view, because it is the only system of government that prevents a permanent hierarchy of rulers from imposing their rigid, class-bounded notion of the good life onto other people, either intentionally or not.

Popper's friend, the economist Friedrich Hayek, shared many of Popper's epistemological beliefs, including the belief that knowledge can't always be ranked, especially because it's impossible to know in the present which theories will turn out to be discredited or disputed in future.

But Hayek's epistemological radicalism ran even deeper than Popper's, in many ways, leading Hayek to pioneer important ideas about the utility of market mechanisms in enabling goods and services to be priced more efficiently than a central planner, such as a central government.

And yet, quite ironically, Hayek's stubborn insistence that market mechanisms lead to the most epistemologically effective pricing system evolved into a sort of ideological rigidity on his part that was equally if not far more resistant to theoretical and practical challenges than the 'statist' socialism that he tried to counter.

Hayek accepted that public sector influence could lead to market distortions, but he denied that large private monopolies over information could lead to the exact same result: even when such results were indisputably apparent. He trumpeted the problem of government coercion, but he ignored the problem of private coercion.

The irony of Hayek's stance is that he, perhaps more than any other 20th-century economist – perhaps any economist in history – was the first economist to realize an important point about the fragility of expert knowledge. He even gave his Nobel acceptance speech on this topic, titling it 'The Pretense of Knowledge.'

In this speech and in earlier philosophical essays, Hayek points out that much articulated knowledge represents only people's narrow understanding of reality, and can't necessarily reflect the whole truth of a situation, much of which lies beyond the grasp of individual consciousness.

It's a good point. And it's a similar point to Popper's criticism of 'know-it-all' forms of authoritarian rule. It's also similar to my criticism, throughout this book, of the idea that 'rule by knowers' leads to more knowledgeable rule.

And yet, while Hayek appeared to be someone committed to the importance of the unknown – while he seemed like an 'unknower' in the same laudable way that J.S. Mill and Harriet Taylor were unknowers – in reality, Hayek was something different. He wasn't even comparable to the distinction that I suggested could be made between Bentham and Mill.

Mill, I suggested, was an 'unknower' to Bentham's 'knower.' Bentham tended to operate in good faith, but as Mill suggested, he was blind to the problem of truths that he couldn't see. He underestimated the problem of not simply his own ignorance, but of human ignorance in general.

The same could not be said of Hayek, who realized, perhaps more than any other major economist over the 20th century, that the problem of human ignorance is an unavoidable one. In the same way, if not more so, than scholars on the left who are often maligned for being social constructivists, Hayek was a committed believer in the social construction of truth.

But he was also certain, with a sort of zealotry that seemed to border on Arendtian 'pseudo-mysticism,' that markets could somehow perform acts of arbitration and decision-making far better than humans ever could. Hayek seemed to believe in the market's oracular judgements while forgetting that the market, like any oracle, is merely human too.

Hayek shifted over his life from being an open-minded unknower to becoming a deliberate agnotologist.

The irony of the legacy of the one of the greatest economists of the 20th-century is that while he made his name making excellent points about 'pretence of knowledge,' he was quietly creating ignorance alibis for himself and his friends. Hayek was always trying to avoid a paper trail. He constantly tried to make it seem as if he and his peers were not dependent on corporate funding, even when they were.

Hayek was right, in some ways. The pretence of knowledge *is* a problem. But so is the pretence of ignorance, and the discipline of economics, and the social sciences more broadly, still haven't grappled enough with this second problem.

Even right-wing economists who had helped to push the University of Chicago's economics department into new, pro-market directions over the 1940s and 1950s grew irritated by Hayek's wilful blindness to the same market 'distorting' activity that Hayek would loudly attack whenever it hailed from the public sector or a labour union.

Chicago economist Jacob Viner was one of Hayek's fiercest critics in this regard. Viner criticized 'Hayek for excusing private cartels while objecting to unions who monopolized the supply of labour.' Viner wasn't alone: Orwell made a similar point about Hayek.[17]

Hayek and his friends also cherry-picked from history when it came to the legacy of enlightenment thinkers, including one of Hayek's great heroes: Alexis de Tocqueville.

DISSERVICE TO HEROES

Hayek is believed to have named his influential book, *The Road to Serfdom*, in honour of his hero Tocqueville's worries about the rise of servitude in democratic societies. But much like Stigler, Hayek read copiously but with a penchant for ignoring what he didn't like. Hayek mostly ignored Tocqueville's worries about the rise of 'new corporate bodies' and the belief 'industrial classes, more than other classes, need rules, supervision, and restraint.'[18]

Hayek and his friends didn't simply ignore their heroes' belief that government regulations were needed in many instances. Rather, they attacked any pro-regulation views head on, insisting that such beliefs were 'anomalies' of their general faith in free markets rather than legitimate, deeply felt concerns.

Whether Hayek *purposely* distorted the legacy of people like Tocqueville or not, I don't know. I simply know that he and other mid-century economists *did* distort the legacy of late enlightenment and classical liberal scholars, helping to displace the strong importance that Tocqueville and others placed on the need for checks and balances on *both* public sector and private sector concentrations of power.

Hayek's pro-market dogmatism had unintended effects, leading to his own robust ideas for social protection to be denigrated and jettisoned over the years.

When Hayek called, for example, in *The Constitution of Liberty* for universal healthcare and the provision of social housing, even people sympathetic to government intervention were quick to chastise him for his apparent inconsistency, for having the temerity to defend positions seen as insufficiently 'libertarian.' Sure, it might work in practice, the old joke goes, but what about in theory?

STOP SEEING

The steps that Hayek and his peers took to obscure their dependence on corporate funders didn't simply stop at obscuring paper trails. When it came to cartel-building and anti-competitive behaviour, they began studying the economy as if monopoly power wasn't creating asymmetries in information happening in plain sight. Their theories, too, had to pretend to ignore.

The best example of this is Milton Friedman's celebrated 'as if' dictum: the argument that markets should be treated by policymakers *as if* they were actually competitive – even though in reality large concentrations of corporate power proved that they weren't.

Not all of their friends agreed with the value of this move. Just as Jacob Viner, for example, resolutely refused to depart from 18th and 19th-century concerns about monopoly power during his exchanges with Hayek, Viner also criticized Friedman's fantasy modelling approach, insisting that to discuss the merits of the free competitive market as if that were what we were living with or were at all likely to have the good fortune to live with in the future seem to me academic in the only pejorative sense of that adjective.[19]

THE REVIVAL OF CHECKS AND BALANCES

As insider disputes between scholars such as Viner, Hayek and Friedman make clear, there are obviously important differences among the methodological stances of major mid-20th-century economists.

But in general, the most influential economists of the past 50 years have tended to share Hayek's anti-government, pro-market bias. The evenhandedness of their 18th and 19th-century heroes – thinkers such as Smith and Tocqueville who saw that both 'big' government and 'big' industry can lead to despotic concentrations of power – fell to the wayside of the economics academic mainstream.

That is, until recently.

Jacob Viner's concern is just one of countless examples over the years of a growing counter-challenge to the doctrinaire tenets within neoclassical economic theory, and especially the anti-regulation approach of the Chicago School. These challengers argue that the Chicago School economists have strayed too far from the discipline's early roots as an empirical social science, committed to studying actual economic processes.

At the forefront of this new awakening is a broad, interdisciplinary group of economists, philosophers and sociologists studying the relationship between regulation, tax policies, capital flows and growing inequality.

Their work is contributing to new policy efforts aimed at mitigating the problem of corporate impunity and the harm it causes. Throughout this book, I have pointed to some of the practical ideas they raise, ideas that could help to mitigate interrelated problems of economic inequality, racial injustice and corporate exploitation if they were to be more widely adopted. This includes Mariana Mazzucato's call to challenge the rigidity of economics teaching; Charles Mills, Pankaj Mishra and Utsa Patnaik's call for the history of economic liberalism to include the history of racial exploitation; Poonam Puri's efforts to hold corporations accountable for human rights breaches; Alexander Sarch's call for 'reckless ignorance' provisions in US courts. To name just a few powerful ideas.

And yet, even reasonable, fair and achievable proposals – rooted in enlightenment notions of the value of open inquiry; in longstanding recognition of the value of democratic checks and balances – can strike many people as hopeless or unachievable when the threat that Tocqueville feared, the possibility of 'one irresponsible man or body of men' seizing power indefinitely, seems more real than ever.

When political polarization deepens, when corporate–government cronyism seems so intertwined and unfixable that any solution seems either too pedestrian or too extreme to mitigate problems without worsening them, we need more than policy proposals to inspire hope.

We need to remember a truth that is rarely obvious when it is most needed. I noticed this truth from reading Tocqueville's work, not from what he stated explicitly but from what I realized about his own ignorance. From his ignorance it's possible to see the conclusion that I have promised: an illumination of the ways that ignorance can be emancipatory.

CONCLUSION: THE GREAT ENLARGEMENT

The unknown requires humility. We should be wary of any ideology that pretends to have arrived at the end of history, claiming to have permanently silenced critics, to have won the battle of ideas for once and for all.

Only the hubristic think otherwise. 'To judge from the climate of opinion, we have won the war of ideas,' Milton and his wife Rose Friedman wrote in a memoir published late in life.[1]

Friedman died in 2006. Signs of the great financial crisis of the early 21st century were mounting, but he missed it by one year, never forced to confront its devastation: the crescendo of home foreclosures, the unmeasurable number of suicides across the US and the world, unmeasurable because we don't know for certain how many people took their life directly because of the financial crisis. But we can picture how it might feel, placing ourselves on the street with an evicted family, imagining the last moments when the key to the door was ours.

It's never possible to know for certain the cause of an individual's suicide (ignorance is always greater than knowledge, especially when it comes to this). But we do know, thanks to statistics released in 2018 by the Centers for Disease Control and Prevention (CDC), that the rate of death by suicide has grown in America by roughly 25 per cent over the last two decades. For young people between the ages of 15 to 24 in that country, suicide is now the second leading cause of death.[2]

I'm not blaming the financial crisis on one man, but I am blaming it on the anti-regulatory zealotry that stupefied the American public, persuading them the root of all misery lay with government. Misery rarely rests with one group, not with government, or with industry, or with the public, but rather with the 'rotary motion' Paine pointed out: the ability to use blame-shifting and ignorance alibis to avoid liability for causing harm and suffering to less powerful groups.

People don't need enlightenment now: they have it already, bearing witness to injustice happening in plain sight. They need accountability now.

When I read government data indicating that suicide in America has risen by 25 per cent in 20 years, I think of Paine, the great British revolutionary who urged Americans to fight for a free government. His dream has not yet been fully realized. The vote in America has long been restricted in different ways. From the era of slavery through Jim Crow to the worsening problem of a two-tiered justice system today, one system for the rich and another one for the poor, the individual right to equal justice has long been curbed.

It's this reality – too little democracy and not too much – that is leading to a new awakening, to a new demand for economic justice, to the dawn of a new age of democratic enlargement.

Tragic suicide statistics like this are underpinning growing calls for policies that echo Paine's idea – his proposal for a cross-generational tax that would ease tensions between rich and poor, young and old, by ensuring injustice at birth didn't bind some children to hardship while others feel entitled to rule.

But other factors hinder such proposals, like the assumption that billionaire benevolence is a fair substitute for economic justice.

Today, billionaire charity is treated in a way that would have stunned Paine and other enlightenment radicals who suggested that unequal laws create the need for private charity in the first place.

'Having the resources to practice such beneficence,' Immanuel Kant wrote, 'is, for the most part, a result of certain human beings being favoured through the injustice of government, which introduces an inequality of wealth that makes others need their beneficence. Under such circumstances, does a rich man's help to the needy, on which he so readily prides himself as something meritorious, really deserve to be called beneficence at all?'[3]

Kant was one of the pioneers of democratic theories of checks and balances, including the need to establish education systems that enabled students and teachers to challenge the received wisdom of the past.

What is enlightenment, he asks, but the ability to question the assumptions of the powerful? He grappled with elite ignorance in his day, and this book has grappled with the same problem. When doctrines become unchallengeable, when a theory like 'marginal productivity of income distribution' takes on the irrefutability of gospel, are we living in enlightened times or something else?

When the social sciences were first developing in the 19th century, early visionaries saw it as the measure of a good scientist to be cautious about generalizations. 'No man on earth can affirm, absolutely and generally, that the new state of societies is better than the old,' Tocqueville writes in *Democracy in America*.[4]

But since then, new ideologies have solidified, calcifying the hubris of people who think they know more than they do, that the whole world is fine because *their* world is fine, that any problems rest with the ignorance of others and not the limits of their own ideological positions. Hannah Arendt warned about this problem: 'Ideologies pretend to know the mysteries of the whole historical process – the secrets of the past, the intricacies of the present, the uncertainties of the future – because of the logic inherent in their respective ideas.'[5]

This excerpt from Arendt is the non-fiction sister statement to Orwell's warnings about all-knowing rulers in his novel 1984, where he points out that it is the capacity to monopolize human greatness and to appear all-knowing that enables authoritarianism to take hold: 'Big brother is infallible and all-powerful. Every success, every achievement, every victory, every scientific discovery, all knowledge, all wisdom, all happiness, all virtue, are held to issue directly from his leadership.'

For anti-democratic 'rule by knowers' to entrench itself today, it's necessary for narrow history to reign.

Deliberately circumscribed retellings of complex political and historical events enable a group of 'knowers' to convince others that any single test or set of tests of knowledge can be used as a criterion to judge human intelligence or perceptiveness. Self-proclaimed 'epistocrats' want voters subjected to a test of their political and economic knowledge to be eligible to vote, but who judges the knowers? Who has the capacity to point out a test is flawed when any failure of the test is a sign of one's inferiority to question the test?

This is the great importance of Smith's call for 'suspicious attention' to any group which purports that its own monopoly over a set of resources will serve the common good, whether it's a monopoly over the economic resources or a monopoly over political knowledge.

Smith's own life story is one of the clearest illustrations of the error of epistocracy because the reception of his work shows the hazard of using any academic test to 'prove' that someone is more knowledgeable than another person. Which version of Smith is likely to turn up on a test of voter knowledge in the 2020s, or 2040s, or 2060s? No matter what that question is, it is easy to imagine the 'right' answer: that he disapproves of government regulation, but is it true?

The answer is: sometimes. The lie is that he sides with either an anti-regulatory or pro-regulatory stance exclusively – that he could see only one side of the truth.

Throughout this book, I have repeated his phrase 'suspicious attention' a lot because I think it's necessary to illuminate the seriousness of the ironic way his work has been treated over the years.

One really couldn't make up fiction like this. It's perhaps *the* greatest academic hoax in modern western history: the way that Smith's point about wealthy businessmen tricking the public into presuming *their* self-interest *is* the public interest morphed into the basis of a 200-year-old academic industry selling exactly that idea and doing so in Smith's name.

In the centuries after his death, his ideas have been invoked countless times to justify deep cuts to government services, misappropriation that violates the legacy of a man who believed that a nation's wealth should be used to protect its citizens from impoverishment and premature death.

It wasn't even Smith's greatest insight, the fact that businessmen can lie and cheat to get ahead. His bigger point is that we all do it, convincing ourselves that an action or a truth is morally righteous when it's not. And his *greatest* insight was that the problem can be countered – that it's possible for individuals to expand their own narrow understanding, deliberately enlarging our perspective to understand how our behaviour affects others.

Even before path-breaking scholars like American sociologist W.E.B. Du Bois and John Rawls used the metaphor of the 'veil' to understand the limits and the potential

of human understanding, Smith called for a similar mechanism, using the image of the 'spectator' to call on people to
use the greatness of their imagination to see a problem in a
multifaceted way.

Wollstonecraft went a step further than him, suggesting the state should provide public education in a way that
increased the opportunity for one's narrow worldview to be
enlarged. Through mixed-education, she insisted, through
boys and girls sharing a classroom together, they can come to
see one another as equals: 'only by the jostlings of equality can
we form a just opinion of ourselves.'[6]

Wollstonecraft and Smith were two of the first *greats* of
the modern age, countering the *smarts* and *strongs* in their day
(check out Smith, for example, on the quality of scholarship
at Oxford).

They were among the first modern greats, but not the last.

As this book shows, greats are everywhere, toiling in
underrecognized jobs, striving to help others, striving, most of
all, to understand where the power to dominate and to exploit
other people comes from. A great may be you and she may be
me. She may be the stranger or the friend or the child beside
you now. Greats are defined by perspectival enlargement, by
the capacity to imagine one's circumstances differently and
the human will and capacity to do so.

Strongs or smarts may hold or seize political power,
but they can never be 'greats' because they deny other people
their capacity for free will. Smarts and strongs appreciate
the value of human liberty but only for themselves, or for
people who look like them or who act like them. This is why

strongs and smarts often prefer a narrow reading of history, because recognition of the greatness of others threatens the intactness of their ideology.

GREATER HISTORY

As feminist scholars have long pointed out, how human beings see the past and the future is always a matter of judgement.

Oracular power – the ability to speak believably about the boundaries of ignorance and knowledge – tends in practice to be controlled by people in positions of political or economic leverage who are able to espouse a narrow history that reinforces the inevitability of a future they wish to create.

When challengers point out this narrowness, the dominant group often reacts violently to the new knowledge, even when it is true. Especially when it is true.

Consider the example of Black Lives Matter and affiliated global protest movements who have called for the removal of statues that commemorate racist figures from history: people like Cecil Rhodes, the British colonizer, and John A. Macdonald, the Canadian leader who oversaw the starvation of native groups.

White people have often reacted angrily and violently to this effort, leading to the death in 2017 of an American woman named Heather Heyer, who was intentionally struck by a car at a rally organized by neo-Nazis. Her terrible killing reveals a terrible truth: her death is indefensible, but to treat it as incomprehensible would be a disservice to her memory.[7]

The violence signals the white supremacists' irrational and bigoted terror at losing monopoly control over representations of the past. When the violence is framed as reaction to the loss of control over oracular power, it becomes clear that individual statues are irrelevant to their real concerns. It is not simply statues that worry them the most, it's the fact that their detractors have made a successful oracular claim on the future – and won.

When Donald Trump plaintively cries, 'who's next? Washington, Jefferson, so foolish!', what he really means is, how far can they take this? Because Trump recognizes the loss for what it is. It was never about felled statues – it was about a lost competition over which voices should be listened to, which voices have the power to decide whose histories should be ignored – as the memorial-less victims of white lynching were ignored for so long – and which to honour. Trump and his allies lost their effort to ensure the statues of their ancestors stand in perpetuity, and this loss terrifies them, because with their loss comes a weakening of their dominion over the future.[8]

'You … can't change history, but you can learn from it,' Trump tweeted, around the same time that his team chose to gloss over his bigotry by removing any mention of his involvement with the Birther movement from his corporate biography.[9] Of course you can change history. Guys like Trump do it all the time.

What Trump really means is *you* can't change it: the little 'you,' the people without the same resources to shift the historical record in their own favour. And for the most part, he is right. Once a dominant historical narrative takes shape, efforts to challenge it are fiercely and successfully refuted, even when the earlier narrative is misleading or grossly inaccurate. The powerful have long had the power to ignore inconvenient facts and voices. Indeed, elite power functions *through* strategic ignorance – through the ability to select which voices to acknowledge and which to dismiss.

FROM STRATEGIC IGNORANCE TO EMANCIPATIVE IGNORANCE

The fact that strategic ignorance drives political and corporate decision-making can be alarming, but it can also be forcefully inspiring and positive for dominated groups as well, because although ignorance can be exploited for long periods, it can never be entirely monopolized.

For a period, some groups *do* have greater ability to control and to benefit from ignorance than others, a point that I emphasized in case studies explored throughout this book.

The more power that any particular group accumulates, the more they tend to necessarily rely on strategic ignorance in order to meet various goals, exploiting different types of 'ignorance alibis' that enable the powerful to maintain that their power does not cause harm to other groups even when it does.

And yet, the superior capacity to exploit strategic ignorance cannot be maintained forever, because the inescapable fact of elite ignorance means that the less powerful have an inalienable ability to question the knowledge of the few. The oracular power to determine the boundaries of what 'counts' as knowledge is powerful but not impregnable, because knowledge itself is always imperfect. Knowledge is always a pretence of sorts: Hayek was right about that.

The powerful and the weak always both unknow, and it is only autocracies – only 'rule by knowers' – that insist otherwise, claiming wrongly that a ruler has a special right to rule based on special enlightenment. This claim is always false, because elites also unknow, often in ways they don't realize.

Elite ignorance is valuable for the less powerful. This might strike some people as a surprising point or even an excuse for bad behaviour, especially given how often the powerful can and do exploit ignorance to avoid liability for actions that harm others. But seen in a different light, ignorance can become a tool of emancipation. Ignorance can be emancipative because it reminds us that to *not know* is incontestably a universally shared human trait.

The fact that ignorance grows in tandem with new knowledge is the reason why we are, at the individual level, *equal unknowers*. People *do* have more or less knowledge or intelligence than other people, but often it is this very strength, one's superior knowledge, that can be the main hindrance to perceiving one's own ignorance.

It is not possible to either measure or to rank individual ignorance.

It is not possible, for example, to rank objectively whether Burke was more 'unknowing' than Wollstonecraft. They both had their blind-spots; they both unknew.

I mentioned that Burke's opponents sometimes relied on bigotry to challenge his right to hold office in England, but I didn't say specifically who did this. It was Wollstonecraft who did this, taking jabs at his religion. The idea that women are 'naturally' less bigoted than men is as questionable as the idea that men are 'naturally' smarter than women, but that doesn't stop us from falling into the same traps of glorifying one group at the expense of another.

This may seem cynical, but it's not, because while the terrible problem of our ignorance can undermine the effort to perceive and to treat each other as equals, it's also the power of human ignorance that guarantees that no one person or group can ever maintain their dominance over others in perpetuity. The ignorance of a dominant group always shows – a ruler's ignorance always shows – permitting a weaker group to exploit that ignorance to their advantage. The inalienable nature of human ignorance is emancipatory because it furnishes for all the ability to question the wisdom of the few.

Does this mean that illuminating the ignorance of a dominant group is easy? Of course it isn't. As pioneering black scholars such as Audre Lorde and Charles Mills point out, it can be dangerous to speak out in societies that want nothing better than one's silence, whose entire edifice rests on the unwillingness to pierce a dominant ideology's truths.

THE NEW AND THE OLD

Audre Lorde is an American feminist thinker who was active in women's rights and black rights movements in the late

20th century. Contrary to how her school of feminist thought is sometimes perceived and maligned today, it is actually Lorde's work that best exemplifies today the enlightenment spirit of progress, free-thinking and equal rights for all.

I indicated I would conclude this book with a discussion of the way that ignorance can be emancipatory. Lorde's earlier writing enables such an argument to be made. I saved the best for last in a way, for a few reasons.

The main reason is that I wanted to show commonalities between contemporary feminist writing and the thought of 18th-century radical thinkers, and doing so meant exploring aspects of 18th-century enlightenment thinkers that tend to be side-lined. Not simply Wollstonecraft, who contemporary feminists are often linked to, but people like Burke or Smith who are sometimes upheld as the antithesis to feminism today.

I'm not trying to vindicate the importance of contemporary feminist scholarship by tying it to 18th-century thought. Feminist theory doesn't need any such vindication.

Nor am I trying to offer some apologetics for the short-sightedness or blatant bigotry and classist elitism of someone like Smith or Burke. Both Burke and Smith *were* class elitists. Neither of their theories, nor Wollstonecraft's, for that matter, should be transplanted to the present in some wholesale way.

We should study the past for cautionary lessons, not blueprints for the present or oracular assessments of an unknowable future.

Look at Kant's terrible 'own goal,' for example. He was one of the challengers to notions of divine providence theories in his day. His work helped to break the yoke of providential theories which entrenched and legitimated gross gender and economic inequality. But his own prejudice and racism also led to early social scientific classifications of human worth that were later 'refined' and enlisted in the service of full-blown systems of scientific racism: to the rise of equally abhorrent and, in ways, even more inhumane treatments of enslaved peoples than in earlier eras. They were more inhumane because the new, flourishing social sciences of the 19th century conferred 'scientific' respectability on slavery that earlier eras lacked. Kant and his friends fought religious oppression only to bequeath the world new forms of racial categorization and subjugation. What comes after a revolution is not always 'better' than the system that prevailed before.

Why then, is there value in insisting upon a lineage that many people – including many feminist thinkers today and status quo populists alike – might object to?

The answer is both simple and obvious: because the enlightenment quest for universal human rights is unfinished.

What happened to Smith's dream of 'perfect justice'? To Wollstonecraft's hope that the 'jostlings' of equality can lead people to recognize our shared humanity? To Burke's insistence that 'their morality is equal to ours'? To Maria Stewart's appreciation of the role of labour in creating economic value? To Paine's idea for a shared wealth fund?

Audre Lorde is what happened. Decades of half-won struggles for racial, gender and economic justice are what happened. It is not Pinker's audience who needs enlightenment now. It is Pinker who needs it. He needs to read Audre Lorde's work.

THE UNFINISHED CHALLENGE

Much like Adam Smith, Lorde thought it was possible to acknowledge and to celebrate that human difference inevitability exists, and should exist, while still insisting on the inalienability of equal rights and individual liberty for all.

Is equality through difference possible? They both thought yes, but they both also recognized that the path to 'perfect justice' would be unwaveringly hard, a never-finished quest, because suffering always exists, and silence about that fact doesn't eradicate its reality.

If the similarities between Lorde and Smith aren't clear, consider the words of feminist scholar Keeanga-Yamahtta Taylor, who argues that 'solidarity is standing in unity with people even when you have not personally experienced their oppression.'[10]

For all his many limitations, Adam Smith was capable of this type of solidarity, and it led him to consider the subjugation of workers, including their lack of a right to education, in a new light. He and Wollstonecraft were among the first greats of the modern age to call on the state to provide public education at a time when the 'right' to education was considered a laughable, impossible indulgence.

Think too about Smith's comment, that only an ignorant person can maintain that collusion among business merchants doesn't exist as long as it's not seen. His solution was to look harder. And Lorde's point was to talk louder. She argued that silence is not an option, even when one's life is at threat, even when the future implications can't be known, because that's usually when speaking out is needed most – when the danger is most unknowable.

Smith and Lorde's points are similar to each other because both recognized that the greatness of being human is to see and to speak when it is least in one's self-interest to do so, even when others may deride or try to harm you, which is a constant danger given that it's typically those articulating uncomfortable truths who tend to be most resented in any given social setting.

It is the courage of the unsilent that pierces the ignorance alibi of the few, making an ignorance alibi untenable over the long term.

INCONVENIENT TRUTHS

Sometime it takes years, if not centuries, for an ignorance alibi to dissipate, in part because scholars are not perpetuating untruths or partial truths on purpose. When students of the present or the past get things wrong, often it is not always intentionally, but rather because the entrenchment of dominant ideologies veils alternatives from emerging.

To combat this problem, scholars should stress our capacity for error, resisting the spell of Plato by searching for the ways we are wrong.

I tried to do so by stressing that neither the right nor the left have all the answers, that it's possible to disagree with Bastiat while admiring his support for free speech, possible to cite Wollstonecraft while disavowing her prejudice.

Indeed, she should be cited more, out of sociological faithfulness to the facts. She pioneered theories of confirmation bias and her originality should be more widely known.[11]

What I mean by sociological faithfulness to facts is not some sort of academic triumphalism, I mean simply that the least a sociologist can do is to try to explain social change without relying on supernatural or godly explanations for social progress – as well as avoiding the other extreme, relying on provable facts but only the facts that prove one's thesis, ignoring all counter-evidence. Tocqueville, for example, tried but failed to avoid his own blind-spots, and from his unwitting ignorance it is possible to see a truth about individual power and social transformation that even he, a brilliant and conscientious scholar, was incapable of seeing.

BLAME GOD?

It's an important truth, and it is a truth that makes other more localized forms of political accountability and economic justice more achievable.

There is a little discussed aspect to Tocqueville's classic book, *Democracy in America*, that doesn't get acknowledged much today in the social sciences. That is the fact that throughout *Democracy in America*, Tocqueville relies on God to explain things that he can't explain, including his amazement at the triumph of democracy in America and the ripple effect it had on European nations: his shock that against all odds, when the power of the aristocracy seemed at its most insurmountable, when the wealth of monarchs and their allies was at its heights, the nobles were toppled by a weaker force.

He reaches the only possible conclusion in his eyes. God, he surmises, *must* be on the side of the people. How else to explain it? He tried to make his case with a social scientist's earnest, methodical rigour. Just look at the facts, he insists: the powerful were once all-mighty, with control over tax collection, over the courts, over all land, over the people, and yet the people overcame. He concludes that God *must* desire 'not the particular prosperity of the few, but the greater well-being of all.'

He admits that this truth might be unpalatable to his aristocratic friends and family and even to himself, but he begs them to look past their own narrow class interests: 'What seems to me decay is thus in His eyes progress; what pains me is acceptable to Him. Equality may be less elevated, but it is more just, and in its justice lies its greatness and beauty.'[12]

I'm not religious nor a believer in God, but I can see how the belief that equality must be godly might be uplifting to many people.

I hope, for example, that if my mother reads this book and if she reaches the end (which isn't certain, she gave up on my last book halfway through) that, if nothing else, Tocqueville's words bring her some comfort in a politically volatile time, that she can be uplifted by something that she already believes but might like to see reinforced: that equality must indeed by godly.

Certainly I admire her belief in God even if I don't share it, just as I admire the fact that the democratic separation of church and state protects the human right to religious difference – just as I admire the courage of a philosopher like Karl Popper, his stated willingness to give his life for democracy, his dedication to my mother's right to liberty, his commitment to a future stranger's freedom to worship whatever God she likes.

But I'm not religious, nor as a social scientist can I accept Tocqueville's own fatalism, his assumption that incomprehensible things can only be explained through God's will.

I did the only thing a sociologist can do. I gave Tocqueville the benefit of my doubt, and I read further into his future, curious to learn whether he grew more empirical as he got older. And that's when, reading his *Recollections*, a political memoir written about 20 years after he wrote *Democracy in America*, I noticed in his writing the important truth that he had failed his whole life to see.

You can see it too: I mentioned it in an earlier chapter.

Is it obvious? The truth that he failed to see? The power that he couldn't perceive?

It's easy to miss, especially during times of desperate certainty that political tensions will worsen, and indeed, they might. But even if or when they do, even when the future seems at its bleakest, even if a new class takes more control of the courts, more control of the land, more control of women's and men's bodies, and more control of democratic governments, it is then that the power that Tocqueville overlooked will rise: the truth that he couldn't recognize, the greatness that was there all along, if only he could have seen her. She was right before his eyes. She was sitting right next to him at dinner. *'I loathe women who write.'*

Tocqueville's blind-spot, in a sociological sense, is that he underestimates the power of women, and the power of men too. He underestimates any person who didn't speak with the same accent as he did, or who didn't look like him, or who didn't sit in the National Assembly as he did. People like Madame Sand.

Orwell: it's the familiar that's always hardest to see.

Smith: *Look harder.*

Lorde: I'm right here.

It's the eternal credibility deficit: to misrecognize the strength and the power of those who are 'weak.'

Tocqueville failed to recognize, in the people he rarely encountered, a capacity for greatness so immense that it could topple slave masters, imperialists, despots, kings, queens, oligarchs, tyrants, nobles, billionaires; in every era, in every region, in every culture, time and time again, new greats unite, drawing strength from the hatred of being despised and the love of an inalienable right: the right to individual freedom.

Tocqueville couldn't see this because he was blinded by his own class and racial privilege, and to his credit, he does admit it: how little he understood about the struggle of workers in France until, over 1848, they brought their legitimate grievances to the streets.

'I was strongly prejudiced against Madame Sand,' he admits, 'for I loathe women who write.'

To give him his due, he sat and he listened. 'Madame Sand depicted to me, in detail and with singular vivacity, the condition of the Paris workmen, their organization, their arms … I thought the picture overloaded, but it was not, as subsequent events proved.'[13]

He quotes her warning to him verbatim: 'Try to persuade your friends,' she said, 'not to force the people into the streets by alarming or irritating them. I also wish I could instill patience into my own friends; for it if comes to a fight, believe me, you will all perish.'[14]

In the spring and summer months of 1848, a workers' insurrection erupted, with women fighting alongside the men. The militancy of women is something that Tocqueville is amazed by but doesn't try to hide. 'Women took part in it as well as men,' he admits, 'and when at last the time had come to surrender, the women were the last to yield.'[15]

THE LORDE PRINCIPLE

This is a book about strategic ignorance, but also other types of ignorance too, the most pernicious of which isn't necessarily the deliberate will to ignore, but rather the slow, unwitting hardening of assumptions into false beliefs.

I was faced about 15 years ago with what I saw as an impoverished language for describing the unknown and so I developed new terms worthy of a new conceptual framework. The meanings of 'micro-ignorance,' 'macro-ignorance' and 'useful unknowns' might seem obvious when pointed out, but the terms were not coined before this book.

I mention this because I'm staking a claim to originality and offering another thinker the last word. My suggestion is that her name should be attached to a truth about rational ignorance that she discovered long before me. Political scientists do this all the time: Downs' principle of ignorance or Rawls' principle of the veil of ignorance. It's usually the names of men.

But I think there is a historical rationale, a scholarly rationale, and quite unexpectedly, a somewhat serendipitous poetic justice to using Audre Lorde's name to denote a historical principle that can stand next to Tocqueville's godly principle for explaining revolutionary change.

The Lord(e) principle is this: the power of human unknowing is unlimitable and will break even the strongest oppression.

The Lorde principle explains why emancipatory struggles that seem impossible or improbable eventually come to pass. For years, for decades, even for centuries, a powerful group might find ways to discount a grievance as 'irrational' or 'illusory' or 'ungrateful,' but eventually a new generation of greats – a new enlargement of knowledge – pierces stubborn ignorance alibis, exposes useful unknowns as illusory, and reclaims the equality denied.

It is possible to take comfort in the assumption that Madame Sand was mistaken, that she was exaggerating her perilous times. But I think that her warning was right: that she was right to implore Tocqueville and his friends in power to recognize the suffering of others, to recognize their grievances as fair.

Not simply because right now, just like in her day, legitimate grievances about racial injustice and economic inequality are leading new greats to rise and to demand their rights.

But also because it is clear that Tocqueville was mistaken. It's possible to see this easily; it's written on the page. The problem is his use of the past tense. He assumes the women and the men rested their weapons and pens, he assumes they ceased their struggle, he assumes the women *yielded* – but he was wrong.

NOTES

Introduction: The power to ignore

1   Alexandra Topping, 2018. 'Home Office misled court about treatment of child refugees from Calais, judges find' (*The Guardian*, July 31).

2   Ibid.

3   The same problem affects the effort to study deception by government actors in domestic and international politics. See John Mearsheimer, *Why Leaders Lie: The Truth about Lying in International Politics* (Oxford: Oxford University Press, 2011); Grégoire Mallard and Linsey McGoey, 2018. 'Strategic ignorance and global governance: an ecumenical approach to epistemologies of global power.' *The British Journal of Sociology* 69(4): 884.

4   See Garrity Hill, 2018. 'Engagement for (climate?) change: The movement against unconventional gas in Victoria, Australia.' Unpublished PhD thesis, Swinburne University of Technology.

5   Ron Chernow, *Titan: The Life of John D. Rockefeller, Sr.* (New York: Vintage Books, 2004), 209.

6   John Gray, *Straw Dogs* (New York: Farrar, Straus & Giroux, 2002), 95.

7   Linsey McGoey, 2009. 'Pharmaceutical controversies and the performative value of uncertainty.' *Science as Culture* 18: 151–164.

8   In Smith's words, 'To expect, indeed, that the freedom of trade should ever be entirely restored in Great Britain, is as absurd as to expect that an Oceana or Utopia should ever be established in it.' Adam Smith, *Wealth of Nations*. Ed. Mark Spencer (Ware, Herts: Wordsworth Classics, 2012), 460; 'suspicious attention' quote is from Spencer (ed.), page 258. I draw on two separate editions of *Wealth of Nations*, one edited by Spencer (2012); the other edited by Sutherland (1997).

9   J.S. Mill, *Autobiography of J.S. Mill* (New York: Signet Classics, 1964), 180.

10 Stuart Firestein, *Ignorance: How It Drives Science* (Oxford: Oxford University Press, 2012); Jerome Ravetz, 'From Descartes to Rumsfeld: The rise and decline of ignorance-of-ignorance' in M. Gross and L. McGoey (Eds), *The Routledge International Handbook of Ignorance Studies* (London: Routledge, 2015); Michael Smithson, *Ignorance and Uncertainty: Emerging Paradigms* (New York: Springer, 1989).

11 Andrew Abbott, 2010. 'Varieties of ignorance.' *American Sociologist* 41: 174–189.

12 Robert Proctor and Londa Schiebinger, *Agnotology: The Making and Unmaking of Ignorance* (Palo Alto, CA: Stanford University Press, 2008). See also Steve Rayner, 2012. 'Uncomfortable knowledge.' *Economy and Society* 41(1): 107–125; Mathias Girel, *Science et territoires de l'ignorance* (Paris: Quae, 2017); Matthias Gross, *Ignorance and Surprise: Science, Society and Ecological Design* (Cambridge, MA: MIT Press, 2010).

13 The terms macro-ignorance and micro-ignorance are my coinage, building on earlier work from science and technology studies (STS) and allied disciplines. See A. Kinchy, S. Parks, K. Jalbert, 2016. 'Fractured knowledge.' *Environment and Planning C: Government and Policy* 34: 879–899; Scott Frickel and Abby Kinchy, 'Lost in space: Geographies of ignorance in science and technology studies' in Gross and McGoey, *The Routledge International Handbook of Ignorance Studies*, 174–182; Claudia Aradau and Rens van Munster, *Politics of Catastrophe: Genealogies of the Unknown* (Abingdon: Routledge, 2011); Tom Slater, 2012. 'The myth of "broken Britain": Welfare reform and the production of ignorance.' *Antipode* 46: 948–969; Nora Stel, 2016. 'The agnotology of eviction in south Lebanon's Palestinian gatherings.' *Antipode* 48: 1400–1419.

14 Stephanie Savell, 2018. 'The wars no one notices: Talking to a demobilized country' (*Vox*, February 20).

15 Mona Chalabi, 2017. 'Over a third of enlisted US military personnel are racial minorities' (*The Guardian*, October 19).

16 Dennis Laich and Lawrence Wilkerson, 2017. 'The deep unfairness of America's all-volunteer force' (*The American Conservative*, October 16).

17 See also my treatment of 'liminal ignorance' in 'On the will to ignorance in bureaucracy.' *Economy and Society* 36(2): 212–236.

18 Thomas Paine, 'Common Sense' in *Rights of Man, Common Sense and Other Political Writings*. Ed. Mark Philp (Oxford: Oxford University Press, 1995), 17.

19 Cathy Booth, 2006. 'Can Lay and Skilling win on appeal?' (*Time*, May 25).

20 Katie Thomas and Michael Schmidt, 2012. 'Glaxo agrees to pay $3 billion in fraud settlement' (*The New York Times*, July 12).

1 Narrow history

1 Quoted in Jamie Doward, 2017. 'The chronicle of a tragedy foretold: Grenfell Tower' (*The Guardian*, June 17); see also Dawn Foster, 2017. 'People died thinking "they didn't listen," says ex-Grenfell residents' group chair' (*The Guardian*, June 15).

2 Rachel Roberts, 2017. 'Grenfell Tower blogger threatened with legal action by council after writing about safety concerns' (*Independent*, June 16).

3 The 'playing with fire' blog post is available here, and has been shared tens of thousands of time since the Grenfell fire: https://grenfellactiongroup.wordpress.com/2016/11/20/kctmo-playing-with-fire/.

4 'Wilful ignorance of experts' comes from Jason Sayer, 2017. 'London tower block fire occurred due to countless ignored fire safety warnings' (*The Architect's Newspaper*, June 15). See also Divya Ghelani, 2017. 'Grenfell Tower: "there are only the deliberately silent, or the preferably unheard"' (*Media Diversified*, June 22).

5 Miranda Fricker, *Epistemic Injustice* (Oxford: Oxford University Press, 2007).

6 James Daschuk, *Clearing the Plains: Disease, Politics of Starvation, and the Loss of Aboriginal Life* (Regina, Saskatchewan: University of Regina Press, 2013).

7   Niigaanwewidam James Sinclair, 2013. 'Clearing the plains: A double review' (*Canada's History*, September 12); see also Colin Samson, *A World You Do Not Know: Settler Societies, Indigenous Peoples and the Attack on Cultural Diversity* (Washington, DC: Brookings Institution Press, 2014).

8   Jesse B. Staniforth, 2014. 'James Daschuk rewrites Canada's uncomfortable indigenous history' (*The Nation*, November 15).

9   Jeffrey Simpson, 2015. 'Judge leaders by the standards of their time' (*Globe and Mail*, January 4); for a counterargument, see Dru Oja Jay, 2013.'What if natives stop subsidizing Canada?' https://intercontinentalcry.org/what-if-natives-stop-subsidizing-canada/.

10 The cartoon is from Daschuk, *Clearing the Plains*. See also T. Pearce, 2015. 'Old chieftain or old charlatan? Assessing Sir John's complex legacy through political cartoons' (Activehistory.ca, January 6).

11 Tim Harford, 2017. 'The problem with facts' (*Financial Times*, March 9).

12 Ian Black, 2006. 'Secrets and lies at the heart of Britain's Middle Eastern folly' (*The Guardian*, July 11).

13 Quoted in David Runciman, *The Confidence Trap* (Princeton, NJ: Princeton University Press, 2014), 85.

14 Paul Bignell, 2011. 'Secret memos expose link between oil firms and invasion of Iraq' (*Independent*, April 18); for a longer discussion of oil theft following the invasion, see Dave Whyte, 2006. 'The crimes of neo-liberal rule in occupied Iraq.' *The British Journal of Criminology* 47(2): 177–195.

15 Greenspan's quote is from A. Juhasz, 2013. 'Why the war in Iraq was fought for big oil' (CNN, April 13); see also N. Ahmed, 2014. 'Iraq invasion was about oil' (*The Guardian*, March 20).

16 I. Goldin, 2018. 'The limitations of Steven Pinker's optimism' (*Nature*, February 16).

17 L. Elliot, 2016. 'The World Bank and the IMF won't admit their policies are the problem' (*The Guardian*, November 9).

18 Pierre, Pénet, 'The IMF failure that wasn't: Risk ignorance during the European debt crisis.' *British Journal of Sociology*. https://doi.org/10.1111/1468-4446.12602 (2018); J. Best, *Governing Failure: Provisional Expertise and the Transformation of Global Development Finance* (Cambridge: Cambridge University Press, 2014).

19 Albert Hirschman, *The Rhetoric of Reaction: Perversity, Futility, Jeopardy* (Cambridge, MA: Harvard University Press, 1991).

20 See Steven Pinker, *Enlightenment Now: The Case for Reason, Science, Humanism and Progress* (New York: Penguin, 2018), 63, for Pinker's discussion of the 'sin of ingratitude,' and p. 113, for a discussion of the 'tradeoff.'

21 J.S. Mill, *'Utilitarianism' and 'On Liberty': Including 'Essay on Bentham'* (London: Wiley, 2003), 67.

22 Gerd Gigerenzer and Rocio Garcia-Retamero, 2017. 'Cassandra's regret: The psychology of not wanting to know.' *Psychological Review* 124(2): 179–196.

23 For an overview, see Ralph Hertwig and Christoph Engel, 2016. 'Homo ignorans: Deliberately choosing not to know.' *Perspectives on Psychological Science* 11: 359–372. Recent work on deliberate ignorance under decision-making differs from earlier psychological work on cognitive biases from scholars such as Daniel Kahneman. For an introduction to recent challenges to mainstream economic perspectives on ignorance, see Henk van Elst and Ekaterina Svetlova, 2015. 'Decision-theoretic approaches to non-knowledge in economics' in Gross and McGoey, *Routledge International Handbook of Ignorance Studies*, 349–360.

24 Gigerenzer and Garcia-Retamero, 'Cassandra's regret.'

25 See, for example, *New York Times* journalists Susan Chira and Catrin Einhorn's study of decades of sexual harassment and discrimination suffered by blue-collar workers at Ford plants. 'When you speak up,' one woman they interviewed said. 'You're like mud in the plant.' Susan Chira and Catrin Einhorn, 2017. 'Blue-collar women ask, "what about us?"' (*New York Times*, December 20). See also Joanne Roberts, 2015. 'Organizational ignorance' in Gross and McGoey, *Routledge International Handbook of Ignorance*, 361–369.

26 See also the work of Everett Hughes, 1963. 'Good people and dirty work.' *Social Problems* 10(1): 3–11.

27 Arnold Meagher, *The Coolie Trade: The Traffic in Chinese Laborers to Latin America 1847–1874* (Bloomington, IN: XLibris, 2008).

28 Karl McDonald, 2018. 'Millions of working-class men got the vote 100 years ago too' (*INews*, February 6).

29 Selina Todd, *The People: The Rise and Fall of the Working Class* (London: John Murray, 2014).

30 Ian Jack, 2016. 'The *History Thieves* by Ian Cobain review: How Britain covered up its imperial crimes' (*The Guardian*, October 6); Ian Cobain, *The History Thieves: Secrets, Lies and the Shaping of a Modern Nation* (London: Portobello Books, 2016).

31 See also Jack Goody, *The Theft of History* (Cambridge: Cambridge University Press, 2007); Akala, *Natives: Race and Class in the Ruins of Empire* (London: Two Roads, 2018); Richard Seymour, *The Liberal Defence of Murder* (London: Verso, 2008).

32 Paul Mason, 2018. 'Ink it onto your knuckles: Carillion is how neoliberalism lives and breathes' (Novaro Media, January 1). http://novaramedia.com/2018/01/15/ink-it-onto-your-knuckles-carillion-is-how-neoliberalism-lives-and-breathes/.

33 Wajahat Ali and Pankaj Mishra, 2018. 'Empire's racketeers' (*The Boston Review*, November 7); see also Shubhra Chakrabarti and Utsa Patnaik, *Agrarian and Other Histories: Essays for Binay Bhushan Chaudhuri* (New Delhi: Tulika Books, 2018).

34 See, for example, Reni Eddo-Lodge, 2017. *Why I'm No Longer Talking to White People about Race* (London: Bloomsbury, 2017); Dermot Feenan, 2007. 'Understanding disadvantage partly through an epistemology of ignorance.' *Social and Legal Studies* 16: 509–531, 516.

35 See W.E. Moore and M.M. Tumin, 1949. 'Some social functions of ignorance.' *American Sociological Review* 14: 787–795; Linda Martin Alcoff, 'Epistemologies of ignorance: Three types' in Sharon Sullivan and Nancy Tuana (Eds), *Race and Epistemologies of Ignorance* (New York: SUNY Press, 2007), 39–57; Michael Taussig. *Defacement: Public Secrecy and the Labor of the Negative* (Palo Alto, CA: Stanford University Press, 1999).

36 Charles Mills, 'White ignorance' in Sullivan and Tuana, *Race and Epistemologies of Ignorance*, 11–39, 33; Charles Mills, *The Racial Contract* (Ithaca, NY: Cornell University Press, 2007).

37 Hannah Arendt, *On Violence* (New York: Harcourt Brace, 1969), 88.

38 For important criticism of the limitations of rational ignorance theories in political science, see the work of Friedman and Bennett, such as Stephen Earl Bennett and Jeffrey Friedman, 2008. 'The

irrelevance of economic theory to understanding economic ignorance.' *Critical Review* 20(3): 195–258.

39 Quoted in Ilya Somin, *Democracy and Political Ignorance* (Stanford,
CA: Stanford University Press, 2013).

40 David Gillborn, 2016. 'Softly, softly: Genetics, intelligence and
the hidden racism of the new geneism.' *Journal of Education Policy*
31(4): 365–388. See also G. Evans, 2018. 'The unwelcome revival
of "race science"' (*The Guardian*, March 2).

2   Seeing ignorance differently

1 Anahad O'Connor, 2015. 'Coca-Cola funds scientists who shift
blame for obesity away from bad diets' (*The New York Times*,
August 19).

2 https://en.wikipedia.org/wiki/There_are_known_knowns.

3 Gillian Tett, *Fool's Gold* (London: Abacus, 2010).

4 Quoted in Michael Lewis, *The Big Short: Inside the Doomsday
Machine* (New York: W.W. Norton and Company, 2011), 263.
These paragraphs draw on L. McGoey, 2012. 'The power of igno-
rance and the problem of abundance' (Open Democracy, July 5).
See also McGoey, 'On the will to ignorance in bureaucracy'; and
W. Davies and L. McGoey, 2012. 'Rationalities of ignorance: On
financial crisis and the ambivalence of neoliberal epistemology.'
Economy and Society 41(1): 64–83.

5 A. Schwartz, 2009. 'Man without a plan' (*The New York Times*, July 25).

6 Taussig, *Defacement*, 9.

7 S. Cohen, *States of Denial: Knowing about Atrocities and Suffering*
(Cambridge: Polity, 2000), x; see also D. Thiel, 2015. 'Criminal
ignorance' in Gross and McGoey, *The Routledge International
Handbook of Ignorance Studies*, 256–265.

8 Audre Lorde is one of the first scholars to use the term 'historical
amnesia,' in the influential essay 'Age, race, class and sex: Women
redefining difference.' See Lorde, *Your Silence Will Not Protect You*. Ed.
Reni Eddo-Lodge and Sara Ahmed (UK: Silver Press, 2017). For further discussion, see Mariana Ortega, 2006. 'Being lovingly, knowingly
ignorant: White feminism and women of color.' *Hypatia* 21: 56–74.

9   See Nadine El-Enany, who suggests that the UK's 'unredressed colonial past haunted the recent EU referendum and prophesied its outcome,' (http://blogs.bath.ac.uk/iprblog/2017/05/02/things-fall-apart-from-empire-to-brexit-britain/), as well as writing from Gurminder Bhambra, especially Bhambra, 2017. 'Brexit, Trump, and "methodological whiteness": On the misrecognition of race and class.' *British Journal of Sociology* 68: 214–232.

10 Kristie Dotson, 2011. 'Tracking epistemic violence, tracking practices of silencing.' *Hypatia: A Journal of Feminist Philosophy* 26(2): 236–256. See also Boaventura de Sousa Santos, *Epistemologies of the South: Justice against Epistemicide* (London: Routledge, 2014) on the need for a sociology of 'produced absences' in order to mitigate the problem of cognitive blindness with western legal and political theory. My reading of Santos is indebted to Zara Bain, 2016. 'Responding to cognitive injustice: Towards a 'southern' decolonial epistemology.' *Global Justice: Theory Practice Rhetoric* 9(2): 220–223. See also J. Schiff, 2008. 'Confronting political responsibility: The problem of acknowl-edgment.' *Hypatia* 23: 99–116.

11 See L. McGoey, 2012. 'The logic of strategic ignorance.' *British Journal of Sociology*. https://doi.org/10.1111/j.1468-4446.2012.01424.x; see also Sandya Hewamanne's (2016) exploration of taboo and the unutterable among female factory workers. *Sri Lanka's Global Factory Workers: (un)Disciplined Desires and Sexual Struggles in a Post-Colonial Society* (Routledge, 2016).

12 Sophia Rosenfeld, 2008. 'Before democracy: The production and uses of common sense.' *The Journal of Modern History* 80: 1–54, 1.

13 Akwugo Emejulu and Leah Bassel. 2015. 'Minority women, austerity and activism.' *Race and Class* 57(2): 86–95, 90.

14 George Tavlas, 2013. 'Anna Jacobson Schwartz: in memoriam.' *Cato Journal* 33(3): 321–332.

15 Political philosopher and legal scholar Cass Sunstein points out the similarities between *On Liberty* and Taylor's earlier work, but he doesn't mention Mill's insistence on their co-authorship. See Cass Sunstein, 2015. 'John & Harriet: Still mysterious' (*New York Review of Books*, April 2).

16 For an excellent study of oracles in Greek life, see Michael Scott, *Delphi: A History of the Centre of the Ancient World* (Princeton, NJ: Princeton University Press, 2014).

17 See Katja Vogt's compelling explorations of Socratic reflections on knowledge and ignorance. Katja Vogt, *Belief and Truth: A Skeptic Reading of Plato* (Oxford: Oxford University Press, 2015).

18 See ibid.

19 As I describe in my previous book, private philanthropic foundations more than doubled between 2000 and 2015. See McGoey, *No Such Thing as a Free Gift* (London and New York: Verso, 2015).

20 L. Colley, *Britons: Forging the Nation, 1707–1837* (New Haven, CT: Yale University Press, 2005).

21 Quoted in D. Olusoga, *Black and British: A Forgotten History* (London: Pan Books, 2016), 11.

22 Quoted in Keeanga-Yamahtta Taylor, *From #BlackLivesMatter to Black Liberation* (Chicago, IL: Haymarket Books, 2006), 29.

23 Ibid., 29.

24 See 'Jason Brennan: The right to vote should be restricted to those with knowledge.' http://blog.press.princeton.edu/2016/09/29/jason-brennan-the-right-to-vote-should-be-restricted-to-those-with-knowledge/.

25 David Wallechinsky, 2016. 'Is George Bush guilty of war crimes … and who cares?' (*Huffington Post*, July 8). See also Lisa Stampnitzky, 2016. 'The lawyers' war: states and human rights in a transnational field.' *Sociological Review* 64(2): 170–193; Nisha Kapoor, *Deport, Deprive, Extradite: 21st Century State Extremism* (London: Verso, 2017).

26 Tamsin Shaw, 2016. 'The psychologists take power' (*The New York Review of Books*, February 25).

27 As US lawyer Clive Stafford Smith writes: 'torture did not secure reliable information in 1600 (when witches "confesse"); it was no more helpful in 2001.' See C.S. Smith, 2012. '*Cruel Britannia* by Ian Cobain – A Review' (*The Guardian*, November 23).

28 J. Arlidge, 2009. 'I'm doing "God's work": Meet Mr Goldman Sachs' (*The Times*, November 8).

29 Quotes are from E. Burke, *Thoughts on Details on Scarcity* (Franklin Classics, 2018 [1795]).

30 My point here draws on discussions with Darren Thiel; I'm indebted to him for ongoing insights and discussions on the market's god-like authority. See also L. McGoey and D. Thiel, 2018. 'Charismatic violence and the sanctification of the super rich.' *Economy and Society* 47(1): 111–134. Heterodox scholars who call attention to the religion-like aspects of capitalist economic orthodoxy are often presumed to be speaking metaphorically. But when an economist such as Yanis Varoufakis calls economics a 'religion with equations,' he is being more literal than people sometimes perceive. See Yanis Varoufakis, *Talking to My Daughter about the Economy* (London: Bodley Head, 2017; Harvey Cox, *The Market as God* (Cambridge, MA: Harvard University Press, 2016).

3   Elite agnotologists

1 See Victoria Saker Woeste, *Henry Ford's War on Jews and the Legal Battle against Hate Speech* (Stanford, CA: Stanford University Press, 2012).

2 Neil Baldwin, *Henry Ford and the Jews: The Mass Production of Hate* (New York: Public Affairs, 2001), 173.

3 V. Woeste, 2013. 'Henry Ford: Behind the myth' (*Huffpost*, August 7).

4 Woeste, *Henry Ford's War on Jews*, 282.

5 Kevin Williamson, 2016. 'The father-führer' (*National Review*, March 28).

6 N. Carnes and N. Lupu, 2017. 'It's time to bust the myth: Most Trump voters were not working class' (*Washington Post*, June 5).

7 Sarah Smarsh, 2016. 'Dangerous idiots' (*The Guardian*, October 13); see also Ta-Nehisi Coates, 2017. 'The first white president' (*Atlantic*, October).

8 G. Wodtke, 2012. 'The impact of education on inter-group attitudes: A multiracial analysis.' *Social Psychology Quarterly* 75(1). doi: 10.1177/0190272511430234.

9 C. Cadwalladr, 2017. '"Dark money" is threat to integrity of UK elections, say leading academics' (*The Guardian*, April 1); C. Cadwalladr, 2017. 'The Great British Brexit robbery: How our democracy was hijacked' (*The Guardian*, May 7).

10 Joshua Green, 2015. 'This man is the most dangerous political operative in America' (*Bloomberg Businessweek*, October 8).

11 P. Scraton. *Hillsborough: The Truth* (Edinburgh and London: Mainstream Publishing, 2016), 173.

12 http://www.politifact.com/punditfact/statements/2016/jul/01/daily-mail/what-google-trends-tell-us-and-doesnt-about-brexit/.

13 Zoe Williams, 2016. 'Think the north and the poor caused Brexit? Think again' (*The Guardian*, August 17). See also Bhambra, 'Brexit, Trump, and "methodological whiteness."'

14 Satnam Virdee and Brendan McGeever point out that the 'invisible driver of the Brexit vote and its racist aftermath has been a politicization of Englishness.' Part of this invisibility has been the tendency to see Brexit as the kneejerk reaction of the poor, rather than a jingoistic affirmation of white British identity spearheaded by the wealthy. See S. Virdee and B. McGeever, 2017. 'Race, crisis, Brexit.' *Ethnic and Racial Studies*, doi: 10.1080/01419870.2017.1361544.

15 Spencer Ackerman, 2016. 'Obama claims US drone strikes have killed up to 116' (*The Guardian*, July 1). See also C. Friedersdorf, 2013. 'Dianne Feinstein's outrageous underestimate of civilian drone deaths' (*The Atlantic*, February 11); E. Schweiger, 2015. 'The risks of remaining silent: International law formation and the EU silence on drone killings.' *Global Affairs* 1(3): 269–275.

16 Civilian death tolls are notoriously hard to determine in most wars, something that can contribute to 'official forgetting,' Naomi Klein's term for strategies that obfuscate government wrongs. See *No Is Not Enough: Defeating the New Shock Politics* (London: Penguin, 2017), 195. See also Brian Rappert, *How to Look Good in War* (London: Pluto Press, 2012).

17 C. Crain, 2016. 'The case against democracy' (*The New Yorker*, November 7).

18 J. Brennan, 2016. 'Can epistocracy, or knowledge-based voting, fix democracy?' (*LA Times*, August 28). See also Jason Brennan, *Against Democracy* (Princeton, NJ: Princeton University Press, 2016).

19 Somin, *Democracy and Political Ignorance*, 182–183. See also Tilley's discussion of race, racism and the problem of scientific

testing on the African continent over the late 19th and early 20th centuries. Helen Tilley, *Africa as Living Laboratory* (Chicago, IL: University of Chicago Press, 2011).

4   The Murdoch strategy

1   See N. Davies, *Hack Attack: How the Truth Caught Up with Rupert Murdoch* (London: Vintage Books, 2014); and M. Hickman and T. Watson, *Dial M for Murdoch* (London: Allen Lane, 2012).

2   http://www.publications.parliament.uk/pa/cm201012/cmselect/cmcumeds/903/903i.pdf, 70.

3   D. Rushe and M. Sweeney, 2013. 'News Corp reaches settlement with shareholders' (*The Guardian*, April 22).

4   A. Whittam Smith, 2011. 'If we don't act now, worse will follow' (*Independent*, July 7).

5   Jack Mirkinson, 2015. 'The fall and rise of Rupert Murdoch: How the world's most ruthless mogul salvaged his media empire' (*Salon*, June 12).

6   Davies, *Hack Attack*, 4. Davies' work has been indispensable to my discussion, and I draw on it throughout this chapter.

7   Ibid., 5.

8   Information Commissioner's Office, 2016. *What Price Privacy? The Unlawful Trade in Confidential Personal Information*, 28.

9   Ibid., 27.

10   http://webarchive.nationalarchives.gov.uk/20140122145147/http:/www.levesoninquiry.org.uk/wp-content/uploads/2011/11/Transcript-of-Afternoon-Hearing-30-November-2011.pdf, 29.

11   Quoted in James Robinson and Lisa O'Carroll, 2011. 'Former information commissioner: We were right not to prosecute newspapers' (*The Guardian*, December 9). http://www.theguardian.com/media/2011/dec/09/former-information-commissioner-leveson-inquiry.

12   Andreas Whittam Smith, 2013. 'How the Leveson Report stopped the press in its tracks: One year on, the forensic cataloguing of media bullying retains its power to shock' (*Independent*, November 28). http://www.independent.co.uk/news/media/

press/how-the-leveson-report-stopped-the-press-in-its-tracks-one-year-on-the-forensic-cataloguing-of-media-bullying-retains-its-power-to-shock-8971015.html.

13 For a longer discussion of 'anti-strategies,' see McGoey, 'On the will to ignorance in bureaucracy.'

14 Information in this paragraph is taken from Nick Davies, 2014. 'Phone hacking: Met had the evidence' (*The Guardian*, July 2). http://www.theguardian.com/uk-news/2014/jul/02/phone-hacking-met-evidence-operation-caryatid-trial-police-news-international.

15 D. Ponsford, 2013. 'Sun journalists "treated as criminals for doing what company expected" have Murdoch's 'total support' (*Press Gazette*, July 4).

16 R. Greenslade, 2015. 'Rupert Murdoch's News UK shamed by failure to pay legal costs' (*The Guardian*, July 17).

17 D. Rushe and M. Sweeney, 2013. 'News Corp reaches settlement with shareholders' (*The Guardian*, April 22).

18 MMIC = Main motherfucker in charge.

19 Isabel Sawhill and Edward Rodrigue, 2015. *Wealth, Inheritance and Social Mobility*. Brookings Institute, January 30.

20 Rachel Sherman, 2017. 'What the rich won't tell you' (*The New York Times*, 8 September). https://www.nytimes.com/2017/09/08/opinion/sunday/what-the-rich-wont-tell-you.html.

21 R. Khurana, *From Higher Aims to Hired Hands* (Princeton, NJ: Princeton University Press, 2007); see also M. Parker, *Shut Down the Business School: What's Wrong with Management Education* (London: Pluto, 2018). There are exceptions to this problem. In the UK, there is robust scholarship within the field of criminology that explores corporate harms, such as work by Nigel South, Dave Whyte and Vickie Cooper. But for the most part, business schools have failed to place corporate crime at the centre of teaching and research.

22 R. Martin, 2011. 'Rupert Murdoch and Rebekah Brooks scandal: management by willful ignorance' (*Daily Beast*, July 21).

23 S. Young, 2011. 'Corporate governance 101: The buck stops with Rupert Murdoch' (*The Conversation*, July 21).

24 K. Krawiec, 2018. 'The return of the rogue.' *Arizona Law Review* 51: 127–174.

25 B. Hutter and M. Power, *Organizational Encounters with Risk* (Cambridge: Cambridge University Press, 2005), 14. See also M. Stein, 2000. 'The risk taker as shadow: A psychoanalytic view of the collapse of Barings Bank.' *Journal of Management Studies* 37: 1215–1229.

26 Smith, Book 5 in *Wealth of Nations*. Ed. Spencer, 854.

5   Suspicious attention

1 For an important recent analysis of unpaid labour and its social effects, see L. Pettinger, *What's the Matter with Work?* (Bristol: Policy Press, 2019). For an illuminating analysis of Smith's work that resonates with points made in this chapter, see also J. Norman, *Adam Smith: What He Thought and Why It Matters* (London: Allen Lane, 2018).

2 A. Smith, *Wealth of Nations*. Ed. K. Sutherland (Oxford: Oxford World Classics, 1997), Vol. 11, p. 188.

3 Smith, *Wealth of Nations*. Ed. Spencer, 753.

4 Ibid., 753.

5 See J. Montgomerie, *Should we Abolish Household Debts?* (London: Polity Press, 2019).

6 Smith, *Wealth of Nations*. Ed. Spencer, 609.

7 Ibid., 754.

8 Both quotes in George Orwell, 1939. 'Not counting niggers.' http://orwell.ru/library/articles/niggers/english/e_ncn (accessed December 2018).

9 Quoted in Patricia Hill Collins, *Black Feminist Thought* (London: Routledge, 2008), 4.

10 Michael Hudson, 2015. 'Rewriting economic thought' (Counterpunch Radio, Episode 19, September 21).

11 See F. Moseley, 2012. 'Mankiw's attempted resurrection of marginal productivity theory.' *Real-world Economics Review* 61: 115–124; L. McGoey, 2017. 'The elusive rentier rich: Piketty's data battles and the value of absent evidence.' *Science, Technology, and Human Values* 42(2): 257–279.

12 Gregory Mankiw, 2013. 'In defence of the one percent.' *Journal of Economic Perspectives* 27(3): 21–34, 30.

13 J. Stiglitz, 'Inequality and economic growth' in Michael Jacobs and Mariana Mazzucato (Eds), *Rethinking Capitalism: Economics and Policy for Sustainable and Inclusive Growth* (London: Wiley, 2016).

14 J. Robinson, 1953–1954. 'The production function and the theory of capital.' *Review of Economic Studies* 21(2): 81–106, 81.

15 Quoted in G. Stigler, 1980. 'Economics or ethics? Tanner Lectures on Human Values,' 166. Accessed December 19, 2016. http://tannerlectures.utah.edu/_documents/a-toz/s/stigler81.pdf.

16 Samuelson 1966: 1577, quoted in A. Sen, *On Economic Inequality* (Oxford: Oxford University Press, 1997), 101.

17 Pinker, *Enlightenment* Now, 102.

18 Ibid., 13.

19 Pinker, *Enlightenment Now*, 80.

20 See N. Phillips, 2017. 'Power and inequality in the global political economy.' *International Affairs* 93(2): 429–444.

21 J. Hickel, *The Divide: A Brief Guide to Global Inequality and Its Solutions* (London: Penguin, 2017); S. Reid, *The Political Origins of Inequality* (Chicago, IL: University of Chicago Press, 2015).

22 Smith, *Wealth of Nations*. Ed. Sutherland, 155.

23 Ibid, 156.

24 Ibid, 156.

25 Ibid, 157.

26 Ibid, 65.

27 Ibid, 65.

28 For further discussion, see A.H. Kelly and L. McGoey, 2018. 'Facts, power and global evidence.' *Economy and Society* 47: 1–26.

29 Smith, *Wealth of Nations*. Ed. Sutherland, 668.

30 Smith, *Wealth of Nations*. Ed. Sutherland, 614.

31 'Introduction,' in Smith, *Wealth of Nations*. Ed. Sutherland, x.

32 Author interview, conducted via email.

33 B. Harcourt, *The Illusion of Free Markets* (Cambridge, MA: Harvard University Press, 2011), 111.

34 E. Burke, *Reflections of the Revolution in France* (London: Penguin, 1987 [1790]).

35 All quotes in this passage are taken from Mary Wollstonecraft's *Vindications of the Rights of Men*. 'The game laws,' 44; 'An honest mechanic,' 45; 'You have shown, Sir,' 45.

36 Paine, *Rights of Man*, 126.

37 Wollstonecraft, *Vindications of the Rights of Men* in *The Vindications: The Rights of Men and the Rights of Woman*. Ed. D.L. Macdonald and K. Scherf (Peterborough, Ontario: Broadview Press, 1997), 38.

38 Quoted in D.L. Macdonald and K. Scherf, 'Introduction' in Wollstonecraft, *The Vindications*, 11.

39 Wollstonecraft, *Vindications of the Rights of Men*, 90.

40 See Dimitrios Nomidis, 2018. 'The mistakes of the marginal productivity theory of income distribution' (June 20). https://ssrn.com/abstract=3199738 or http://dx.doi.org/10.2139/ssrn.3199738.

41 The discipline of sociology is not exempt from problems surrounding wilful ignorance that are visible in the history of economic thought. Aldon Morris' study of the historical dismissal of pioneering work by the black scholar W.E.B. Du Bois is a good example; as is Mary Jo Deegan's influential study of the unacknowledged debt that Chicago School sociologists such as Parks and Burgess owe to the earlier scholar, Jane Addams.

6   Know-it-all epistocrats

1 J.S. Mill, *Autobiography* (New York: Signet Classics, 1964), 126.

2 J.S. Mill, *The Subjection of Women*, in *On Liberty, Utilitarianism and Other Essays* (Oxford: Oxford World Classics, 2015).

3 See D. Schwan, 2013. J.S. Mill on coolie labour and voluntary slavery. *British Journal for the History of Philosophy* 21(4): 754–766.

4 A. Briggs, 'Preface,' in Mill, *Autobiography*, xix.

5 Mill, *Autobiography*, 164.

6 Ibid., 180.

7 Briggs, 'Preface,' xviii.

8 J.S. Mill, *Considerations on Representative Government*, in *On Liberty, Utilitarianism and Other Essays* (Oxford: Oxford University Press, 2015), 405.

9 Mill, *Autobiography*, 67.

10 See Eddo-Lodge, *Why I'm No Longer Talking to White People* for deeper discussion of the problem with phrases such as 'white working class.'

11 On this point, I strongly disagree with David Runciman, who suggests 'Epistocracy is flawed because of the second part of the word rather than the first – this is about power (*kratos*) as much as it is about knowledge (*episteme*).' Runciman is right about power, but he is far too quick to let epistocrats off the hook for their naïve understanding of epistemology and knowledge. See D. Runciman, 2018. 'Why replacing democracy with experts is reckless idea' (*The Guardian*, May 1).

12 K. Popper, *The Open Society and Its Enemies*, Vol. 1 (London and New York: Routledge, 1995).

13 Ibid., 214.

14 Alexis de Tocqueville, *The Recollections of Alexis De Toqueville* (London: Meridian Books, 1957), 148.

15 See https://www.newstatesman.com/2018/05/psychologist-jordan-peterson-says-lobsters-help-explain-why-human-hierarchies-exist-do-they.

16 J.M. Keynes, *The General Theory of Employment, Interest and Money* (Middletown, RI: BN Publishing, 2008), 383.

17 F. Bastiat, *Economic Sophisms*. Trans. A. Goddard (Foundation for Economic Education, 1996), 134.

18 Ibid., 378.

7 Conflict blindness

1 See D. Rodrick, 2013. 'In truth, mercantilism never really went away' (*The National*, January 11).

2 C. Rampell, 2018. 'Trade policy is stuck in the 80s – the 1680s' (*Washington Post*, June 2).

3 *The Economist*, 2013. 'What was mercantilism?' (August 23). https://www.economist.com/free-exchange/2013/08/23/what-was-mercantilism.

4 Preface, Keynes, *The General Theory of Employment*, viii.

5   John Maynard Keynes 'National self-sufficiency.' *The Yale Review* 22(4) (June 1933): 755–769. http://jmaynardkeynes.ucc.ie/national-self-sufficiency.html.

6   Paine, Preface, 'Agrarian Justice,' in *Rights of Man and Other Essays*, 414.

7   Quoted in C. Monaghan, 2011. 'In defence of intrinsic human rights: Edmund Burke's controversial prosecution of Warren Hastings, Governor-General of Bengal.' *Law, Crime and History* 1(2): 58–107.

8   Quoted in G. Trefgarne, 2006. 'How the first multinational was hijacked by greed' (*The Spectator*, October 25).

9   W. Dalrymple, 2015. 'The East India Company: The original corporate raiders' (*The Guardian*, March 4).

10 Ibid.

11 Ibid.

12 Ibid.

13 Paine, *Rights of Man*, 191.

14 N. Robins, 2006. 'East India Company: The first multinational corporation' (*Ecologist*, November 1).

15 Quoted in ibid.

16 Paine, *Rights of Man*, 127–134.

17 Ibid., 134.

18 Ibid., 92.

19 Ibid., 92.

20 Paine, 'Agrarian justice,' 429.

21 Ibid., 429.

22 G. Tetlow, 2018. 'MPs seek cut in high interest rates on student loans (*Financial Times*, February 18).

23 See M. Paré and T. Chong, 2017. 'Human rights violations and Canadian mining companies: Exploring access to justice in relation to children's rights.' *International Journal of Human Rights* 21(7): 908–932; Les Whittington, 2010. 'Canadian mining firms worst for environment, rights: Report' (*The Toronto Star*, 19 October).

24 M. Patterson, 2016. 'How the U.S. violates international law in plain sight' (*America: The Jesuit Review*, October 24).

25 P. Thiel, 2009. 'The education of a libertarian' (*Cato Unbound*, April 13). https://www.cato-unbound.org/2009/04/13/peter-thiel/education-libertarian.

26 Smith, *Wealth of Nations*. Ed. Spencer, 454.

27 M. Watson, 2017. 'Historicising Ricardo's comparative advantage theory, challenging the normative foundations of liberal international economy.' *New Political Economy* 22(3): 257–272, 259.

28 https://larspsyll.wordpress.com/2017/04/19/david-ricardo-and-comparative-advantage-a-bicentennial-assessment/.

29 Ha-Joon Chang, *Bad Samaritans, The Guilty Secrets of Rich Nations and the Threat to Global Prosperity* (London: Random House, 2007), 47.

30 Eugene Wendler, *Friedrich List (1789–1846): A Visionary Economist with Social Responsibility* (Heidelberg: Springer, 2015), 4; see also David Levi-Faur, 1997. 'Friedrich List and the political economy of the nation-state.' *Review of International Political Economy* 4(1): 154–178. doi: 10.1080/096922997347887.

31 F. List, *National System of Political Economy, Vol. 1: The History* (New York: Cosimo, 2005 [1841]), xx.

32 Ibid., 33.

33 Smith, *Wealth of Nations*. Ed. Spencer, 609.

34 Ibid., 610.

8   Masters of industry, masters of ignorance

1 Christian Parenti, 2014. 'Reading Hamilton from the Left' (*Jacobin*, August 26); see also B. Katz and J. Lee, 2011. 'Alexander Hamilton's manufacturing message.' Brookings Institute, December 5.

2 Mill was not, of course, an unqualified proponent of laissez faire. He flirts with socialism during stages of his life, and introduced notions such as a land tax later embraced by Henry George. See George Stigler, 1980. 'John Stuart Mill.' Working Paper no. 50, Center for the Study of the Economy and the State, University of Chicago. http://www.chicagobooth.edu/assests/stigler/50.pdf.

3   Timothy J. Dowd and Frank Dobbin, 2001. 'Origins of the myth of neo-liberalism: Regulation in the first century of U.S. railroading' in L. Magnusson and J. Ottosson (Eds), *Private Actors and Public Interest: The Role of the State in Regulated Economies* (Cheltenham, UK: Edward Elgar), 61–88.

4   R. John, 1997. 'Elaborations, revisions, dissents: Alfred D. Chandler, Jr.'s, *The Visible Hand* after twenty years.' *Business History Review* 71(Summer): 151–206; see also Robert Knox, 2016. 'Valuing race?' *London Review of International Law* 4(1): 81–126; and R. Stahl, 2018. 'Economic liberalism and the state: Dismantling the myth of naïve laissez-faire.' *New Political Economy*, doi: 10.1080/13563467.2018.1458086.

5   C. Dunlavy, 1991. 'Mirror images: Political structure and early railroad policy in the United States and Prussia.' *Studies in American Political Development* 5: 1–35; C. Dunlavy and T. Welskopp, 2007. 'Myths and peculiarities: Comparing US and German capitalism.' GHI Bulletin 41, Autumn.

6   Howard Zinn, *A People's History of the United States* (New York: Harper & Row, 1980), 394.

7   A. de Tocqueville, *Democracy in America* (New York: Perennial Classics, 1966 [1835]), 556–557.

8   Dunlavy and Welskopp, *Myths and Peculiarities*.

9   Tocqueville, *Democracy in America*, 685.

10 Ibid., 696.

11 Ibid., 684.

12 Ibid, 686.

13 Ibid, 686.

14 Ibid., 693.

15 Ibid., 698.

16 Ibid., 701.

17 For example, David Runciman, in an otherwise superb study of Tocqueville, ignores Tocqueville's remarks about the corrosive effects of private industry on democratic governance. See Runciman, *Confidence Trap*. An exception is Sheldon Wolin, who does explore Tocqueville's concerns about the new business aristocracy. Sheldon Wolin, *Tocqueville between Two Worlds:*

The Marking of a Political and Theoretical Life (Princeton, NJ: Princeton University Press, 2001), 347–353.

18   Ibid., 121.

19   Bastiat, *Economic Sophisms*, 271.

20   Mill, *The Subjection of Women*, 429.

21   Quoted in J. Berke, 2018. 'Bill Gates reads 50 books a year and says this is his all-time favorite: here are his top highlights' (*Business Insider*, March 20).

22   John Dower, 2017. 'America wants peace for the world – by any means necessary' (*The Nation*, March 28).

23   See R. Dunbar-Ortiz, 2014. 'America's foundation myths' (*Jacobin*, November 27).

24   David Nasaw, *Andrew Carnegie* (New York: Penguin, 2006), 106.

25   T. Nace. *Gangs of America: The Rise of Corporate Power and the Disabling of Democracy* (San Francisco, CA: Berrett-Koehler Publishers, 2005), 5.

26   Nasaw, *Andrew Carnegie*, 257.

27   Ibid., 323.

28   Ibid., 325.

29   Ibid., 448.

30   Ibid., 522.

31   See Henry George, 1868. 'What the railroad will bring US.' *The Overland Monthly* 1(4): 297–306.

32   Chernow, *Titan*, 114.

33   Ibid., 114.

34   Ibid., 161.

35   Ibid., 148.

36   Ibid., 148.

37   Nasaw, *Andrew Carnegie*, 257.

38   Quoted in I. Kawachi and P. Howden Chapman, 2004. 'Five American authors on wealth, poverty, and inequality.' *Journal of Epidemiology and Community Health* 58: 738–742. doi: 10.1136/jech.2004.021741.

39   Z. Carter, 2018. 'Trump's tariff war is the final act of a broken system' (*Huffington Post*, July 22).

40   https://www.gatesnotes.com/Books/Enlightenment-Now.

41 Peter Bakvis, 2017. 'Orthodoxy, evidence and action: Labour rights at the World Bank.' *International Union Rights* 24(1): 3–5.

42 Hickel, *The Divide*, 173. See also McGoey, *No Such Thing as a Free Gift*, as well as this article from former World Bank economist Branko Milanovic, who makes similar points about the political way that Gates and Pinker use self-pleasing statistics to defend rigid ideological positions: https://www.globalpolicyjournal.com/blog/11/02/2019/global-poverty-over-long-term-legitimate-issues.

43 Hannah Arendt, *Origins of Totalitarianism* (London: Penguin Classics, 2017), 282.

44 Peter Bakvis, 2018. 'It's time to end the World Bank's biased business regulation ratings' (Inequality.org, January 18).

45 Poonam Puri's quote available here http://www.fondationtrudeau.ca/en/community/poonam-puri (accessed December 2018).

46 Pinker, *Enlightenment Now*, 336.

9 The ostrich instruction

1 I. Robbins, 1990. 'The ostrich instruction: Deliberate ignorance as criminal mens rea.' *The Journal of Criminal Law and Criminology* 81(2): 191–234, 196.

2 Ibid., 197.

3 Ibid., 192.

4 Mohammed Suleh-Yusuf, 2017. 'Corporate criminal liability: Reviewing the adequacy of willful blindness as mens rea.' *International Journal of Law* 3(2): 23–24.

5 M. Heffernan, *Wilful Blindness: Why We Ignore the Obvious at Our Peril* (New York: Simon & Schuster, 2012); J. O'Brien, *Redesigning Financial Regulation: The Politics of Enforcement* (Chichester: John Wiley, 2007); see also J. Rakoff, 2014. 'The financial crisis: Why have no high-level executives been prosecuted?' (*New York Review of Books*, January 9).

6 Author interview, 2017.

7 A. Sarch, 2016. 'Equal culpability and the scope of the willful ignorance doctrine.' *Legal Theory* 22: 276–311, 278.

8   See also Max H. Bazerman et al., 2002. 'Why good accountants do bad audits.' *Harvard Business Review* 80(11): 96–102, 99 and Donald C. Langevoort, 2006. 'Reflections on Scienter (and the securities fraud case against Martha Stewart that never happened).' *Lewis and Clark Law Review* 10: 1–17, 15.

9   Sarch, 'Beyond Wilful Ignorance,' *University of Colorado Law Review* 88: 97–177, 105.

10 Ibid., 108.

11 Ibid., 100.

12 Z. Carter, 2015. 'House bill would make it harder to prosecute white-collar crime' (*Huffington Post*, November 16).

13 Lisa Graves, 2015. 'Koch self-interest in criminal justice reform, exposed' (PRWatch, December 16).

14 M. Apuzzo and E. Lipton, 2015. 'Rare White House accord with Koch brothers on sentencing fray' (*The New York Times*, November 24).

15 S. Davies, 1998. 'The jurisprudence of wilfulness: An evolving theory of excusable ignorance.' *Duke Law Journal* 48(3): 341–427. See also Mark C. Winings, 1993. 'Ignorance is bliss, especially for the tax evader.' *Journal of Criminal Law and Criminology* 84(3): 575–603.

16 Davies, 'Jurisprudence of wilfulness,' 347.

17 'Swift and Sweeping,' 2016 working paper, Lawyers' Committee for Civil Rights under Law.

18 Brennan, *Against Democracy*, 147.

19 Rena Steinzor, 2016. 'Trump-era criminal justice "reform" won't help stop mass incarceration' (*The Hill*, December 19).

20 Smith, *Wealth of Nations*. Ed. Sutherland, 156.

21 Quoted in Robert Van Horn, 2018. 'Corporations and the rise of Chicago law and economics.' *Economy and Society* 47(3): 477–499, 481.

22 For path-breaking analysis of this shift, see Harcourt, *The Illusion of Free Markets.*

23 For astute analysis of similiarites and differences between economists associated with the 'Virginia' and 'Chicago' schools, see Melinda Cooper, *Family Values: Between Neoliberalism and the New Social Conservatism* (New York: Zone Books, 2018).

24 D. McCloskey, 1998. 'Other things: The so-called Coase Theorem.' *Eastern Economic Journal* 24(3): 367–371, 367.

25 G. Stigler, 1980. 'Economics or ethics?' Tanner Lectures on Human Values. http://tannerlectures.utah.edu/_documents/a-to-z/s/stigler81.pdf (last accessed December 2018).

26 For further discussion of Mandeville, see McGoey, *No Such Thing as a Free Gift*, 90–93.

27 See William Novak, 2013. 'A revisionist history of regulatory capture' in Daniel Carpenter and David Moss (Eds), *Preventing Regulatory Capture: Special Interest Influence and How to Limit It* (Cambridge: Cambridge University Press, 2014), 25–48.

28 William Black, 2013. 'Discrediting regulation: From George Stigler to Tyson's fraud-free carbon tax fantasy' (neweconomicperspectives. org, July 8).

10 Good experts

1 Author interview, February 2005. See also Linsey McGoey and Emily Jackson, 2009. 'Seroxat suppression of clinical trial data: Regulatory failure and the uses of legal ambiguity.' *Journal of Medical Ethics* 35(2): 107–112. See also C. Medawar and A. Hardon, *Medicines Out of Control? Antidepressants and the Conspiracy of Goodwill* (Amsterdam: Aksant, 2004).

2 C. Whittington, T. Kendall, P. Fonagy, D. Cottrell, A. Cotgrove and E. Boddington, 2004. 'Selective serotonin reuptake inhibitors in childhood depression: Systematic review of published versus unpublished data.' *The Lancet* 363: 1341–45. See also Allison Bass, *Side Effects: A Prosecutor, a Whistleblower and a Bestselling Antidepressant on Trial* (Chapel Hill, NC: Algonquin Books, 2008), and David Healy, *Let Them Eat Prozac: The Unhealthy Relationship between the Pharmaceutical Industry and Depression* (New York and London: New York University Press, 2004).

3 Katie Thomas and Michael Schmidt, 2012. 'Glaxo agrees to pay $3 billion in fraud settlement.' (*New York Times*, July 2).

4 B. Goldacre, 2010. 'Drug firms hiding negative research are unfit to experiment on people' (*The Guardian*, August 14). See also Peter

C. Gøtzsch, 2012. 'Big pharma often commits corporate crime, and this must be stopped.' *BMJ* 2012;345:e8462

5 Harold Evans, 2012. 'Thalidomide's big lie overshadows corporate apology' (*Reuters*, July 12).

6 Michael Brewster Folsom, 1979. 'Upton Sinclair's escape from *The Jungle*: The narrative strategy and suppressed conclusion of America's first proletarian novel.' *Prospects*, 4: 237–266. doi:10.1017/S0361233300002891.

7 Andrew Ward, 2015. 'Frances Kelsey, drug regulator who barred Thalidomide, 1914–2015' (*Financial Times*, August 14).

8 Leila McNeill, 2017. 'The woman who stood between America and a generation of "Thalidomide babies"' (Smithsonian.com, May 8).

9 Quoted in Ward, 'Frances Kelsey.'

10 Robert McFadden, 2015. 'Frances Oldham Kelsey, who saved U.S. babies from Thalidomide, dies at 101' (*The New York Times*, August 7).

11 Benjamin Kentish, 2016. 'Donald Trump could be like John F Kennedy, says Bill Gates' (*Independent*, December 14).

12 J. Avorn, 2006. 'Dangerous deception: Hiding the evidence of adverse drug effects.' *New England Journal of Medicine* 355 (November 23): 2169–2171, 2169.

13 H. Krumholz, J. Ross, A. Presler and D. Egilman, 2007. 'What have we learned from Vioxx?' *British Medical Journal* 334: 120–123.

14 E. Topol, 2004. 'Failing the public health: Rofecoxib, Merck, and the FDA.' *New England Journal of Medicine* 351: 1707–1709.

15 R. Horton, 2004. 'Depressing research.' *The Lancet* 363: 1287.

16 R. Horton, 2004. 'Vioxx, the implosion of Merck, and aftershocks at the FDA.' *The Lancet* 364: 1995–1996.

17 Quoted in Krumholz et al., 'What have we learned from Vioxx?,' 121.

18 C. Bombardier, L. Laine, A. Reicin, D. Shapiro, R. Burgos-Vargas et al., 2000. 'Comparison of upper gastrointestinal toxicity of rofecoxib and naproxen in patients with rheumatoid arthritis.' *New England Journal of Medicine* 343(21): 1520–1528; J. Lisse, M. Perlman, G. Johansson, F. Shoemaker, J. Schechtman et al., 2003. 'Gastrointestinal tolerability and effectiveness of rofecoxib

versus naproxen in the treatment of osteoarthritis.' *Annals of Internal Medicine* 139: 539–546.

19 D. Michaels, 2005. 'Doubt is their product: Industry groups are fighting government regulation by fomenting scientific uncertainty.' *Scientific American* June: 96–101, 100.

20 A. Berenson, 2005. 'For Merck, Vioxx paper trail won't go away' (*The New York Times*, August 21).

21 Matthew Herper, 2014. 'Face of the Year: David Graham' (*Forbes*, December 13).

22 Author interview.

23 Cite G. Harris, 2007. 'Potentially incompatible goals at F.D.A.' (*New York Times*, June 11).

24 Daniel Carpenter, 2006. 'Reputation, gatekeeping and the politics of post-marketing drug regulation.' *Virtual Mentor: Ethics Journal of the American Medical Association* 8: 404. See also Daniel Goldberg, 2016. 'On physician–industry relationships and unreasonable standards of proof for harm: A population-level bioethics approach.' *Kennedy Institute of Ethics Journal* 26(2): 173–194.

25 Daniel Carpenter, *Reputation and Power* (Princeton, NJ: Princeton University Press, 2010), 610. He adds that during the Vioxx tragedy, high-ranking FDA officials 'engaged in an organizational motivated embrace of the status quo by defending randomized controlled trial and by disparaging pharmacoepidemiology.'

26 Author interview.

27 Author interview.

28 André Brink, *A Dry White Season* (Vintage, 2011), 234.

29 See K. Hundley, 2007. 'Drug's chilling path to market: How a broken FDA approved a cold antibiotic despite a wide trail of alarms' (*St. Petersburg Times*, May 27); D. Ross, 2007. 'The FDA and the case of Ketek.' *New England Journal of Medicine* 356: 1601–1604; G. Harris, 2006. 'Approval of antibiotic worried safety officials' (*New York Times*, July 18).

30 See Hundley, 'Drug's chilling path to market'; Ross, 'The FDA and the case of Ketek'; Harris, 'Approval of antibiotic worried safety officials.'

31 G. Harris, 2006. 'Halt is urged for trials of antibiotic in children' (*New York Times*, June 8)

32 The meeting with von Eschenbach is described by Ross during his testimony before the subcommittee hearing into Ketek. When he was later called before the subcommittee himself, von Eschenbach said that he had been trying to impress on staff that the FDA was a place where, like a pre-game locker room, 'completely different perspectives on an issue or problem can come together with mutual respect and vigorously, even aggressively, debate and discuss those issues.' See https://www.gpo.gov/fdsys/pkg/CHRG-110hhrg35502/html/CHRG-110hhrg35502.htm (last accessed December 2018).

33 Harris, 'Potentially incompatible goals.'

34 Ann Marie Cisneros and Douglas Loveland's testimony available here: https://www.gpo.gov/fdsys/pkg/CHRG-110hhrg48587/pdf/CHRG-110hhrg48587.pdf (accessed December 2018).

35 Hundley, 'Drug's chilling path'; McGoey, 'Logic of strategic ignorance.'

36 See Loveland's testimony here: https://www.gpo.gov/fdsys/pkg/CHRG-110hhrg48587/pdf/CHRG-110hhrg48587.pdf.

37 Casey Sullivan, 2015. 'Health plans lose class action over risky antibiotic Ketek' (Findlaw.com, November 17).

11   The pretence of ignorance

1 D. Stipp, 2005. 'Trouble in Prozac' (*Fortune*, November 28).

2 Bass, *Side Effects*.

3 Medawar and Hardon, *Medicines Out of Control?*

4 See Sarah Boseley, 2004. 'Drug safety agency accused of cover-up' (*The Guardian*, March 13).

5 Quoted in ibid.

6 Quoted in ibid.

7 Author interview.

8 Author interview.

9 J. Lenzer, 2004. 'Secret US report surfaces on antidepressants in children,' *British Medical Journal* 329: 307.

10 Ibid., 307.

11 Joel Bakan, *Childhood Under Siege: How Big Business Targets Your Children* (New York: Free Press, 2011), 76.

12 Author interview.

13 See McGoey and Jackson, 'Seroxat and the suppression of clinical trial data.'

14 J.-P. Sartre, *Being and Nothingness: An Essay on Phenomenological Ontology* (Abingdon: Routledge, 2003), 91.

15 Ellen Meiksins Woods, *Citizens to Lords: A Social History of Western Political Thought from Antiquity to the Late Middle Ages* (London: Verso, 2008), 39.

16 Ibid., 39.

17 Nicholas Wapshott, *Keynes/Hayek: The Clash That Defined Modern Economics* (New York: W.W. Norton), 222.

18 See, for example, Hayek's growing tolerance for monopoly power, discussed extensively in *The Constitution of Liberty*. Hayek is willing to tolerate far higher degrees of monopoly power than Smith, and he also ignores Tocqueville's insistence that corporate regulation is valuable for avoiding preventable human death. F. Hayek, *The Constitution of Liberty* (London: Routledge Classics, 2006).

19 Quoted in Van Horn, 'Corporations and the rise of Chicago law and economics,' 494.

Conclusion: The great enlargement

1 Milton Friedman and Rose Friedman, *Two Lucky People: Memoirs* (Chicago, IL: University of Chicago Press, 1998), 582.

2 S. Scutti, 2018. 'US suicide rates increased more than 25% since 1999, CDC says' (CNN, June 22).

3 Quoted in Rob Reich, *Just Giving: Why Philanthropy Is Failing Democracy and How It Can Do Better* (Princeton, NJ: Princeton University Press), 111–112.

4 Tocqueville, *Democracy in America*, 704.

5 Arendt, *Origins of Totalitarianism*, 616.

6 Wollstonecraft, 'The Rights of Woman,' in *The Vindications*, 317.

7   See Carol Anderson, *White Rage: The Unspoken Truth of our Racial Divide* (New York: Bloomsbury, 2016).

8   The first memorial to the lives of American individuals who were lynched opened in Montgomery, Alabama in 2018, established by Bryan Stevenson of the Equal Justice Initiative.

9   Shehab Khan 2017. 'Donald Trump's corporate biography drops Barack Obama birther reference' (*Independent*, September 13).

10 Taylor, *From #BlackLivesMatter to Black Liberation*, 215. The notion of 'solidarity' is re-emerging as a central problem in social theory and distributive justice. For a compelling discussion, see Barbara Prainsack and Alena Buyx, *Solidarity in Biomedicine and Beyond* (Cambridge: Cambridge University Press, 2016).

11 Currently, for example, Wollstonecraft's name doesn't appear on the Wikipedia page on 'confirmation bias,' which lists only male authors in a short section on the history of the concept.

12 Tocqueville, *Democracy in America*, 704.

13 Tocqueville, *Recollections*, 149.

14 Ibid., 149.

15 Ibid., 151.

INDEX

Ackerman, Spencer, 91
agnotology, 11, 29–30, 39,
    188–9, 221
Andrews, Samuel, 210–11
antidepressants: dosage level
    concerns, 283–5; FDA black box
    warning, 288; FDA investigations,
    281, 287–8; information
    dissemination, 285–6; lack of
    effectiveness for children, 250,
    251–2; MHRA reviews, 282–6;
    off-label prescribing for children,
    250–1, 292; patient information
    labels, 281, 282; popularity, 280,
    290; suicide and other side effects,
    280–1, 282, 287–90; unpublished
    trials data, 250, 281, 286–7
Arendt, Hannah, 45, 62, 179,
    220–1, 309
Arthur Anderson, 235
auditors, 234–5
Aventis, 269–77

Bacevich, Andrew, 13–14, 68–9
Bachelet, Michelle, 221–2
Bain, Alexander, 159–60
banks, corporate ignorance, 120
Bannon, Stephen, 34–5, 87, 93–4, 175
Barings, 120
Bassel, Leah, 59

Bastiat, Frédéric, 168, 200–1
Bentham, Jeremy, 8, 37, 155, 299
Bernanke, Ben, 55
Bignell, Paul, 32
black Americans, 196, 237, 238, 241
Black, Eugene, 219
Blair, Tony, 31–2
Blankfein, Lloyd, 76–7
Brandeis, Louis, 65
Breitbart, 34, 85–6
Brennan, Jason, 93–4, 95–6, 243;
    Against Democracy, 66–7, 96
Brexit vote: Cambridge Analytica
    Leave campaign assistance,
    86; half-truths, 89–90; Leave
    campaign claims, 30–1; and low-
    income voters, 19; support from
    wealthy, 90; supposed ignorance
    of leave voters, 82–3, 89–90, 162;
    voter turnout, 31
Briggs, Asa, 159–60
Brink, André, *A Dry White Season*,
    268–9
Britain, nation of shopkeepers, 192
Brook, Richard, 283–5, 295
Brooks, Rebekah, 100, 103, 113–14
Buchanan, James, 246–7
Buffett, Warren, 55, 67
Burke, Edmund, 9, 317; background,
    148; condemnation of French

Revolution, 149–51, 182; and the divine, 77; and East India Company, 10, 122, 175, 176, 180–1; government regulation, 20–1; Warren Hastings prosecution, 180, 182
Bush, George W., 72–3
business: collusion, 141–2; economics teaching, 205, 215–16, 304; government intervention, 43; labour practices, 13; preoccupation with self-interest, 139–40; strategic ignorance, 20; useful unknowns, 51–6, 277; *see also* regulation
business schools, 118–19

Cadwalladr, Carole, 86
Calais Jungle, 1–3
Cambridge Analytica, 86
Cambridge University, 67–8
Canada: indigenous groups, 26–9, 58; mining companies, 185, 222–4
Carnegie, Andrew: belief in self-made competitive success, 205, 214; beneficiary of laissez-faire business practices, 205–6; beneficiary of steel industry tariffs, 206, 210; deception and lies, 207, 209; Edgar Thomson strike, 208; master of ignorance, 20; philanthropy, 204; professed support for workers' rights, 207–8, 210, 215; stock market trading, 206–7; strategic ignorance of Homestead crisis, 208–10, 214
Carpenter, Daniel, 263–4, 265
Carter, Zachary, 217, 236

Caryatid Operation, 112–14
Chandler, Alfred, *The Visible Hand*, 195
Chang, Ha-Joon, 187–8
Chernow, Ron, 211, 212, 213–14
Chicago, meat plants, 255
Chicago School, 246–7, 300, 303
children: Canada's indigenous children, 27, 58; family reunions, 2–3; obesity, 51–2, 65; *see also* antidepressants
Chile, 221–2
Cisneros, Ann Marie, 271–2, 274
Clark, John Bates, 133–4
Clark, Maurice, 210–11
Clinton Foundation, 87
Clive, Robert, 177–8, 179, 205
Cobain, Ian, *The History Thieves*, 42
Coca-Cola, 51–2, 65
Cohen, Stanley, 57
colonialism: Britain's defence of American colonies, 191–2; and Canada's indigenous groups, 26–9; destruction/falsification of files, 42, 58; in India, 44; indigenous rights, 28–9; *see also* East India Company
confirmation bias, 37–8, 151
conscription, 14–15
contingency, 6
corporate veil, 46, 222–3, 311–12
Coulson, Andy, 102–3, 113
credibility deficits/excess, 25–6, 77

Dalrymple, William, 177, 178
Daschuk, James, *Clearing the Plains*, 26–7
Davies, Nick, 103–6
Davies, Sharon, 239–40

The Dearborn Independent, 79–81

deaths, workplace, 218, 219, 238

democracy: choice by algorithm, 66–7; and disenfranchisement, 16, 66, 70, 96, 156, 174; epistemological strengths, 297–8; Greek democracy, 296–7; low-income voters, 19, 78; male enfranchisement, 42; online campaign infringements, 86; *see also* voter ignorance

Deng, Wendi, 101

denial, 56, 57, 120

Dewdney, Edgar, 28

disenfranchisement, 16, 66, 70, 96, 156, 174

displaced people, 202–3

divine providence, 67–9, 174, 176, 318–19, 322–4

Dobbin, Frank, 194–5

Dowd, Timothy, 194–5

Dower, John, 202–3

Dowler, Milly, 19, 100

Downs, Anthony, 46

drone strikes, 91–2

drug trials: Ketek, 271–2, 274–7; testing methods, 264–7; Vioxx, 262; Vioxx/naproxen, 259–60

drugs: naproxen, 259–60; patient information labels, 273, 281, 282; rare adverse effects, 265–7; rational response to adverse effects, 266–7; Thalidomide, 254, 256–8; Vioxx, 258–62, 269, 270; *see also* antidepressants; Ketek

Dunlavy, Colleen, 194

East India Company: monopoly privileges, 128–9, 145; parliamentary accountability efforts, 175, 176, 179, 180–1; public-private hybrid, 176–7, 178; state protection, 5; tax collection, 178; territorial control, 177–8; treatment of Indians, 10, 122, 127, 161, 176, 180; wealth extraction, 178, 180

economic justice, 174–5, 184–6

economics teaching, 205, 215–16, 304

Economist, 165, 171

Eden, Anthony, 31

Edgar Thomson steel works strike, 208

Eli Lilly, 280

elite ignorance, 18–19, 41, 43, 90–4, 160–1, 166; *see also* epistocracy; wealth

Elliot, Larry, 34

Emejulu, Akwugo, 59

Enlightenment, 9, 148, 150, 173, 175, 183, 186

Enron, 21–2, 230–1, 234–5

environmental groups, 3–4

epistocracy, 17, 93, 95–6, 163, 165, 267–70

equal culpability thesis, 233–5

Eritrea, Bisha Mining, 223–4

Ernst, David, 261

expert ignorance, 24–5, 33–4, 64–6, 266–70, 275–7, 295

experts, not necessarily better leaders, 97

Exxon Mobil, 214

fake news, 79–81, 88–90

FDA *see* Food and Drug Administration (FDA)

Federal Reserve Board, 53–4, 55

feminist theory, 317–18

financial advisors, 67

financial crisis (2007-8), 33, 52–6, 306–8

Fitzgerald, F. Scott, *The Great Gatsby*, 85

Food and Drug Administration (FDA): antidepressant black box warning, 288; antidepressant investigations, 281, 287–9; Aventis investigation, 274, 275, 276; employee concerns, 269–70; establishment, 255–6; fear of reputational damage, 263–4; fees from pharmaceutical companies, 263; Ketek safety concerns ignored, 272–4; negative response to problem exposure, 269–70; Office for New Drugs, 265–6; Thalidomide, 254, 256–8; useful unknowns, 51; and Vioxx, 258, 259, 262

Food and Drugs Act (1906) (US), 255

Forbes, 262, 293

Ford, Henry, 10, 79–81, 97–8

Frank, Anne, 50

free trade, 17–13, 44, 57, 200–1

French Revolution (1789), 149, 181, 182, 183–4

French Revolution (1848), 201, 325–6

Frick, Henry Clay, 210

Fricker, Miranda, 25, 77

Friedman, Milton, 54–5, 59–61, 302–3, 306

futility thesis, 35–6

Galbraith, John Kenneth, 40

Garcia-Retamero, Rocio, 38–9

Gates, Bill, 136, 202, 203, 218, 258

gender: female economists, 146; J.S. Mill's co-authorship, 7, 60–1, 153, 157–60; progress, 166–7; Wollstonecraft's legacy, 151–2

gender realism, 48

Geneva Conventions, 72–3, 185

Gigerenzer, Gerd, 38–9

GlaxoSmithKline, 22, 250–2, 282, 290, 291–2

globalization, 175

Goldacre, Ben, *Bad Pharma*, 11, 253

Goldin, Ian, 33

Goldman Sachs, 76, 87

Goodman, Clive, 104, 105, 106

Google Trends, 89

Gould, Jay, 211

governance: epistocracy, 17, 93, 93–4, 95–6, 163, 267–70; *see also* regulation

Graham, David, 258, 261–3, 266, 267, 269–70, 293

Graves, Lisa, 237–8

Gray, John, 13, 163; *Straw Dogs*, 5–6

greatness, 81, 97

greats, 312–13

greats (social movements), 17–18

Greek democracy, 296–7

Greek oracles, 62–4

Green, Joshua, 87

Greenspan, Alan, 32

Grenfell Tower fire, 23–5, 59

Hamilton, Alexander, 193–4

Handlin, Mary and Oscar, 195

Harford, Tim, 30–1, 33–4, 221

Hastings, Warren, 180, 182

Hayek, Friedrich: dependence on corporate funding, 246, 300, 302; disdain for government regulation,

248, 301, 303; on fragility of expert knowledge, 298–300; *Road to Serfdom*, 164, 301; and social protection, 301–2

Heffernan, Margaret, *Wilful Blindness: Why We Ignore the Obvious at Our Peril*, 230–1

Heilbroner, Robert, *The Worldly Philosophers*, 216

Heyer, Heather, 313

Hickel, Jason, *The Divide*, 137

Hillsborough disaster, 88–9

Hirschman, Albert, 35

historical amnesia, 57, 202

history: presentism, 28; sanctioned ignorance, 40–2; statue removal protests, 313–14; unintentional misunderstandings, 169

Hitler, Adolf, 50, 80

Homestead steel mill strike, 208–10

Huffington Post, 217, 236

human contingency, 6

Hume, David, 176

Hurcombe, Linda, 288–90

identity politics, 138–9

ignorance: enduring myths, 81–4; first acknowledgement, 154; greater than knowledge, 47, 49; psychology of, 38–42; rational ignorance, 46–7; snowmobile fallacy, 241–3; useful unknowns, 51–6, 257, 277; *see also* elite ignorance; reckless ignorance; strategic ignorance; voter ignorance; wilful ignorance

ignorance alibis, 12, 56–61, 87, 210

ignorance cycles, 225–6; *see also* macro-ignorance; micro-ignorance

ignorance doesn't excuse principle, 231–3, 239–40

ignorance pathways, 167–8, 175–6

ignorantia legis principle, 231–3

IMF, 33–4, 137

imperialism, 68, 179; *see also* colonialism

income, minimum income, 183

income inequality, 216, 220

India, 10, 122, 127, 131, 160–1; *see also* East India Company

indigenous peoples, 26–9, 58

Information Commissioner's Office (ICO): failure to pursue journalists, 109–12; hindrances to effective operation, 106–7, 108, 109; Operation Motorman, 107–8; regulatory agency, 106–7; *What Price Privacy?*, 108–9

inherited privilege, 182–4

inherited wealth, 200

institutional ignorance, 33–4, 294–5

International Monetary Fund, 33–4, 137

Iraq war, 17, 31–2, 52

Jews, anti-Semitism, 79–81, 97–8

Johann-Liang, Rosemary, 273

judiciary, 199

Kant, Immanuel, 9, 308–9, 318–19

Kelsey, Frances Oldham, 254, 255–8

Kendall, Tim, 249–52, 286–7

Kerviel, Jérôme, 120

Ketek, 269–77; adverse reactions, 253–4, 271, 272–4; drug trial irregularities, 271–2, 274–7; FDA failings, 269–70, 272–3; labelling,

273; reliance on expert ignorance, 276–7; withdrawal, 253

Keynes, John Maynard, 31, 167, 170, 172–3

Khurana, Rakesh, 118–19

Kim, Jim Yong, 219–20

Kirkman-Campbell, Anne, 270–2, 274–6, 276–7

Knight, Frank, 133–4, 152

knowledge: derived from torture, 74–5; equal unknowers, 47–9; low desire for knowledge of life events, 38–9; political knowledge, 66–7, 95–6

known unknowns, 52

Koch, Charles and David, 65, 237, 238, 244

Kuttner, Stuart, 103–4

labour: Adam Smith's wage labourers, 139; domestic labour, 125; exploitation, 129–30; weakened labour protection, 134, 137, 218–20; see also servitude; slavery

laissez-faire economy, 20, 21, 126–7, 194–5, 200

The Lancet, 252, 259, 286

language, in ignorance pathways, 168, 169, 200–1

Lay, Kenneth, 235

Leeson, Nick, 120

Leveson inquiry, 109, 110–11

Lippmann, Walter, 16

List, Friedrich, 188–91

Liverpool Football Club, 88–9

Lorde, Audre, 18, 163, 317–18, 319–21, 326–8

Loveland, Douglas, 274, 275

Macdonald, John A., 26–7, 28, 313

McIntosh, Glenn, 288–90

macro-ignorance, 12–15, 169, 225–6

Madison, James, 47

Mandeville, Bernard, 248

Mankiw, Gregory, 132; *Macroeconomics*, 152–3, 216

marginal productivity theory, 76, 130–5, 152–3

market fundamentalism, 4–5, 6–7, 13

Mason, Paul, 43

Mazzucato, Mariana, 152, 304; *The Value of Everything*, 134–5

meat industry, 255

medical experiments, 72

Medicines Act (1968) (UK), 291–2

Medicines and Healthcare Products Regulatory Agency (MHRA): antidepressant reviews, 282–6; dependence on pharmaceutical companies, 278, 284–5; GlaxoSmithKlein investigation, 252, 290, 291–2; non-prosecutions, 252, 253, 278, 291, 292; unpublished medical trials, 251–2, 286; useful unknowns, 51

Meikson Woods, Ellen, 296

Mens Rea Reform Act (US), 236–44

mental health: National Collaborating Centre, 249–50; see also antidepressants

Mercer, Robert, 85–6, 87

Merck, 258–61

Merrell, 256, 257

Meyer, Eugene, 219

MHRA *see* Medicines and Healthcare
Products Regulatory Agency
(MHRA)
micro-ignorance, 12–15, 141–2, 168,
225–6
Middle East, 14–15, 68–9, 202–3
Mill, George, 159
Mill, James, 161
Mill, John Stuart, 37, 41; as an
'unknower', 156–7, 162, 299;
Autobiography, 157–60; Britain's
peaceful global dominance, 202,
203; co-authorship with wife and
stepdaughter, 7, 60–1, 153, 157–60;
*Considerations on Representative
Government*, 161; and the coolie
trade, 155–6; *On Liberty*, 7, 60–1,
153, 158, 166; *Principles of Political
Economy*, 158; *The Subjection of
Women*, 202, 203; voter franchise
limitations, 156
Mills, Charles, 45, 304
mining companies, 185, 222–4
Miranda, Lin-Manuel, 193
Mishra, Pankaj, 44, 304
Monod, Jacques, 6
Montesquieu, Albert de Secondat, 29
Mosholder, Andrew, 287–8
Mulcaire, Glenn, 104, 105, 106,
112–13
multinational companies, 185, 219,
222–4
Murdoch, Elisabeth, 101, 115–16, 117
Murdoch, James, 100, 102
Murdoch, Lachlan, 102
Murdoch, Rupert: ignorance of phone
hacking, 19; and racist news outlets,
85–6; select committee appearance,
99, 100–1, 114; *Sun* office meeting,
114–15; wilful blindness, 101–2
Muttitt, Greg, 32

Nasaw, David, 207, 208, 210
Nazism, 72, 74
neoclassical theory, 130–3, 303
Nevsun Resources, 223–4
New York Times, 54–5, 87, 238
News Corporation, 115–16, 117,
119–20, 274–5; *see also* phone
hacking
News of the World: Gordon Taylor
lawsuit, 105–6; phone hacking,
19, 99, 101, 102–3; use of private
investigators, 103–4
Nobel prize, 60–1
Nuremberg Code, 72

Obama, Barack, 82, 91–2, 148–9
oil companies: and Iraq war, 31–2;
Standard Oil, 4, 211–14
On Liberty (Mill), 7, 60–1, 153,
158, 166
Open Society (Popper), 164
Operation Motorman, 107–8
oracular power: Brennan's 'simulated
oracle' test, 66–7, 95–6; concept,
16, 61–2; divine providence, 67–9;
financial advisors, 67; historical
context, 62–4; mainstream
economic theories, 217; natural
and social scientists, 64–7
Orwell, George, 129, 131–2, 164,
168, 225, 309–10
Ostrich instruction, 21, 228, 231–2;
see also wilful ignorance
Owens, Alec, 109–11

Paine, Thomas: 'Agrarian Justice', 183–4; blame-shifting, 180, 307; on divine providence, 174; and elite ignorance, 18–19; on hereditary privilege, 182–4, 308; *Rights of Man*, 149, 183

Patnaik, Utsa, 44, 304

pharmaceutical industry: damage settlements, 261; distortion of evidence, 11–12, 75; fear of reputational damage, 263–4; fraud, 22; medical trial data, 250–2, 259–60, 262; Merck settlement, 261; presumption of innocence, 291, 292–3; regulation seen as barrier to progress, 257–8; UK's weak regulatory system, 252–3, 278, 291, 292; useful unknowns, 51, 257; Vioxx and heart failure, 258–62; *see also* drug trials; drugs

philanthropy, 97–8, 204, 308

phone hacking: Caryatid Operation, 112–13; and corporate ignorance, 19; Culture, Media and Sport Committee report, 99–101; Gordon Taylor lawsuit, 105–6; ICO failure to pursue journalists, 109–12; method, 104–5; *News of the World*, 19, 99, 101, 102–3; victims, 19, 100, 105–6, 112

Pinker, Steven: Bannon-Pinker conundrum, 34–5; *Enlightenment Now*, 20, 36, 37, 135–6, 142, 202, 203, 224; globalization, 175; information avoidance theories, 37–8; poverty and in-country inequality, 36–7; on wealth distribution, 147–8

Plato, 164, 296, 297

plausible deniability, 56, 120

political deceptions, 30–1

political liberalism, 41

Popper, Karl, 163–5, 297–8; *Open Society*, 164

positive-sum theory, 123, 136, 147

Powell, Enoch, 68

press freedom, 199

Preston, Lewis, 219

prisoners of war, 72–3

private investigators, 103–4, 107–8

Proctor, Robert, 11

The Protocols of the Elders of Zion, 79–81

Prozac, 280–1, 289, 290

Pulquero, Ramiro Obrajero, 272

Puri, Poonam, 222–3, 304

race realism, 48

racial exploitation, 304

racism, 45, 48, 84–7, 319

Rampell, Catherine, 171, 217

rational ignorance, 46–7

Rawls, John, 'veil of ignorance', 8–9, 46

Reagan, Ronald, 68

reckless ignorance, 54–6, 235, 304

regulation: Adam Smith legacy, 20–1, 121, 126–7, 136–7, 140–1; anti-regulation stance, 246–8, 258, 303, 307; Hayek's disdain, 248, 301, 303; pharmaceutical industry, 252–3, 257–8, 278, 291, 292; Tocqueville's recommendations, 20–1, 197–200, 301

rent, 128

rent-seeking, 127–8, 131, 132

Rhodes, Cecil, 313

Ricardo, David, 186–7

Robbins, Lionel, 146

Robins, Nick, 180–1

Robinson, Joan, 133, 135, 147, 152

Rockefeller, John D.: belief in self-made success, 205, 214; beneficiary of laissez-faire practices, 205–6; deceitful opposition to anti-monopoly legislation, 4; master of ignorance, 20; new cooperation principle, 215; philanthropy, 204; secretive railroad deals, 211–13; South Improvement Company cartel, 213; Standard Oil, 4, 211–14; strategic ignorance of business takeovers, 213–14

Roosevelt, Franklin D., 196

Rosenfeld, Sophia, 58

Ross, David, 269–70, 272–3

Rumsfeld, Donald, 52

Samuelson, Paul, 134, 152

sanctioned ignorance, 40–2

Sand, George, 166–7, 324–6

Sanofi-Aventis, 269–77

Sarch, Alexander, 231–2, 233–5, 304

Sartre, Jean-Paul, 293–4

Schiebinger, Londa, 11

Schwartz, Anna, 54–5, 59–61

science, 8, 64–7

scientific racism, 48, 319

Scotland Yard, 112–14

Scott, Tom, 207, 212

Securities and Exchange Commission (SEC), 53–4

self-interest, 125–6, 126, 136, 139–40

Seroxat, 250–2, 282

servitude, 41–2, 44, 155–6

Shapiro, Aaron, 79

shared prosperity theory, 123, 136, 147

Sherman, Rachel, 117–18

Shine lawsuit, 115–16, 117

Simons, Henry, 246

Simpson, Jeffrey, 28

Sinclair, Niigaanwewidam James, 27

Sinclair, Upton, *The Jungle*, 255

slavery, 43–4, 205; *see also* servitude

Smarsh, Sarah, 84

smarts *see* strong/smart groups

Smith, Adam, 9; Britain a nation of shopkeepers, 192; criticism of monopoly protections, 127–9; criticisms of merchants, 247, 320; economic classes of society, 138–40, 143; and economic inequality, 136; on government regulation, 20–1, 121, 126–7, 136–7, 140–1; his mother's influence, 125; inevitability of conflict, 186; misrepresentation of his ideas, 142–6, 310–12; on relative poverty, 142–3; on self-interest, 126, 136; strategic and wilful ignorance of, 122–3; tiered justice system, 121; timing and motives for helping the poor, 245; trade protectionism, 186, 190–1; on wealth distribution, 142–4, 191; *Wealth of Nations*, 6–7, 121, 125–6, 136, 169, 189, 245; *Wealth of Nations* abridged versions, 144–6

Smith, David, 109–10

snowmobile fallacy, 241–3

social silence, 53

Société Générale, 120

Socrates, 45, 63

Somin, Ilya, 94–5, 96

Sorel, Georges, 17

Soviet Union, uncomfortable facts, 5, 13

Spivak, Gayatri, 40–1

SSRI drugs *see* antidepressants

Standard Oil, 4, 211–14

Steinzor, Rena, 244–5

Stewart, Maria W., 130–1

Stigler, George, 133, 246–7, 248

strategic ignorance: autocratic exploitation, 69–71; business practices, 20, 205; Carnegie, 208–10; corporate anonymity, 45–6; definition, 3; of drone strikes, 91–2; economic theory, 122–3; emancipatory nature, 315–17; exposure efforts treated as inexcusable, 269–70; Ford, 79–81, 98; MHRA's non-prosecution record, 291–2, 293–4; and political networks, 22; Rockefeller, 213–14

strong/smart groups, 16–17, 69–71, 77, 173–4, 312–13

student loans, 185

Suez crisis, 31

suicide rates, 307

Sun, 114–15

Sutherland, Kathryn, 145–6, 159

Syll, Lars, 187

Symons, Baroness, 32

taxation, Paine's proposals, 184, 308

Taylor, Gordon, 105–6

Taylor, Harriet, 7, 60–1, 153, 157–60, 166, 299

Taylor, Helen, 157–60

Taylor, Keeanga-Yamahtta, 68

Teicher, Martin, 280

Temple, Robert, 287–8

Tett, Gillian, 53

Thalidomide, 254, 256–8

think tanks, 65

Thomas, Richard, 110, 111

Tillerson, Rex, 214

tobacco industry, 51

Tocqueville, Alexis de: *Democracy in America*, 197–200, 309, 322–3; and divine providence, 322–4; French workers, 325–6; government regulation of industry, 20–1, 197–200, 301; prejudice against women, 166–7, 324–6

torture, 72–5

trade: free trade, 17–13, 57, 200–1; mercantilism, 169–70, 171; protectionism, 186, 188, 190–1; Ricardo's comparative advantage theory, 186–8; US policy, 171, 188, 190, 217

Trefgarne, George, 179–80

Trump, Donald: class myths of voter support, 81–4, 162, 163; elite ignorance, 90–1, 93–4; on history, 314; on Obama, 82, 148–9; presidential election, 19; selective use of facts, 92–4; on torture, 73–4; and truth, 17; wealthy backers, 83–4

truth, liberating potential, 9–10

United Kingdom: male enfranchisement, 42; market interventionism, 43–4; military interventions, 14–15; Suez crisis, 31; trade policies, 44, 57, 186, 190–1; weak regulation of pharmaceutical companies, 252–3, 278, 291–2

United States: conscription, 14–15; drone strikes, 91–2; in-country inequality, 14–15, 36–7; labour oppression, 129–30; laissez-faire policies, 194–5; military interventions, 14–15, 68–9, 185; New Deal, 196; origins myths, 169; suicide rates, 307; trade policies, 171, 188, 190, 217; War Crimes Act (1996), 73; workplace deaths, 219–20

United States Department of Justice, 102, 238, 252, 261

Unser, Bobby, 242–3

unwitting ignorance, 42, 122–3

useful unknowns, 51–6, 257, 277

utilitarianism, 8, 155

'veil of ignorance', 8–9, 46

Viner, Jacob, 300, 302–3

Vinson and Elkins, 235

Vioxx, 258–62

von Eschenbach, Andrew, 273

voter ignorance: Brexit, 82–3, 89–90, 162; collective, shared problem, 243–4; definition, 94; justification for disenfranchisement, 70, 156, 174; political knowledge test, 66–7, 95–6; solutions, 94–5; Trump election, 19, 162; see also democracy, and disenfranchisement

War Crimes Act (1996) (US), 73

Washington Consensus, 34

Washington Post, 89, 171, 217, 257

Watkins, Sherron, 235

Watson, Mathew, 187, 188

wealth: evidence of intelligence, 77, 81; financial oligarchy, 65; ignorance and inherited wealth, 139; inherited wealth, 117–18; and morality, 162–3; and racism, 84–7; US voter support for Trump, 83–4, 162, 163

wealth inequality: effect on social wellbeing, 135, 147; God's will, 75–7; growth, 137; in-country inequality, 36–7; India-England, 129; legitimisation, 75–6; as natural law, 71; relative poverty, 143

Wealth of Nations (Smith), 6–7, 121, 125–6, 136, 169, 189; abridged versions, 144–6

Weber, Max The Protestant Ethic and the Spirit of Capitalism, 67

welfare systems, 185–6

wellbeing, and inequality, 135, 147

whistle-blowers, 40, 262–3

White, William Allen, 81, 97, 111–12

white-collar crime, Mens Rea Reform Act, 236–44

Whittam Smith, Andreas, 102

Whittamore, Steve, 107–8, 109, 110

wilful ignorance: definition, 21–2, 228–9; difficult to prove, 22; Enron, 21–2; equal culpability thesis, 233–5; financial law, 239–40; first court appearances, 227–8; Grenfell Tower fire, 24–6; 'ignorance doesn't excuse'

principle, 231–3, 239–40; News
International, 274–5; and reckless
ignorance, 235; Rupert Murdoch,
101–2; suspected fraud Ketek
trials fraud, 271–2, 274–7
Williams, Zoe, 90
Williamson, Kevin, 83
Wollstonecraft, Mary, 20–1, 163,
317; economic fairness, 122;
family background and social
norms, 268, 269; legacy, 151–2;
on mixed education, 312; 'Rights
of Men' rebuttal of Burke, 149,
150–1

women: domestic violence, 59;
ignorance of co-authorship, 7,
60–1; minority women, 59
Woods, Kent, 285–6, 290–1, 292
workplace health and safety, 217,
218–19, 238
World Bank: disputed assumption
of neutrality, 221–2; Employing
Workers Indicator, 225;
institutional ignorance, 33–4;
presidents, 219–20; weakened
labour protection, 137, 218–20

Zinn, Howard, 196

ZED

Zed is a platform for marginalised voices across the globe.

It is the world's largest publishing collective and a world leading example of alternative, non-hierarchical business practice.

It has no CEO, no MD and no bosses and is owned and managed by its workers who are all on equal pay.

It makes its content available in as many languages as possible.

It publishes content critical of oppressive power structures and regimes.

It publishes content that changes its readers' thinking.

It publishes content that other publishers won't and that the establishment finds threatening.

It has been subject to repeated acts of censorship by states and corporations.

It fights all forms of censorship.

It is financially and ideologically independent of any party, corporation, state or individual.

Its books are shared all over the world.

www.zedbooks.net
@ZedBooks